GLAD TO THE BRINK OF FEAR

GLAD TO THE BRINK OF FEAR

A PORTRAIT OF RALPH WALDO EMERSON

JAMES MARCUS

PRINCETON UNIVERSITY PRESS

PRINCETON & OXFORD

Published by Princeton University Press
41 William Street, Princeton, New Jersey 08540
99 Banbury Road, Oxford OX2 6JX

press.princeton.edu

All Rights Reserved

ISBN 9780691254333
ISBN (e-book) 9780691254357

British Library Cataloging-in-Publication Data is available

Library of Congress Cataloging-in-Publication Data

Names: Marcus, James, 1959– author.
Title: Glad to the brink of fear : a portrait of Ralph Waldo Emerson / James Marcus.
Description: Princeton : Princeton University Press, 2024. | Includes bibliographical
    references and index.
Identifiers: LCCN 2023036672 (print) | LCCN 2023036673 (ebook) |
    ISBN 9780691254333 (hardback ; acid-free paper) | ISBN 9780691254357 (ebook)
Subjects: LCSH: Emerson, Ralph Waldo, 1803–1882—Criticism ad interpretation. |
    BISAC: LITERARY CRITICISM / American / General | PHILOSOPHY /
    Movements / Transcendentalism | LCGFT: Literary criticism.
Classification: LCC PS1638 .M288 2024 (print) | LCC PS1638 (ebook) |
    DDC 814/.3—dc23/eng/20230824
LC record available at https://lccn.loc.gov/2023036672
LC ebook record available at https://lccn.loc.gov/2023036673

Editorial: Anne Savarese and James Collier
Production Editorial: Jaden Young
Text and Jacket/Cover Design: Karl Spurzem
Production: Erin Suydam
Publicity: Alyssa Sanford and Carmen Jimenez
Copyeditor: Leah Caldwell

Jacket image: Engraving of Ralph Waldo Emerson by Stephen Alonzo Schoff.
Based on the drawing by Samuel Worcester Rowse. 1878. Library of Congress.

This book has been composed in Arno Pro with Greycliff CF

Printed on acid-free paper. ∞

Printed in the United States of America

10 9 8 7 6 5 4 3 2 1

For my parents,
Deana and Aaron,
and for my daughter, Nat

CONTENTS

GLAD TO THE BRINK OF FEAR

INTRODUCTION

At every family gathering, there is an uncle you are desperate to avoid. He is full of advice you don't want, and despite your efforts to slip away, he always pins you down on the sofa or in that narrow space next to the refrigerator. Sometimes he appears feeble, but mostly he is inexhaustible in his moralizing. This harmless individual smells of witch hazel and shoe polish. Sometimes he asks you questions, but he never listens to the answers. You are simply the unwilling receptacle for his wisdom, all of which sounds terribly familiar.

At first glance, Ralph Waldo Emerson seems to be the irritating uncle at the feast of American letters. *Trust thyself*, he keeps telling you. It sounds like the Victorian version of self-help—which is why it ends up on coffee mugs to this very day. What's more, his insistence on self-realization has made him into a mascot for big business. His image has been enlisted to sell typewriters, cardboard boxes, Turkish cigarettes. The insurance industry, too, has found him an irresistible branding tool: Emerson "was the voice of the American dream," declared a copywriter for John Hancock Mutual Life in 1961, while also giving him a pat on the head for arriving at his lecture engagements on time. In this way, our great apostle of nonconformity has been transformed into a cheerleader for the most conformist aspects of American life.

In fact, Ralph Waldo Emerson is anything but a Victorian relic. Nearly a century and a half after his death, he remains a visionary figure, who speaks to our cultural moment with tremendous urgency. So many of the conundrums of modern American life—identity, race, inequality, ecological apocalypse, and the endless tug-of-war between the individual and the tribe—were anticipated by this slope-shouldered prophet in his rocking chair. This should surprise nobody. He was, after all, the first great American writer. He was also among the first to articulate what we have come to think of as our national character: self-reliant, self-conscious, scornful of institutional pomp and with a built-in bullshit detector. We are, in Emerson's view, theoretically modest but plainly superior to our mummified Old World counterparts. We are reflexively pragmatic but with a deep vein of spiritual yearning and, yes, spiritual confusion.

Born in Boston in 1803, when the United States was a backwater with a population of fewer than four million, Emerson insisted that we shed the inferiority complex of the ex-colonial. Europe, he insisted, was the past. The future was *here*, in what Emerson conceived of as the vast vacancy of the North American continent. Of course this was a mytho-logical view of the place, which happened to be tenanted by several hundred thousand Native Americans, even after the genocidal decades preceding Emerson's birth. It was poetry, not policy. Yet Emerson's sense that the invention of America marked a deep rupture with the Old World, and not simply a small-town, stump-clearing continuity, was correct—and bracing. "Our day of dependence," he wrote in 1837, "our long apprenticeship to the learning of other lands, draws to a close."

Casting off the cultural yoke of Europe was a major act of rebellion. But Emerson was a rebel in other aspects of life, too, the most dramatic being his abandonment of organized Christianity. This was a radical act for a man in his position. Like seven generations of his family before him, he was a clergyman. Indeed, an Emerson baby was more or less a pastor-in-miniature, lacking only divinity classes and a clerical collar. Emerson's pulpit, too, was a historic one: the Second Church of Boston, which had previously housed the heavy-hitting Puritan divine Cotton Mather.

By the time Emerson was appointed, in 1829, the congregation had shucked off its Puritan rigidities in favor of Unitarianism. This was the most mild-mannered of Protestant creeds, which denied that Christ was the son of God and rejected the Calvinist doctrines of original sin and predestination. Surely such an elastic system of belief would give the young pastor plenty of room for his own uncertainties. Yet Unitarianism, just thirty years after it had gained a toehold in a rapidly developing nation, was already a little calcified. It was now the faith of well-heeled Bostonians—it was a belief system with a powdered wig on its head and silver buckles on its shoes.

It was besieged, as well, on two sides. The Congregationalists, from whose midst the Unitarians had sprung, were infuriated by the transformation of Jesus into a mortal man and human beings into free agents. Meanwhile, there was the explosive rise of evangelical Christianity in the United States, which began in the early decades of the nineteenth century. The Methodists, the Baptists, the Disciples of Christ—along with a wild profusion of splinter sects, buzzing like mayflies through the bright air of belief—would soon swamp both New England creeds.

Emerson's exit from the pulpit in 1832 cannot be understood outside of this context. The Second Great Awakening, that tsunami of evangelical fervor, had been building in the United States for the past three decades. Half the country had decided that the old forms of worship were empty. They wanted something more real, more visceral. They wanted to speak directly to God, and have Him respond in kind. Emerson was never an evangelical: his temperament and training inclined him in the opposite direction. Yet he, too, was eager to knock down any barrier to direct communication with the divine. A pastor in this sense was a middleman—a broker of spiritual goods. Why not simply mothball the old faiths and, as Emerson put it, "enjoy an original relation to the universe?"

He paid a price, of course, for walking away from the Second Church. He lost his job and an ironclad position in the very society his ancestors had helped to create. (Six years later, a visitor to an upper-crust Boston household noted that his hosts had been taught "to abhor and abominate R. W. Emerson as a sort of mad dog.") It was only by breaking with the church, however, that Emerson was able to discover his true vocation. He would be an essayist—a creator of secular sermons, you could say, whose ecstatic, icon-smashing prose grabbed readers by the lapels and left them shaken, tickled, transformed. "The maker of a sentence," he once wrote, "launches out into the infinite and builds a road into Chaos and Old Night, and is followed by those who hear him with something of wild, creative delight." As a description of both Emerson the writer and his eventual audience, this can hardly be bettered.

. . .

Ah, Emerson's prose! What needs to be said, first of all, is that he wrote some of the greatest American sentences—hundreds, maybe thousands of them. His golden hits have been quoted so many times that they are hard to view with a fresh eye. Yet they have lost little of their snap, vigor, and residual sadness:

> A foolish consistency is the hobgoblin of little minds, adored by little statesmen and philosophers and divines.

> An institution is the lengthened shadow of one man.

> In every work of genius we recognize our own rejected thoughts: they come back to us with a certain alienated majesty.

> There is a kind of contempt of the landscape felt by him who has just lost by death a dear friend.

> Every spirit builds itself a house; and beyond its house, a world; and beyond its world, a heaven.

> A strange process too, this, by which experience is converted into thought, as a mulberry leaf is converted into satin.

> I pack my trunk, embrace my friends, embark on the sea, and at last wake up in Naples, and there beside me is the stern Fact, the sad self, unrelenting, identical, that I fled from.

> Tobacco, coffee, alcohol, hashish, prussic acid, strychnine, are weak dilutions: the surest poison is time.

> Crossing a bare common, in snow puddles, at twilight, under a clouded sky, without having in my thoughts any occurrence of special good fortune, I have enjoyed a perfect exhilaration.

The sentence was Emerson's unit of thought. He called each one an "infinitely repellent particle," meaning that it was constructed to stand on its own, not lean lazily against its neighbors. If he had come clean and billed himself as an aphorist, that would have been dandy. Yet he was an essayist, who looked both to Michel de Montaigne and to the homily-speckled format of the sermon for his model. This created an odd friction in his work. The essayistic form usually depended on logic and linearity, while the self-sufficient nature of his sentences worked in the opposite direction. Emerson glued them together, and they kept flying apart.

This is all by way of saying that the essays, for which he is best known, can be tough sledding for a modern reader. They move in mysterious ways. They decline to hold your hand or pat you on the back. They revel in pretzel-shaped paradox. They practically invite you to pry loose the incandescent material—to make up a private anthology of the most explosive bits and leave the rest behind. No wonder Emerson himself described his creations as "anecdotes of the intellect, a sort of Farmer's Almanac of mental moods."

It's worth persisting. These are, let's recall, the essays that electrified Henry David Thoreau, Walt Whitman, Margaret Fuller, Friedrich Nietzsche, Emily Dickinson, and William James (for whom Emerson was not merely a spiritual godfather but an actual godfather). A prolonged dip into "The American Scholar" or "Self-Reliance" or "Circles" remains an adventure. You get the glimmers of ecstasy, the tonic zing of the best sentences, and a superb dose of Yankee swagger as Emerson dispatches one sacred cow after another, often by the herd.

All of those sentences required time. Emerson's method was to pile them up in his journals, which he kept for six decades. Here was an enormous catchment for whatever he thought, dreamed, read, experienced, lamented. He once described the journals as a "savings bank," but they were more like an open-pit mine—a giant deposit of unprocessed ore that supplied most of the rhetorical gold in his published work. In many cases he buffed and reshaped this raw material before embedding it in an essay. But often he transplanted it intact—and just as often, the original formulations were superior in terms of speed, immediacy, and self-disclosure. I think Emerson recognized the usefulness of having both a private voice and a public voice. Talking to yourself was a spiritual excavation, full of intensity and acrobatics, while talking to others forced you to connect.

And connect he did. The conventional emphasis on Emerson as a solitary—a man most at home in his America-sized mind—shouldn't blind us to the fact that he was an extremely public figure. For almost fifty years, he was a star of the national lecture circuit. He spoke at theaters, libraries, hospitals, and churches. On other occasions, he plied his trade in ramshackle prairie venues, and sometimes acted as his own booking agent and producer. In a good year he might give as many as eighty lectures, charging from ten to fifty dollars a pop.

Two things should be kept in mind here. First, at the time of Emerson's birth, the United States was still a country starved for entertainment. In part this can be chalked up to the pleasure-hating impulses of the Puritans, who were nonetheless so desperate for titillation that they sought it out in high-minded tracts and sermons. By the 1830s, when Emerson began touring, things had loosened up considerably. Yet the itinerant lecturer remained a primary form of entertainment for most Americans, delivering something halfway between a TED talk and a sermon, with a dash of standup comedy tossed in for good measure. Emerson was among the top attractions, with a sporting attitude toward the often primitive amenities in the American interior, not to mention the brutal winter and some very tough audiences. "The climate and people," he noted, "are a new test for the wares of a man of letters." It was a test he was determined to pass, as he read his latest lecture to one frontier focus group after another.

Some of these listeners felt their patience fraying by the end of the evening. Rutherford B. Hayes, the future U.S. president who attended several of Emerson's lectures during the 1850s, conceded that he held the "undivided attention of his audience"—but that "there is no such thing as one of his thoughts following from another." Yet Emerson's popularity was no fluke. Newspapers regularly described his platform manner in ecstatic terms: he was, in the eyes of one such reviewer, a "spiritual prism though which we see all beautiful rays of immaterial existences."

. . .

What was he talking about, both on the page and on the stage? Emerson addressed a great many topics in his career. He shared his thoughts on nature, beauty, language, ethics, history, politics, friendship, poetry, power, money, slavery, fate. What's more, these topics were fluid—they had a kaleidoscopic tendency to intermingle in the author's mind. This wasn't from lack of focus. No, Emerson believed that grasping the manifold and metaphoric connections *between* things was the whole point of thinking in the first place. "Man is an analogist," he wrote, "and studies relations in all objects. He is placed in the center of beings, and a ray of relation passes from every other being to him."

The urge to trace these relations was, for him, an old one. Emerson had been a metaphor-besotted creature since he was a child. One of his first surviving letters, sent to his brother William when Emerson was eleven years old, consists largely of pictograms—what we would now call emojis. "Hope" is a little man with a hoop. "I" is represented repeatedly by an eye, peering off to the side or straight at the reader.

I don't want to make too much of this youthful frolic. Still, it looks ahead to a mature writer who enshrined metaphor as the primary tool of perception. Everything was itself and something else. The material world, what we agreed to call reality, could never be exhausted, since its every fact pointed to some corresponding fact in the spiritual realm. In the wrong hands (and sometimes those were Emerson's hands), this could turn into a strategy of avoidance. You could dodge difficult questions by alchemizing them into something else—into metaphorical moonshine. For the most part, though, it made his prose magical, with an almost surreal leaping from limb to limb of the author's argument.

That argument, more often than not, was about the self. Emerson certainly wrote about all those topics listed above. But once they went through the spiritual prism, they often turned into sustained conversations about the one and the many, the soul and society. His mightiest topic was "the infinitude of the private man." Every human being, Emerson insisted, should negotiate terms with the great world, and not rely on the standardized contract handed down by the church, the state, or the village elders.

This conviction was not his alone. By the early 1830s, there was a loose network of kindred spirits scattered throughout New England. Many, like Emerson, were Boston clergymen who had grown impatient

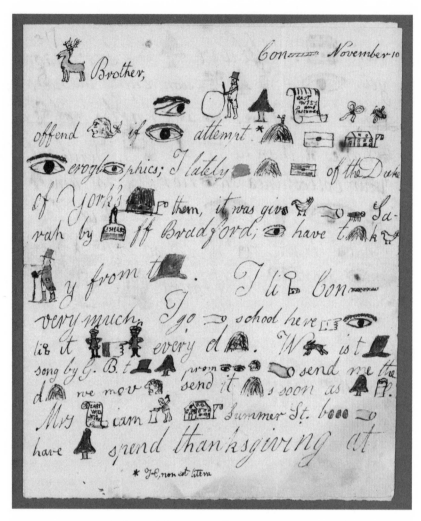

FIGURE 1. First page of RWE's letter to William Emerson, November 10, 1814.
Courtesy of Emerson Family Correspondence, Houghton Library,
Harvard University, MS Am 1280.226 (Box 23: 2012).

fill you in on the nature of reality. You looked at it directly, perhaps squinting a little at that unaccustomed brilliance, and described it in your own words. There was a truth-seeking impulse in every sentence Emerson ever wrote, and that may be his greatest gift to posterity.

. . .

How does one recount Emerson's story? The best idea, I think, is to take a leaf from the man himself. Emerson, an insatiable devourer of books, eventually concluded that most of them could be boiled down to a few key passages. "I read for the lusters," he confessed—for the most brilliant and revealing snippets, which contained the essential character of the book in miniature.

He came to view human lives in the same way. A handful of episodes, and not necessarily the most conventional or melodramatic ones, told you all that you needed to know. "So much of our time is preparation," he wrote, "so much is routine, and so much retrospect, that the pith of each man's genius contracts itself to a very few hours." The task of the biographer, then, is to locate those golden hours, using one's own sensibility as a kind of divining rod.

There is always a place for the giant chronicle, with its exhaustive piling up of incident and atmosphere—an alp of actuality. Indeed, I have relied on several such books to produce my own, have stood on the shoulders of many excellent predecessors. But my method has been different. I have gravitated toward those elements of Emerson's life that spoke to me most directly. Sometimes these were biographical episodes: his abandonment of the pulpit, for example, or his first marriage, or his trip to Egypt in the wake of a disastrous house fire in 1872. Other times I have proceeded thematically, tracing the filament of friendship or love or political activism throughout the length of Emerson's life.

And sometimes, of course, I have zoomed in on what he wrote. My approach to Emerson's work, like my approach to his life, has been selective. I have walked the reader through the essays and lectures that electrified me the most. I wanted to convey not just the meaning of these magnificent texts but the feeling of them. I wanted to get down the sensation of Emerson's language pouring into your brain, the elation and puzzlement and playfulness, and also the communion: the eerie sense that he is speaking *to* you and *through* you. But here too, I was guided by instinct, and felt free to omit much. I have read him, in other words, for the lusters.

Being selective, I should note, is not the same thing as damage control. I have not papered over Emerson's failures. I have tried to explore his foibles, his blind spots, his complacencies, especially because some of them crept into the culture-at-large. What fascinates me, though, is what we can actually learn from those failures.

A conspicuous example would be Emerson's attitude toward the abolitionist movement, which he initially dismissed as a soapbox for virtue-signaling egomaniacs. His early disdain for such activism is enough to make the contemporary reader cringe. What we observe in the end, though, is the slow awakening of a political conscience—Emerson's dawning recognition that he could no longer stay on the Transcendental sidelines. It is, I think, a lesson for our own cultural moment. We are all implicated in the agonies of the age. How we cope with them is an individual matter—some plunge right in, others test the water endlessly with a timid toe—but sooner or later every one of us will be immersed. To quote Emerson, speaking during the annus horribilis of 1851, when the Fugitive Slave Act had cemented the role of New England as human chattel's accomplice and enabler: "The last year has forced us all into politics, and made it a paramount duty to seek what it is often a duty to shun." He did his duty. Will we do ours?

None of this is to suggest that Emerson was a plaster saint. Nor did he conceive of biography as a cosmetic exercise—quite the opposite. In an 1839 letter to Margaret Fuller, he encouraged his dear friend to work on her abandoned life of the German polymath Johann Wolfgang von Goethe. Emerson insisted that a writer must never be intimidated by her subject. No, she should regard him as a peer, or as a hostile witness whose testimony must be taken with several large grains of salt. Some "wicked twitting and whipping" might be required. "On these conditions," he assured Fuller, "no subject is dangerous: all subjects are equivalent."

Despite this call to arms, Fuller never wrote her life of Goethe. Emerson did write his. It's the final chapter of *Representative Men* (1850), in which Goethe brings up the rear after Plato, Swedenborg, Montaigne, Shakespeare, and Napoleon have been thoroughly frisked by the author. Emerson sees Goethe as a spiritual stenographer, put on earth to notate the sublimities and follies of his era.

Indeed, argues Emerson, such a writer has a symbiotic, yin-and-yang relationship to his subject, and to the entire cosmos. "A man is the faculty of reporting," he declares, "and the universe is the possibility of being reported." No writer could ask for a bigger canvas, or for a more ambitious task. But as I hope to show, it is Emerson himself who is ripe for a fresh report.

1

FINDING A VOICE

When do you become yourself? The question is trickier than it sounds. At birth, we are presented with the raw materials of identity. But these are almost random. They are winnings from a game of genetic roulette, just waiting to be cashed out. What comes next is a long trek down the wind tunnel of childhood, the buffeting impacts of family and society and religion, the sculpting of a generic human being into an individual soul: the square peg that will suddenly fit into no hole but its own. This is a gradual process, to be sure. It may take years, or even decades, before the beauty and strangeness of a personality begin to shine through the chrysalis of the ordinary. You may need to surrender to everybody else's notion of yourself—a kind of informal, spirit-squashing referendum—before you can figure out who you are.

That was certainly the case with Ralph Waldo Emerson. The expectation, from the moment he was born in 1803, was that he would become a minister. It was more or less the family business. The Emersons, as well as the Bulkeley and Bliss and Moody clans, all of them related by marriage, had supplied the pulpits of New England for seven generations. Waldo, as he was usually called, had an impressive pantheon peering over his shoulder, many of them vigorous participants in the theological disputes of the era.

There was, for example, the towering figure of Peter Bulkeley, the founder of Concord and a major architect of Puritan society, who set down the contractual relationship between God and man in *The Gospel-Covenant* (1646). There was Samuel Moody, who gave away his wife's only pair of shoes to a beggar and loudly upbraided any parishioner who dared to sneak out of church early: "Come back, you graceless sinner, come back!" There was Daniel Bliss, who invited the volcanic British evangelist George Whitefield to speak from his Concord pulpit in 1741. Bliss was described as a "flame of fire," and it's fair to say that the Great Awakening, which saw Whitefield preaching to enraptured crowds with a sobbing Jonathan Edwards at his feet, did not favor tepid personalities.

In this sense, Waldo might easily be viewed as a culmination: an heirloom product bred from the finest cultivar in the New World. That's how he was seen by Henry James, a generation younger than Waldo and a family friend. "There is an inner satisfaction in seeing so straight, although so patient, a connection between the stem and the flower," the novelist wrote.

What is remarkable, then, is how close Waldo came to dodging the entire enterprise. He spent years engaged in a kind of passive, foot-dragging resistance to the ministry. Why? For one thing, he had a strong ambivalence toward the ancestor cult so common in New England. Much of his family history was conveyed to him by his aunt, Mary Moody Emerson—an amazing figure in her own right, a keeper of the Calvinist flame, and her nephew's most profound spiritual interlocutor for years to come. In her view, the best way to celebrate the family's past was by extending it. You did that by becoming a clergyman.

In Waldo's day as in ours, this kind of pressure had a tendency to backfire. The more he heard about his ancestors, whose piety and vanished perfection he was unlikely to match, the more he recoiled. Not too many years later, he would elevate this distaste for the past into a philosophical principle—into an American credo, which had us living in an eternal present. But in an 1825 journal entry, he mostly sounds bored by his glorious forebears. "It is my own humor to despise pedigree," he writes. Conceding that his aunt had drilled him thoroughly on the topic of family history, he adds: "The dead sleep in their moonless night; my business is with the living."

There was also a real question as to whether Waldo was cut out for the job. He was the second oldest of five Emerson brothers, the others being William, Edward, Charles, and Bulkeley. (Another brother, John

Clarke, had died in 1807 at the age of eight, while Emerson's two sisters, Phebe and Mary Caroline, both perished as toddlers.) Aside from Bulkeley, who had a learning disability and spent much of his life farmed out to relatives and institutions, all of the brothers were viewed as prodigies. Waldo, however, struck many as the runt of the litter. He had a sort of precocious gravity that impressed adults, but his peers found him dreamy and withdrawn.

At Harvard College, which he entered in 1817 at the age of fourteen, the tall, skinny, sandy-haired Waldo was an indifferent student. The accolades he did win, such as class poet, often came to him by default: a half dozen other students had already declined the post. He had recently begun his journal—the massive project that would serve him for six decades as a sounding board, confessional, and prose laboratory. For now, however, he filled its pages with the sort of self-excoriation that would have gratified his Puritan ancestors. As he gloomily wrote on October 25, 1820: "I find myself often idle, vagrant, stupid, & hollow. This is somewhat appalling & if I do not discipline myself with diligent care I shall suffer severely from remorse & the sense of inferiority hereafter."

At college, he already had a sense of vocation: he wanted to be a writer. This flew in the face of his family's wishes. Yet it seemed as though he might get a reprieve, since the Emersons had already pinned their hopes on Waldo's industrious older brother William.

It should be noted that the Emersons were strapped for cash. The Reverend William Emerson, the paterfamilias and pastor of Boston's First Church, had died in 1811 at age 42, leaving the family with little means of support. It would have been cheaper for William to attend the pokey and provincial Harvard Divinity School, which had been founded just a few years earlier. Instead, the clan scraped together all its pennies and sent him off to what was then the powerhouse of theological studies, the University of Göttingen, in Germany.

There William would study a novel academic discipline, the so-called Higher Criticism. This was an attempt to treat the Bible as a literary and historical artifact—to compartmentalize its status as a sacred text and assume it had been written by regular people. Its leading light, the tireless scholar Johann Gottfried Eichhorn, dismissed the "merely theological use of the scriptures." He argued that the prophetic authors of the Old Testament, who had supposedly taken dictation from the Almighty, were in fact "altogether human." Here was a thumb in the eye of traditional Christianity, even if its adherents still regarded themselves as fact-finding believers.

Göttingen rubbed William the wrong way. He soon tired of the filth in the streets and the indolent, bearded, billiards-obsessed students, who periodically launched uprisings against the faculty. More to the point, he felt himself sliding into a spiritual crisis. Eichhorn's lectures were all too effective. They had made William doubt the very truths that his Göttingen education was supposed to set in stone. In September 1824, wondering if he would ever be suited to the ministry, he took the obvious step: he set off for Weimar, on foot, to confer with Goethe.

The poet, statesman, and dramatist was then 75, and still served as something of an oracle-at-large. Presented with William's visiting card, he invited him to return later that day. For thirty minutes, he politely listened as William aired his doubts. Then Goethe told him not to worry about the situation—he should simply work out his theological complexities in private, without tipping off his parishioners. How would they ever know? This pragmatic advice was likely shocking to William. In any case, he soon returned to America, his faith further undermined by a stomach-churning ocean voyage, and threw in the towel. The eldest of the Emerson brothers moved to what is now Staten Island, New York, in 1826 and became a lawyer.

. . .

Now it was Waldo's turn. He had been inching in this direction, however reluctantly, for some time. It wasn't an uptick in piety that made him more willing to consider the ministry. It was his hatred of teaching, which he had been doing since his graduation from Harvard in 1821.

The schools tended to the ad hoc and fly-by-night. Sometimes the students were boys, sometimes they were girls, and sometimes the classes took place in the Emerson household. Generally speaking, Waldo was not good at the job. Lacking any gift as a disciplinarian, he was especially shy around the young women whose minds he was supposed to be molding. When they misbehaved, he sent them to the purgatory of his mother's bedroom. As he later recalled, he "had grown up without sisters, and, in my solitary and secluded way of living, had no acquaintance with girls. I still recall my terrors at entering the school; my timidities at French, the infirmities of my cheek, and my occasional admiration of some of my pupils."

Waldo still viewed himself, somewhat apologetically, as a writer. He had yet to abandon the role of the "mock-Poetic Junior" (as he identified himself at Harvard) and aspiring essayist. In November 1822, a year after graduation, he saw his work in print for the first time: an essay on medieval religion in the *Christian Disciple and Theological Review*.

Yet the pressure to mount the pulpit continued, even before the news of William's washout in Göttingen reached the family. Eventually, Waldo was persuaded. In a journal entry on April 18, 1824, he resolved to "dedicate my time, my talents, & my hopes to the Church." Yet he followed up with a long, sober, intensely self-critical assessment of his prospects, which suggests that he took to the ministry by default.

Waldo recognizes that he has a strong imagination, amply documented in the early volumes of his journal. Yet he lacks the sort of raw analytical power he so admires in the British empirical philosophers John Locke and David Hume. They could start with a basic idea—say, Locke's insistence that perception was "the first step and degree toward knowledge, and the inlet of all the materials of it"—and spend an entire book teasing out its implications. Waldo's mind was more wayward and poetical in its workings. Luckily, he argues, a preacher need not possess this mulching-machine level of logical rigor.

So far, so good. But having suggested that his metaphor-making intelligence is suited to the pulpit, he rounds on himself again and ticks off a brutal list of character flaws. He is afflicted with "a sore uneasiness in the company of most men and women, a frigid fear of offending and jealousy of disrespect." Even worse, he has a "propensity to laugh, or rather, snicker." He eats too much. He lacks self-control. These and other flaws make him unsuitable for the law and medicine. By process of elimination, he is left with a single vocation: the ministry. "In Divinity," he writes, "I hope to thrive."

At certain moments, the whole thing reads like a parody of Puritanical self-scrutiny—an effort to rack up bonus points with the Creator, to Whom nothing was more suspicious than an unblemished soul. But Waldo was in earnest, never more so than when he resisted the temptations of pious diction and spoke plainly: "What is called a warm heart, I have not." There is nothing stagey about that sentence. No—for a moment, Waldo simply sounds sad.

He concludes this rueful résumé on a more hopeful note. The ministry, he envisions, will be "my regeneration of mind, manners, inward and outward estate." It will allow him, too, to "put on eloquence as a robe, and by goodness and zeal and the awfulness of Virtue to press and prevail over the false judgments, the rebel passions and corrupt habits of men."

The tone, with its talk of regeneration and virtue, is exactly what the occasion called for. Yet Waldo, whose recent correspondence with his Aunt Mary had been filled with theological jousting, sounds like he's trying to convince himself—to close the deal. Eloquence, that magical ease with language, is something he already possessed, at least in its rudimentary form. But here the word does double duty, standing in for the elegant sermonizing that the Unitarians in particular had made their stock-in-trade. This sort of eloquence Waldo was determined to don like a ministerial robe. If the garment was initially too grand, too roomy, well, he would grow into it.

. . .

Within months of writing those words, Waldo closed the latest School for Young Ladies. He had told Aunt Mary of his intention to study divinity at Harvard, and in theory, this should have warmed the old Calvinist's heart. But she associated the place with the watered-down creed of the Unitarians. It was also infected, she believed, with the twin pestilences of German Idealism and the Higher Critics. The "deep and high theology will prevail," she insisted, in a letter that Waldo carefully copied into his journal, "and the German madness may be cured."

On February 16, 1825, he was officially admitted to the divinity school. The institution itself was still so new that there was hardly any formal curriculum to speak of. Nor did the school grant any degrees. Students mostly read, attended lectures, and got a handle on up-to-date Unitarian thought. The de facto dean, after all, was the pugnacious Andrews Norton, often referred to as the Unitarian Pope, who stoutly rejected the concept of the virgin birth but insisted on the veracity of all the other Biblical miracles.

Almost at once, Waldo's health failed. First a hip problem made him lame—possibly a rheumatic complaint, possibly connected to his cold, damp lodgings on the first floor of Harvard's Divinity Hall. He could, at least, limp to lectures and obtain books from the library. But in March, as he later recorded in an autobiographical note, he "lost the use of my eye[s] for study." For all practical purposes, that is, he went blind. Certainly he could no longer continue his studies, which he now postponed.

Given Waldo's middling-at-best commitment to the ministry, it's hard not to wonder whether his blindness could have been psychosomatic. His first modern biographer, Ralph L. Rusk, speculated in his 1949 life that "an unconscious but positive distaste for formal theology" might have done the trick—a reasonable post-Freudian conjecture. Yet it seems that his maladies were real, and connected to the tuberculosis that afflicted most of his family. Later in 1825, a Boston surgeon operated on one infected eye, then the other. These procedures, which involved puncturing the cornea to relieve the buildup of pressure inside the eyeball, addressed the symptoms rather than the disease itself. Yet they probably offered some temporary relief until the worst of the tubercular episode had passed.

Meanwhile, Waldo withdrew from the divinity school. In what must have struck him as a fantastically dreary development, he retreated in September to Chelmsford, a small village not far from Concord, and resumed his career as a schoolteacher. Squinting from eye strain, limping around the classroom, he oversaw thirty or forty boys. Did he think he was being punished? We don't know, since his vision problems prevented him from writing much in his journal or corresponding.

There were more schools, more pupils, more misery. By the early days of 1826, at least, Waldo's eyes had healed sufficiently for him to resume his journal. "I come with mended eyes to my ancient friend and counselor," he wrote. "Has the interval of silence made the writer wiser?" He included little detail of his daily life, perhaps having nothing to say about the drudgery of teaching. He did, however, begin exploring what he called compensation—the idea that the universe operated on a double-entry system, whereby the books were inevitably balanced.

"Every defect in one manner is made up in another," he declared. "Every suffering is rewarded; every sacrifice is made up; every debt is paid." It was a concept he tinkered with for many years, dedicating an entire essay to it in 1841. In Waldo's mind, it had little to do with the clanking Christian machinery of sin and expiation. Instead he argued that the very universe was self-adjusting, self-correcting, always moving toward a divine equipoise—and that this process trickled down to the tiniest aspects of human life.

No doubt his own misery made this an attractive proposition. We all want to believe that our suffering is somehow useful. We prefer to view it as a karmic or character-building exercise, or a piling-up of raw material that will be transubstantiated into wisdom. Waldo imagined something more. What he envisioned was a cosmic system of checks and balances, and it must have comforted him.

Except when it didn't. He was still prey to what he called the "dangerous empire of human anxieties." He continued his long-distance argument with Aunt Mary about the Higher Critics, whose wrecking-ball effect on his brother's spiritual life had strangely failed to discredit them in Waldo's eyes. The Germans, with the tiny, courteous Eichhorn leading the charge, had revealed some serious cracks in the faith's factual foundations. Their efforts could not be denied, Waldo insisted, even if they encouraged non-believers to write off the Christian tenets as "the most significant testimonies of human folly." It must have been hard for Waldo to keep a foot in both camps—to tip his hat to the Higher Critics while still subscribing to a good many of those Christian tenets. It must have been harder still once he decided to take another shot at the ministry.

To do so, he didn't need a diploma, which Harvard wasn't issuing in any case. He merely needed to be licensed, or "approbated," by the Middlesex Association of Unitarian Ministers, who would examine him and issue a sort of learner's permit. This would allow the fledgling minister, still without any flock of his own, to preach.

His approbation took place on October 10, 1826. A few days later, he preached his first sermon in Waltham, having been invited by his Uncle Samuel Ripley. Just a couple of weeks earlier, he was still agonizing over his chilly pulpit manner. "I was born cold," he lamented in a letter to Aunt Mary. "My bodily habit is cold. I shiver in and out; don't heat to the good purposes called enthusiasm a quarter so quick and kindly as my neighbors." Enthusiasm—meaning those evangelical outbursts of affection for the Creator, but also certainty, commitment, spiritual ardor—would take a while for Waldo to develop. But he delivered a solid performance to an audience generously sprinkled with his relatives.

In fact, Waldo had been mulling over his text ("Pray without ceasing," from Thessalonians) since June. Desires, wishes—these, he told his listeners, were also a kind of prayer. Men's motives, what Waldo called "the character, the secret self," were impossible for their peers to discern. Yet we were more or less broadcasting our cravings to God on a continuous basis. While the Almighty might well be surrounded by a noisy static of such entreaties, He surely heard them all. "We must be aware, then," concluded Waldo, "what we wish."

. . .

What did Waldo wish for? It's fair to say that he desired several things at once. He wanted to be a dutiful son and a resentful apostate. He wanted a pulpit and a way to escape it. He got at least one of these wishes within two weeks of his debut in Waltham, when his health collapsed again.

This time his lungs were afflicted. The family immediately feared consumption, as tuberculosis was then called—and with good reason. The disease was rampant in Boston, where half the population was infected (although many were simply carriers, who suffered none of the debilitating symptoms). Tuberculosis had long tormented the Emerson family, having already killed Waldo's father and his brother John Clarke. For that matter, his brother Edward had recently exhibited some of the telltale signs, and been sent on a recuperative tour of southern Europe.

He returned to Cambridge on October 19, just as Waldo began complaining of chest pains.

These he had sketched out in a letter to William shortly before. "In my vehement desire to preach I have recently taken into my bosom certain terrors," he explained, "not for my hip which does valiantly, nor my eyes which deserve commendation, but for my lungs without whose aid I cannot speak, and which scare me." His panic was genuine. It's possible that some of his chest pains were psychosomatic—a bout of stage fright induced by his first appearances in the pulpit. Quite reasonably, though, the family was taking no chances. Waldo would undergo treatment right away.

What *that* meant was a little fuzzy. Throughout the nineteenth century, tuberculosis was the most lethal ailment in the Western world, accounting for at least a quarter of all adult mortality and quite likely more. It was called the "white plague" or, more poetically, the "captain of death." In 1722, a pioneering English doctor named Benjamin Marten was the first to speculate, in his *New Theory of Consumptions*, that the disease might be caused by "wonderfully minute living creatures." Alas, nobody would follow up on this microbial theory for many decades. It wasn't until 1882 that the *Mycobacterium tuberculosis* cells were actually stained and identified.

In the meantime, the bewildered medical establishment recommended a regimen of bloodletting, expectorants, warm air, and vigorous physical activity. While these measures did help a small fraction of patients, the disease was increasingly shrouded in a Romantic mist. It was billed as the tragic assassin of the young, the bright, the beautiful. Even the supposedly scientific *Encyclopedia Britannica*, in its first edition of 1768, noted that the typical victim possessed a "merry cheerful disposition," as if that had anything to do with the mounting death toll.

Waldo, then, would be packed off to a warmer climate. On November 25 he boarded the *Clematis*, bound for Charleston, South Carolina. From there he moved on to St. Augustine, Florida, which must have struck him as extraterrestrial. Overgrown with the sort of tropical vegetation that plays havoc with a New Englander's nervous system, the muggy little community had been American territory for only six years.

Prior to that, the Spanish had mainly run the place, and the two iron cages in which they had suspended criminals, allowing them to starve to death in full view of the public, still hung by the city gates.

In the streets Waldo saw Spaniards, Blacks, Native Americans, and invalids like himself, who had come for the restorative heat and never left. The houses lacked chimneys. The animals lacked decent hay— "because," Waldo noted, "there is no scythe in St. Augustine, and if there were, no man who knows how to use one." Oranges essentially grew wild, a rebuff to the rigorous habits of Yankee cultivation. As far as Waldo could tell, nobody seemed to have a job:

> The Americans live on their offices. The Spaniards keep billiard tables, or, if not, they send their negroes to the mud to bring oysters, or to the shore to bring fish, & the rest of the time fiddle, masque, & dance. The Catholic clergyman lately represented at a masquerade the character of a drunken sailor with the most laudable fidelity.

In short, it was an anti-Concord, or anti-Boston, where the beams of Protestant goodness had failed to penetrate. His gibe at the Catholic clergy (and there were others) is especially telling. The Irish had yet to arrive in New England in large numbers, and the Pope was regarded as the devil in very fancy dress.

Waldo strolled on the beach, batting at oranges with a stick. He compared himself to a barnacle, unable to move and with no pleasure but imagining the joys of his fellow barnacles. "Sometimes I sail in a boat," he wrote William, "and sometimes I sit in a chair."

He sounds almost as sleepy as the locals, scribbling now and then at sermons he had little hope of delivering. If his health had never improved, perhaps he might have lived out his life there, a scowling, sunburned, Puritan eccentric hobbling around on a cane, lecturing his manservant about the benefits of nonstop prayer. An anti-Emerson— it's an amazing thought. There were, however, a couple of factors that kept him from lapsing too deeply into his tropical stupor.

One was slavery. In his journal, he had denounced the practice since he was a teenager, but in abstract terms—after all, slavery had been outlawed in Massachusetts in 1783, and he had encountered few if any enslaved people. In mid-February, however, he was invited to attend a meeting of the local Bible Society in a municipal building. Thanks to what Waldo called an "unfortunate arrangement," a slave auction was going on in the adjacent yard. He recorded his impressions of the whole queasy-making event in a pocket notebook:

> One ear therefore heard the glad tidings of great joy, whilst the other was regaled with "Going, gentlemen, going!" And almost without changing our position we might aid in sending the Scriptures into Africa, or bid for "four children without the mother" who have been kidnapped therefrom.

His tone is more ironical than outraged, and it would be a mistake to think that this ugly incident turned him into an abolitionist. But my guess is that it lodged in his memory. Surely it's no accident that on the same page, Waldo took the Bible Society to task for its hypocrisy. At its annual meeting, just a week later, two members got into a fistfight and had to be forcibly separated. Also, the society's president had recently been denounced from the pulpit for his foul mouth—and by a Methodist, whose coreligionists, Waldo recorded on the next page, supposedly jumped "about on all fours, imitating the barking of dogs."

. . .

The other factor that kept him afloat was Achille Murat. Waldo met this new friend at the pink boardinghouse where they both took their meals. It would be hard to imagine a human being more radically unlike himself—here, in fact, was the *real* anti-Emerson.

Murat was the twenty-six-year-old nephew of Napoleon Bonaparte. His mother was the emperor's sister, his father an intrepid cavalry officer whose heroics had caused him to be anointed King of Naples. After Waterloo, this nominal monarch was executed by his subjects, and Achille eventually emigrated to the United States, where he spent some time exploring the country. Resembling his uncle, right down to the aquiline nose and high, dome-like forehead, Murat sometimes traveled under an assumed name, not wanting to be pestered by gawking fans (or

foes) of Old Boney. By the time he met Waldo, he had bought a plantation near Tallahassee, Florida—and completed his transformation into
an American by marrying a descendant of George Washington.

But it wasn't only his lineage, with its whiff of comic opera, that qualified Murat as Waldo's opposite number. He was a true eccentric: a habitual
nudist with an aversion to bathing, who didn't like to change his clothes
(when he wore them) or wash his feet until his shoes were literally disin-
tegrating. He slept on a rough mattress filled with Spanish moss and dined
on turkey vulture, owl, crow, alligator, lizard, and the occasional rattle-
snake. Perhaps he considered himself an American Adam, a noble savage
doing what came naturally. But even if the prim and proper Waldo had
been able to take all this in stride—to simply accept his new friend as a
tree-hugging, French-speaking brother from another planet—there was
still something else to deal with. Murat, you see, was an atheist.

Waldo had jousted with Calvinists, Congregationalists, Unitarians.
He had tested his beliefs, even as they diverged from the Christian
mainstream, against those of other believers. Arguing with an atheist,
however, was something new for him.

His affection for Murat is obvious. Indeed, in a letter to Aunt Mary,
he described him in terms that suggest a low-level infatuation. "A new
event is added to the quiet history of my life," he wrote in his journal.
Until now, he confessed, he had regarded atheists as chimerical creatures, on par with unicorns or mermaids. Now he had encountered one
in the flesh—a colorful extrovert who also happened to be a "disbe-
liever in the existence, and of course, in the immortality of the soul. My
faith in these points is strong and I trust, as I live, indestructible."

The two may have broached some of these topics in the pink house.
They certainly did so during their ocean voyage from St. Augustine to
Charleston, which took place at the end of March. And you can sense a
new spirit creeping into Waldo's journals and letters, which owes something to his conversations with Murat.

Not that he became an atheist. His faith was unconventional, he delighted in baiting Aunt Mary with the Higher Critics or with David
Hume's miracle-debunking polemics—but he was seldom tempted by
the abyss of unbelief. It struck him as empty, self-nullifying. Yet the

beautiful thing about Waldo's mind, which was now making a great leap forward into early maturity, was that he would entertain any thought. There was nothing dutiful about this process. He wasn't paying lip service to ideas that he secretly despised. He was ingesting them, putting them in his own words, which themselves had begun to soar beyond the conventional formulations in his earlier journals.

I have already quoted those journals several times, to give a sense of how Waldo's mind worked. Early on, we hear the smart, bookish, anxious, playful sound of a young man's voice—an adolescent's voice, really, although one so thoroughly marinated in the Scripture and the classics that he can *sound* older by dint of ventriloquism. From time to time, there is a glimmer of eloquence, which seems to take even Waldo by surprise. But mostly the tone has something aspirational to it, as though he were standing on tiptoes.

Now that was changing. His homeopathic dose of atheism, and perhaps the warming effect of communion with another person, had shaken something loose. An idea like compensation, which had earlier seemed like a theological parlor trick, turned into a tool for reconciling metaphysical opposites:

> It is a near neighborhood, that of greatness of destiny and lowness of lot; that of mind and matter; that of man and God. It is like our natural existence. Though we be pigmies of a few feet, it is not a dungeon wall which confines us to the earth. There is nothing between us and the infinite Universe.

You can hear more than a touch of self-conscious grandeur, but also a certainty, a sense of power. As his low mood lifted, so did his sense of being marooned.

Here, too, his friendship with Murat may have had a ripple effect. His pain, his ruined hopes, his humiliating dependence on other people—these no longer isolated him but seemed paradoxically to deepen his connection to others, and to the universe. He was more alive to *feeling*, and saw both his emotional and spiritual life irradiated by this new intensity. Sufferings like his own, Waldo wrote, "suggest the possibility of relations more intimate and more awful than friendship and love.

They bring to light a system of feelings whose existence was not suspected before."

The voice is unmistakably his own, right down to the twofold sense of *awful*, with its slight nod to Waldo's old frigidity. It is a marvelous thing to see a writer discover who he is—even an approximation of who he is, or is on the way to becoming. For the reader, the sensation is joyful, uncanny, intimate, perhaps because in understanding somebody so completely, we have the reflexive (if ghostly) feeling of being understood ourselves. The recognition seems mutual. It is, weirdly, like falling in love.

2

THE LIVES OF OTHERS

The two men left St. Augustine for Charleston on March 28, 1827. Waldo's idea was to gradually make his way back to Concord, while Murat was en route to see his uncle, Joseph Bonaparte, in New Jersey. (That's right: Napoleon's brother, the former King of Spain, lived in New Jersey, near Bordentown.) Normally the ocean trip took two days. But a violent storm, followed by a week of eerie calm, meant that the travelers did not arrive in port for nine days.

During that time, Waldo and Murat engaged in nonstop theological debate. There is, alas, no transcript of their conversations—not even some real-time jottings in Waldo's pocket notebook. But it's clear that the topic was God: his presence or absence.

A letter Murat sent a few months later suggests that the argument was a draw, although he confessed he had been moving in Waldo's direction. First, however, they needed to test the limits of "an absolute notion of truth." To that end, Murat planned to write a monograph in November. He meanwhile urged Waldo to open a Unitarian church in Tallahassee, where he could inject some reason and morality into that whirlpool of fanaticism. With that, he vanished from Waldo's life. The two never met again.

Yet the effects of the friendship—the way it had accelerated whatever change was already underway in Waldo's consciousness—were longer lasting. He returned to Charleston with a sort of superhuman confidence. On April 17, he wrote:

The night is fine; the stars shed down their severe influence upon me, and I feel a joy in my solitude that the merriment of vulgar society can never communicate. There is a pleasure in the thought that the particular tone of my mind at this moment may be new in the universe; that the emotions of this hour may be peculiar and unexampled in the whole eternity of moral being. I lead a new life.

From there, he slowly made his way north. His pace was dictated by the weather, since he was trying to protect his lungs from the cold. Whether they were healed was hard to determine. He sent mixed messages to his family, alternately depicting himself as a perfect physical specimen or a feeble, death-haunted wreck.

"I am not sure that I am a jot better or worse than when I left home in November," he wrote Aunt Mary on May 15. True, he had managed to deliver a sermon on Sunday morning without any major difficulty. Yet his breathing remained labored: "I am still saddled with the villain stricture & perhaps he will ride me to death."

Waldo continued his northerly journey through one cold front after another. He passed through Philadelphia and New York City, where he boarded a steamboat for Boston. Off the coast of Rhode Island, he realized that his idol Daniel Webster was on the same vessel.

Webster, whose speeches he had memorized as a child, was just then wrapping up his second term in the U.S. House of Representatives, and would return to the capital as a Massachusetts senator later that year. He was also, at the exact moment Waldo observed him, puking energetically over the ship's rail. Perhaps it shook Waldo up to see this father figure—whose law office happened to employ his brother Edward—in distress. In any case, such ancestral imperatives were clearly on his mind by the time he reached Concord, which he later dubbed "the quiet fields of my fathers." The prodigal son had returned.

His family was temporarily billeted at the Old Manse, the Emersonian mother ship built by his grandfather, the Reverend William Emerson, in 1770. He had spent many a childhood summer there, in the gray clapboard house overlooking the Concord River. Now Waldo was moved by the familiar sights, sounds, scents. He stood beside the "blue wonder" of the river, which was the same and different: "Look, here he is unaltered, save that now / He hath broke his banks and flooded all the vales / With his redundant waves."

The poem, inscribed in his journal on June 27, smacks of William Wordsworth, who struck Waldo as *too* enamored of nature. The English poet, he complained, would pick apart a rose or a moonlit evening "and pounce on the pleasurable element he is sure is in them, like the little boy who cut open his drum to see what made the noise." This analytic impulse turned Waldo off. Like Wordsworth, however, he took his cues from the landscape, which suggested that he, too, was different and the same.

He was wiser, he thought, and had successfully run the gauntlet of illness, depression, and doubt. His new life was before him. And still, there was something infantilizing about his return to Concord. To go home is to be a child again:

> The stream, the trees, the grass, the sighing wind,
> All of them utter sounds of admonishment
> And grave parental love.

. . .

Waldo rented another room at Divinity Hall, but spent much of the summer out in Concord. Sometimes he was joined by William, Edward, and Charles. There he roamed the fields, picked whortleberries along the swampy margins of the sluggish river, lolled on the calico couch, and forced himself to write some new sermons.

For these, he finally had a regular audience. The First Church in Boston—his father's old congregation—had invited him to preach throughout the summer while the regular pastor was away. He turned to his journals for material. Waldo was not prepared to unleash his spiritual epiphanies of the spring upon his unsuspecting listeners. He did manage to sneak his doctrine of compensation into one sermon, noting that "no man can enrich himself by doing wrong, or impoverish himself by doing right." Presumably his audience took this as a spiritual directive, not a description of the real world.

In another sermon, on the virtues of self-mortification, he seemed to allude to his recent ophthalmological woes: "The tender eye of the mind is dazzled by excessive sunshine." Yet Waldo mainly stuck to the company line. Often he stressed the *character* of Jesus—the human qualities, as opposed to the wonder-working powers—which was standard procedure for the hyperrational Unitarians.

In this way the weeks passed. His return to Divinity Hall did not mean that Waldo would immerse himself in theological minutiae. Indeed, as he told Aunt Mary, "My eyes are not so strong as to let me be learned." This may have been a dodge, by a man who was still deeply ambivalent about his unfolding career. In any case, his focus was on preaching rather than immersion in biblical tracts, and his pinch-hitting at the First Church soon led to invitations from other ministers throughout the region, usually for a fee of ten dollars.

He preached in Greenfield, Lenox, New Bedford, Northampton, Waltham, and Harvard (not the college, but the hamlet where his father had begun his career). He was generally well received. By February 1828, his cousin Samuel Ripley was informing Aunt Mary that Waldo was "the most popular preacher among the candidates [for parishes], and all he wants is health to be fixed at once in Boston." He did in fact receive a small flurry of offers during the winter, but declined them all. For just a little longer, he preferred to remain his own man, galloping from one pulpit to the next, then returning to his room at Divinity Hall.

He hadn't, it should be stressed, turned into a showboat. He didn't turn cartwheels or tell jokes to the congregation. In fact, his personality still struck some observers as impressively wooden. Frederic Henry Hedge, a scholar of German literature and Transcendentalist who met Waldo during his Divinity Hall days, recalled that his speech was slow and that he never interrupted. Even his movements, Hedge said, were a little plodding: "No one, I think, ever saw him run."

Any reader of Waldo's letters and journals will find this description hard to believe. Especially when communicating with his brothers, he is warm, wound-up, almost ostentatiously silly. The words pour out of him faster than he can write them down, and there's a fizziness, a kind of tickling carbonation, to his thoughts.

Such a sharp division between inner and outer life, between the private and public personae, is hardly unheard of. What makes it striking is that during these same months, Waldo regarded *himself* as a sucker for frivolity. He liked nothing more, he insisted, than a "gossiping hour where the talk has been mere soap bubbles." Which was the real Waldo? Could the two be reconciled, or were we all divided creatures to the very end, revealing just a fraction of ourselves to other human beings?

He addressed this issue in one of his oddest letters ever, sent to his brother Charles on a frigid night in Northampton. "I will test the force of my love for you, O plaything," he begins, "& see if it can make of myself what true love should, a little heaven below." His endearments can be confusing. We need to bear in mind that male friendship of the era often operated in an effusive and even erotic register. Waldo wasn't flirting any more than his hero Daniel Webster was when he addressed many of his correspondents as "my lovely boy."

In the wake of his encounter with Murat, however, Waldo was certainly wondering what sort of intimacy was possible between two people. Perhaps he wondered whether it even existed. His immersion in the British empiricists George Berkeley and David Hume, who suggested that human beings might well be imprisoned in their separate silos of consciousness, seemed to buttress his own sense of isolation:

> As you exist to yourself & as you exist to me, you are two persons, darling. I, as may be proved, have no knowledge, &, of course, no care of thy real existence, thy consciousness. I know not what thou art. You may be full of pains or hypocrisies or demons. You may be conscious to worlds of thought & being, whose doors are shut on me.

Waldo's sense that other lives were essentially unknowable—even the lives of his brothers, whom he knew better than anybody else—was confirmed by a disaster just a few months later. In May 1828, his brother Edward suffered a nervous collapse. The family had been concerned that he was stretching himself too thin, working himself to a frazzle in

Webster's law office. His tuberculosis scare only deepened these anxieties. Yet they were still shocked when, during the third week of May, Edward came downstairs for breakfast at the Old Manse and launched a stream of mockery at his grandfather-by-marriage Ezra Ripley. He followed this with an elaborate prayer on behalf of his grandfather and mother. They had gone crazy, Edward told the Lord, and he begged for their sanity to be restored.

For a short while, Edward seemed to recover his wits. He was advised to take it easy and "not touch a book for a year" (a scenario that Waldo thought impossible). By the end of June, however, this bookish and brittle figure had unraveled again. Soon Waldo and two companions were transporting him by closed carriage to the McLean Asylum near Boston, which had opened its doors just a decade earlier.

There Edward joined Bulkeley, who had been deposited in the hospital several weeks before by his current custodians. His behavior had evidently improved since then. Still, Waldo must have been struck by the oddity of two Emerson brothers in the same asylum: it was a near neighborhood indeed, that of the golden child and the benighted black sheep. Bulkeley was soon discharged. Edward, meanwhile, remained in a state of frenzy. He threw his clothes and belongings out the window and rolled on the floor with his eyes screwed shut for thirty minutes at a time.

Waldo could not make sense of this transformation. The pathos and perplexity were stunning to him: "Edward the admired learned eloquent thriving boy—a maniac." Compensation was of no use here. Neither was Calvinism: Had Edward really earned his fate? Or worse, had he been written off by a cruelly indifferent Creator as a kind of collateral damage? It is humiliating to be handed the finest cognitive tools of your era and to discover they are worthless.

Yet Waldo felt himself to be strangely inoculated against whatever had destroyed his brother. The Emersonian disease—some combination of ardor, intensity, fanaticism—was unlikely to afflict him. "I have so much mixture of silliness in my intellectual frame," he wrote, "that I think Providence has tempered me against this." He must have known that to some degree, this was a silly argument. His flippant speech, his blushes and giggles and indolent movements, were an unlikely means of salvation.

. . .

On July 14, Waldo wrote William to say that had seen Edward at the hospital and found him calm and pliable. He added that through "the whole of August I supply for an indefinite term Mr Ware's pulpit."

This was Henry Ware Jr., the ginger-haired pastor of the Second Church, who was ailing at the time. At first Waldo hesitated to take the job. He suspected that Ware might not recover and that he would be appointed to the pulpit straightaway—stuck, that is, with a congregation of his own and little latitude for that life-saving silliness. But he was offered sixty dollars for four sermons and reluctantly accepted.

He preached at the Second Church throughout the summer and fall. He visited Edward, finding him one day improved, another in the throes of his own Calvinist calculations: "His present idea is that he is suffering punishment for great offences." By December it seemed likely that Ware would be stepping down to take a post at the Harvard Divinity School. Waldo, in a mixture of scrupulousness and self-preservation, thought he should make himself scarce, not wanting the job by default. Perhaps he didn't want it at all. So he hemmed and hawed, trying to evade his familial fate at the very moment he was about to fulfill it.

But Ware had designated him as heir apparent. On January 17, 1829, Waldo noted in his journal: "I am called by an ancient and respectable church to become its pastor." The Second Church was indeed ancient and respectable. It had been presided over by the Puritan giant Increase Mather, and then by his son Cotton Mather, the pro-vaccination and anti-witch crusader who somehow found time among his pastoral duties to write some 450 books and pamphlets. The church was a substantial, if secondary, pinnacle in the landscape of New England Christianity. It was also, by now, in a slightly down-at-the-heels North End neighborhood. There were saloons, of the type frequented by sailors from the nearby wharves, and there were brothels (ditto).

It was, in other words, a less prestigious post than the one his father William Emerson had occupied at the First Church. No matter. Waldo accepted the job at an annual salary of $1,200, with the understanding that once he became senior pastor, he would receive an additional $600.

He delivered his first sermon as junior pastor, "The Christian Minister," on March 15, five days after his ordination. In this double-decker address, split between the morning and afternoon services, he assured his listeners that his new responsibilities would include both tending to the flock and elevating their souls. The latter goal, crucially, would be accomplished via eloquence—the "mightiest engine," he told his flock, "which God has put into the hands of man." It had taken Waldo nearly twenty-six years to ascend the pulpit. It would take him less than four to step down.

. . .

I had planned to tell the story of Waldo's serpentine, side-stroking progress toward the ministry in fewer words. It seemed like a simple task. He would defy his fate. I'm not talking about predestination. I didn't feel that God had personally picked him out to be a clergyman— although, if we're going to fall back on the language of theology, I'm all for the Arminians. They were a Protestant sect, founded by the Dutch theologian Jacobus Arminius, who believed in free will. In their view, God extended the possibility of salvation to all of His creatures, and they were welcome to run in the opposite direction.

The Arminians called this, quite beautifully, the doctrine of "resistible grace." Well, Waldo would resist. He would delay and dodge and enroll himself, however unwillingly, in the society of the halt and the blind. He would run out the clock. He would flee to Florida, the polar opposite of everything he knew, and hang around with an atheist. And in the end, he would do what his ancestors had always done: put on the ministerial robe and preach.

But I got sucked into the biographical vortex. There were so many facts. "Our life looks trivial, and we shun to record it," Waldo wrote in "Experience." Yet he had recorded his own life in lavish, almost holographic detail, piling up thousands of pages in his journals and enough letters to fill six stout volumes. There was too much information and it seemed wrong to omit it.

So I succumbed to the forensic fallacy and tried to reconstruct what had happened, and when, and where. In an ideal world, the writer could add so much detail, create such a thick impasto of trivia, that it would become an approximation of the life itself. The reader would need as much time to read it as Waldo had required to live it. But that's not a practical plan, is it?

It is also, on a conceptual level, completely nuts. Waldo was right about the inexplicable lives of others. If we can't truly know the person in the same room, how can we know the person who died more than a century ago in another room, etherized and observed by his anxious son?

It doesn't matter how much evidence we have on hand. The papers, notebooks, letters, journals, all resting in their climate-controlled reliquaries—these do not make a life. The biographer aims at an ever deeper level of detail, assembles each molecule of experience, and gets nowhere. Within minutes of Waldo's death, the First Parish Church down the street began tolling its bell, once for each of his seventy-nine years. That was sensible. But if they had rung the bell for each day of his life, or each hour, or each minute—well, that would have been the biographical approach, ending at last in a blurry, bleary tintinnabulation.

Waldo was disturbed in his youth by David Hume's severing of cause from effect, by his insistence that such things were perceptual accidents. Just as troubling was Hume's skepticism about the neat and predictable passage of time. Later on, however, Waldo seemed halfway to accepting these ideas. Experience was a dream, a shining ether: "We wake and find ourselves on a stair; there are stairs below us, which we seem to have ascended; there are stairs above us, many a one, which go upward and out of sight." I would suggest that we compulsively creep up and down those stairs. On certain occasions, we may slide down the banister.

I don't mean this in a literal sense. I'm talking about perception, and memory, and neurology. There is a clock in our brains, made up of oscillating cells in the upper cortex. They set the tempo for us—a tiny coxswain-by-committee. Yet our sense of time passing is remarkably elastic. It is distorted by, for example, our emotions. One recent study found that fear speeds up the cranial clock, elongating what we actually experience. Shame has the opposite effect. Surely this glorious substance, shrinking and expanding to suit our moods, can be cut and reshuffled, too.

What I'm trying to say is that I can't tell Waldo's story in order. I didn't begin with his birth, and will not conclude with his death. He will die along the way, of course, in his room in Concord, struggling to rise from his bed and (as he told his companions) go home. There will be stretches, too, in which one event obediently follows another. But elsewhere, I will go with my instincts and resist the gravitational pull of chronology, its onward-rushing logic and crisp complacency. I will find Waldo where I find him.

And I will leave things out. Biography, as I noted earlier, is the art of omission. Yet I can't help but mention the fate of the brilliant, broken Edward Emerson, whom we last saw at the McLean Asylum. He was eventually released, drifted back to the law, was wrecked again by tuberculosis, and sent off to recuperate. Waldo lobbied for Florida, where his brother could be near Achille Murat. But Edward insisted on Puerto Rico, sailing there on a brig whose main cargo was a load of mules. From his new home in the tropics he wrote letters, in which his voice seemed to flicker in and out like a failing radio signal. In September 1834 he went for a walk and was caught in the rain, exactly as Waldo would be a half-century later. His cough worsened, his lung was found to be riddled with tubercular clots and abscesses, and he died on October 1. His life is the sort you glean from the index of somebody else's biography—his brother's. Yet he deserves a small book of his own. Don't we all?

3

ONE FIRST LOVE

In the midst of calamity, we manage to find happiness. We assume that one is supposed to cancel out the other. Instead they proceed under their own steam, with a kind of delicate stealth. So it was that Waldo, in the midst of his vocational doubts and his brother's disintegration, fell in love and got married.

Always an awkward social presence, he had little experience of romantic love. During the beginning of his senior year at Harvard, in 1820, he noticed "a strange face in the Freshman class whom I should like to know very much." Waldo carefully omitted the freshman's name from his journal, but subsequent scholarship has filled in the blank: Martin Gay. By October 24, Waldo had developed a serious crush:

> I begin to believe in the Indian doctrine of eye-fascination. The cold blue eye of _____ has so intimately connected him with my thoughts and visions that a dozen times a day, and as often by night, I find myself wholly wrapt up in conjectures of his character and inclinations. We have had already two or three long profound stares at each other. Be it wise or weak or superstitious, I must know him.

He followed this entry with a short poem, presumably addressed to Gay, in which he begged him to "grant me still in joy or sorrow, / In grief or hope, to claim they heart." There is also a paper flap attached to the actual page. When lifted, it reveals a sketch of Gay's profile in India ink. Yet this multimedia love shrine may have caused Waldo some discomfort. In his journal entry of the very next day, he gave himself a Puritanical lashing for his idleness and stupidity.

Presumably this schoolboy crush continued throughout the fall. It was at this very moment that Waldo, never an enthusiastic consumer of novels, developed a lifelong affection for Sir Walter Scott's *The Bride of Lammermoor* (1819). In this tale of doomed romance, the spurned lover dies by falling into a pool of Scottish quicksand—what better reading for an infatuated teenager? Yet Waldo and Gay exchanged no more than a few words. A couple of years later, after his graduation, Waldo noted seeing on campus an "ignotum amicum"—an unknown friend, possibly Gay. He also recorded, then heavily crossed out, a shamefaced confession. "I have a nasty appetite," he wrote, "which I will not gratify."

This is generally understood as an allusion to masturbation. Even the most buttoned-up product of Boston Unitarianism must have known something about that. If he didn't, Waldo could turn for enlightenment to his predecessor in the pulpit Cotton Mather, who had published *The Pure Nazarite: Advice to a Young Man, Concerning an Impiety and Impurity Not Easily to Be Spoken Of* in 1723. It was one among several popular pamphlets on the topic, although possibly the kind of thing you hid down in the root cellar.

In any case, Waldo was not comfortable with his homoerotic impulse. He was aware of it as such, declining to smuggle it in under the banner of chaste affection, and fretted in his journal about the possibility of ending up like King James I, whose dalliances with his male courtiers were widely reported. His solution was to suppress it, or sanitize it by merging it with his exalted notion of friendship.

In that sense, his longing for an ideal companion speaks to our current notion of erotic fluidity. Gender was a somewhat incidental factor, at least at first. Male or female would do, with a slight preference for the former, as he wrote to his brother Charles in 1828, during one of his preaching gigs in New Hampshire. He was sorely lacking such a companion, he explained, who would answer to "the fabulous description of a friend." He felt this absence all the time. "Here in the snows, and at Cambridge in the chambers, I want him," Waldo wrote. "A thousand smart things I have to say which born in silence die in silence for lack of his ear."

He stressed, however, that he would settle for such companionship in female form, too. This was a crucial addendum, and it pointed to a recent change of heart. Waldo had experienced no romantic entanglements during his pursuit of the ministry, unless you count his infatuation with Murat. His teaching days were similarly barren—just some stuttering and Indian eye-fascination with his female pupils.

But in December 1827, while delivering a sermon-for-hire in Concord, New Hampshire, he had met a sixteen-year-old girl named Ellen Tucker. She was pale, dark-haired, narrow-waisted, full of poetry and piety. We have no reason to think they communicated after this initial meeting. But when Waldo returned to "the other Concord" in May and June for additional sermonizing, Ellen, now seventeen, made a huge impression on him.

Waldo being Waldo, the initial clues are endearingly oblique. "It is hard to yoke beauty and wisdom," he wrote in his journal in September. He added that beauty turned a theoretically rational creature (i.e., himself) into a klutz. "In her magic presence," he wrote, "reason becomes ashamed of himself and wears the aspect of Pedantry or Calculation." Ellen's stepfather, Colonel William Austin Kent, had ascended from his humble beginnings as a tinsmith to become a merchant, legislator, military man (hence his title), and pillar of the community. His family was also the driving force behind the town's Unitarian Society. Waldo was therefore a frequent visitor to the household during his trips to New Hampshire, and the opportunities for pedantic or botched conversations can be easily imagined.

Yet something was happening. On December 6, he traveled up to Concord to deliver three more sermons. He brought along Edward, who had been released from McLean and was thought to need a change of scenery. He also carried a meaningful item in his baggage: *Forget Me Not*, a collection of sentimental poetry in a fancy leather binding, inscribed "for ELT."

The details of their high-speed courtship are lost to history. We do know that Edward spent an awful lot of time observing the proceedings of the New Hampshire state legislature—perhaps Waldo suggested that he make himself scarce. In any case, the couple got engaged eleven days later. On December 21, back at Divinity Hall, he sent William an exultant letter notifying him of the engagement. Ellen, he promised, was "very beautiful by universal consent. Her feelings are exceedingly delicate & noble—and I only want you to see her."

. . .

Waldo's engagement to Ellen took place right before Henry Ware offered him the job at the Second Church. As I mentioned earlier, he hesitated. He might have hesitated in any case, valuing as he did his whimsical, whortleberry-collecting freedom—but now he had an additional reason. Ellen's family, too, was scarred by tuberculosis. The disease had killed her father and her brother, and by the time Waldo met her, both her sister and mother were occasionally coughing up blood. Ellen, whose beautiful pallor owed something to her consumptive state, was also infected. If her doctors suggested that she seek a warmer climate, Waldo didn't want to be pinned down in Cambridge.

There is some psychological complexity afoot when one consumptive, who has just clawed his way back to health, eagerly marries another consumptive, considerably more advanced in the illness. It seems strange, a little masochistic. You could argue that the sheer pervasiveness of the white plague had the effect of normalizing it. It's also likely that Waldo, having beaten tuberculosis himself, thought he could help Ellen to do the same. He could be her savior as well as her husband.

In a January 28 letter to William, he announced that after consulting with Ellen's doctor, he had decided to accept the job at the Second Church. But this very letter was written from his fiancée's sickroom, since she had "raised blood a week ago." Ellen would die just two years later, on February 8, 1831. In a sense, their entire relationship would be a rehearsal for her death, or at least an attempt to hold it temporarily at bay. Waldo confessed early on to Charles that Ellen was "too lovely to live long," and she too had an oddly sunny sense of her own mortality. And yet they were happy, almost ecstatic.

Soon after their engagement, Ellen and her family spent some time in Boston, so the two lovers could be together. (In fact, it was a carriage ride back from the Old Manse to Boston that had led to Ellen's relapse—they got caught in the rain, often the consumptive's death warrant.) She was too weak to attend Waldo's ordination on March 10, although her future mother-in-law dropped by afterward for tea and a full debriefing. A few weeks later, she felt strong enough to return to New Hampshire and continue her recovery.

No doubt the five-month separation that followed was torture for both of them. Waldo frequently journeyed up to Concord to see her, spending the second half of June by her bedside—for Ellen had once more "taken sick in the old way." When they felt too deprived, they could consult the miniature portraits produced by the painter Sarah Goodridge, which they kept in reddish Morocco-leather cases. (The tiny image of Waldo captured his big Emerson nose, along with a saucily cocked eyebrow.) They also corresponded. This was a godsend, because the four dozen letters Ellen sent are, along with some fugitive notebook jottings and poems and the Goodridge miniature, all that we really have of her.

Waldo's letters to her have vanished. She certainly kept them—she notes at one point that his latest communication is "reposing among its fellows." Most likely he inherited the whole pile when she died, and destroyed them. We do have some of the poems he wrote for her, because he copied them into his journal. They are pretty conventional stuff:

> Dear Ellen, many a golden year
> May ripe, then dim, thy beauty's bloom,
> But never shall the hour appear
> In sunny joy, in sorrow's gloom,
> When aught shall hinder me from telling
> My ardent love, all loves excelling.

Sometimes we suspect emotions that are expressed in conventional terms. It seems more sincere to say these things in your own words, the idea being that you are feeling them *yourself*, not channeling some stuff you read in a book. The originality of the language is supposed to reflect the absolute freshness of feeling, as distinct and recognizable as, say, the scent of newly mown grass.

This is a bad mistake. Not everybody in the grip of an electrical emotion can invent a new language to describe it—certainly not at the same time. We can probably identify the most important sensations we will ever have, the deepest feelings we will ever feel, by the fact that we can't quite identify them. They are too novel, too elusive. So let's not hold these starchy poems against Waldo. And let's pray that he didn't destroy his letters to Ellen, that they will turn up next year at a Concord garage sale, in an old shoebox full of decaying American Express bills.

Meanwhile we have Ellen's. They are so touching, funny, and stamped with her personality that you understand at once why Waldo fell in love with her. Perhaps it was the very fact of her youth that allowed her to be this straightforward. At seventeen, she hadn't yet constructed a persona, whereas Waldo's was already on its way to becoming a comfy sarcophagus. She avoids commas and periods (and sometimes grammar), welding together entire letters with a breathless sequence of dashes. Smart, silly, immersed in books, she is precisely the sort of ideal companion that Waldo required. She recognized how extraordinary he was. Yet she had no difficulty joshing him in her letters, sometimes calling her twenty-six-year-old paramour "Grandpa."

On one occasion she warns him that she will be an unmanageable armful once they are married. In the spirit of full disclosure, she writes:

> Do you remember what I told you one day—which you pshaw'd at furiously—I assured you I was hard hearted and I told you the thermometer would rise often to an alarming height on trifling occasions—therefore if the lover persists in closing his eyes fast—let not the husband & lover start to find his *wify* told true stories of herself.

This is not arty, ornate prose, of the kind that sometimes creeps into Waldo's informal utterances. It is the sound of a person talking. The italicized *wify* is a great touch: she acknowledges her supposedly subordinate role and makes fun of it all at once. Also, you can almost hear Waldo's pshaw.

It's like audio verité. So is this little slice of life, written when Ellen's health had declined again and she was looked after by a nurse: "I write

FIGURE 2. Miniatures of RWE and Ellen Tucker Emerson. Portrait of Ellen Tucker Emerson on ivory by Sarah Goodridge, 1829. Concord Museum Collection, Gift of Dr. Augusta G. Williams; Pi806. Sarah Goodridge's matching portrait of Ralph Waldo Emerson has been lost, but an ambrotype is reproduced here, courtesy of the Houghton Library, Harvard University, MS Am 1280.235 (Box 63: 706.1).

a thousand letters to you [daily] in my head which are only interrupted by Nursey's saying Wan'nt it funny Miss Ellen? an enquiry respecting some yard long story or other which she might as well tell to the rocking chair or Old Morpheus himself."

There are glimpses of Ellen's frail condition throughout, effectively soft-pedaled by her blithe tone. She tells Waldo that she is eager to be free of her medications and hot-water bottles and the nurse's "kind though annoying arm binding her like the supporting hoop of a weak butter tub"—meaning that she is too feeble to walk by herself. She even parodies the endless talk about her health by filing a quasi-official report on the state of her heart: "I am inclined to believe from certain commotions in this restless organ at certain sounds and thoughts that amongst other complaints with which I am afflicted and which entitles me to the most fragile corner on the list of invalids—I have certainly contracted the disease of Love."

The temptation is to quote and quote. It's hard to convey the enchanting mixture of idle chatter and adoring patter and shrewdly phrased observations of the household, along with frequent echoes of Milton, Southey, Thomas Moore, the Bible, and Waldo's earlier poetry, which he had given her to read. But there are also moments of deep, almost desperate feeling.

Grieving over Waldo's long absence, for example, she compares their reunion to the trembling merger of raindrops on a windowpane. At the "instant of meeting," she writes, "there is a universal jar—a thrill—remember and watch your window when the sky weeps—If I were a hundred years old and had been separated from you a month after living with you all my days there would be a chance of frightening the soul from the old shell when we met." The universal jar, the soul frightened from its shell—the phrases have a touch of Emily Dickinson's metaphysical acuity. Who knows what sort of poetry Ellen would have written had she lived a full life. But she did not.

In early August she and Waldo set out on a ten-day trip to the White Mountains in an open chaise. They were accompanied by Ellen's mother and her sister Margaret, who followed in a closed vehicle with the baggage. This vacation, too, was essentially curative. Physicians had long believed that vigorous jostling was good for the consumptive. According to Thomas Sydenham, known to his seventeenth-century contemporaries as the English Hippocrates, there was no better treatment for tuberculosis than "long and continued journeys on horseback," although others opted for the rolling, bouncing, nauseating experience of a sea voyage.

With their dual chaperones in tow, they traveled up to the Shaker community in Canterbury, New Hampshire. There, one resident extolled the "beauty of virginity" to the couple and discouraged them from "living after the way of manhood & womanhood in the earth." Waldo declined to address the virginity issue but did note that he and his fiancée were devoted to good works. The convoy next moved on to Centre Harbor, on Lake Winnipesaukee, where Waldo noted the somewhat ambiguous state of Ellen's health. "Ellen is sometimes smart," he wrote, "sometimes feeble, & hates to say, I am sick, almost as much as Edward."

You do sense some special pleading, an affectionate conspiracy between the two young lovers. Ellen hates to say she is sick and Waldo loves to say she is better. Between these two paragons of denial, it's hard to figure out exactly how feeble she was along the way.

There was also a disagreeable conversation about Ellen's will, whose details are hard to deduce from the scattered references in her letters. Waldo was no gold digger. Perhaps he brought up the topic as a matter of Yankee practicality and then couldn't extricate himself from a bone-headed exchange. Yet the awkwardness didn't end there. Nearly a month after the trip, Ellen was still delaying any relevant discussion with Pliny Cutler, the executor of her father's estate. After her death, this skittish approach would create problems for Waldo, when various family members challenged her will and the settlement was bogged down in litigation for years.

But that was far in the future. For now, they relished their time together. "It is rather delightful to me the progress our affection has made—wrapping us more closely every day in its fairy web of smiles and tears," she wrote Waldo as soon as she was home again. "We have tried a short journey together and like it so well that we think of taking a *longer*."

There was another jostling expedition in early September, equally entertaining for both parties. In a joyful summary, Waldo noted that "we botanize & criticize & poeticize & memorize & prize & grow wise we hope." On September 30, 1829, having previously obtained Colonel Kent's permission, he married Ellen at her family's home in New Hampshire.

Strangely, only a single member of his own family attended the ceremony. This was his brother Charles, who seemed to resent hanging around what he called, in a letter to William, "that big house full of women" while "W. and the fair Ellen were whispering honied words above stairs." He wouldn't have been the first sibling to feel that a spouse was siphoning off the attention that *he* deserved. Perhaps Charles couldn't believe that his gawky brother had landed such a beautiful and intelligent woman. In any case, the newlyweds settled into their new home on Chardon Street in Boston, and Waldo commenced the happiest and saddest period of his life.

. . .

Mostly he was happy. He preached and he read (a dizzying assortment of stuff, including books on insect life, Samuel Taylor Coleridge's *Aids to Reflection*, and the perhaps Murat-related *Antidote to Atheism* by Henry More). He attended to his flock, sometimes with a benign clumsiness. He would mistakenly call on families who happened to share the last name of his parishioners. On one occasion, when he was summoned to the deathbed of a neighbor, he launched into a long riff about glassmaking and was eventually asked to leave. In his journals, he continued to tinker with the ideas that had germinated back in St. Augustine. He meanwhile relished his life with Ellen, however much that life was consumed by fending off her illness.

Within a few months of their wedding, her symptoms began to return. In March, they undertook another jostling journey to Philadelphia, whose slightly warmer climate was supposed to soothe her lungs. The trip itself, which included a storm-tossed boat trip from New Haven to New York City, must have exhausted Ellen even more. Yet her high spirits are evident in a verse chronicle she kept, with rhyming interjections from her husband. Arriving at their final destination, she writes:

> Fair land of bonnets white and neat
> Of taste so pure of streets so clean
> That here the first pigs we have seen
> Lay wallowing in thy muddy streets

A boyhood friend of Waldo's, visiting the young couple at their boardinghouse, found them walking around the parlor in a sort of ambulatory embrace. It was love, it was desire (the Shakers be damned)—and surely it was a protective gesture on Waldo's part. For he had to leave, and Ellen, who had been coughing up what her husband called "red wheezers" during the journey, was once again ailing.

Waldo returned home. His wife remained in Philadelphia. She kept up her marvelous impersonation of a healthy human being, at least in her letters, with their drily comic reports of the "fair unruffled Friends gliding unstained and unspotted through the tumult and dust of fashion." But Waldo knew better. Back in their Chardon Street lodgings, which he had hastily filled with all the objects that made a home—a piano, a bird, a magnet, a pair of dumbbells, a history of enthusiasm—he must have been anxious.

Before the end of May he retrieved Ellen from Philadelphia and moved her to Brookline, within striking distance of Boston, for the summer. There, perversely, the coastal breezes were relentless and (in Ellen's words) "blue & shrill." Then it was back to Chardon Street, for another lethal dose of New England winter.

In a letter to her brother-in-law Edward, who had just fled to the Caribbean in hopes of cleansing the red wheezers from his own lungs, Ellen noted the "thermometer at 6, snow, wind, long icicles blue noses and sad looking invalids." Icicles and invalids: her illness was not something to be cured, not an imperfection, but a fact of nature. It was inseparable from her, had been so for most of her conscious life. In the last letter she ever wrote, to Aunt Mary, she would discuss it in almost heraldic terms: "A drop of vermeil should be the family coat of arms."

Ellen knew that she was now dying, or dying faster. In response, she scribbled a few poems on the blank pages of a diary that had belonged to her brother George, whom the disease had killed in Paris five years earlier. Hope, she wrote, had departed, leaving a "golden feather quivering on the ground—/ Just bright enough to cheat the eager eye / Just strong enough temptation for a lie."

This seems remarkably honest for a nineteen-year-old. She was able to put aside hope while mostly skirting the Romantic blather about tuberculosis and easeful death. I would call Ellen a realist, albeit one who believed that she would go to Heaven, as did her husband, who was meanwhile negotiating his own relationship to death in the next room.

On November 3, he posed a very pertinent question in his journal: "Is it possible for religious principle to overcome the fear of death?" His initial answer was no. Hadn't his own faith, by making life richer and more suffused with holiness, also made it that much harder to let go? "Christianity has done much to increase the fear of death in the world," he declared, "by the general advance it has brought about in the cultivation of the moral powers." Having painted himself into this corner, he quickly whipped up an escape hatch. What *really* mattered, Waldo decided, was a diligent flexing of the moral muscle: the Apostles, never to be bested when it came to piety, had welcomed death, had exalted in it.

Within just a few weeks, he took this dilemma to the pulpit as well. On December 31 he preached a new sermon called "How Old Art Thou?" It was one long riff on universal extinction, not exactly calculated to usher in the New Year with a smile:

> All history is an epitaph. All life is but a progress toward death. It is computed that in ordinary times when the plague is stayed in Asia and War in Europe and only the common causes of mortality operate, 2,400 of the human race die in an hour; so that almost every pulse is the knell of a brother. The world is but a large urn.

On the bright side, he told his parishioners, they could turn to the church, the "true asylum from these apprehensions of mortality." They could escape the world of decay and dissolution. They could take up residence in the Kingdom of God, which was "incorruptible and cannot grow old." I have no doubt Waldo believed every word of it. But I hear, too, a faint uneasiness—a death-fearing man reassuring himself that there was nothing to be afraid of.

"In this world," he insisted, meaning the realm of the spirit, in which Ellen would no longer cough up blood, "we die daily." The citation is from Corinthians; the vision, the happy dream, is of the soul in a perpetual state of regeneration. It is the most comforting vision we have. It is the narcotic that allows us to bear, almost, the loss of everyone and everything we love. Yet the phrase seems to domesticate death at the same time, to make it familiar, habitual. Waldo, despite his description of the planet as an orbiting mortuary, was soothing himself.

Day after day, the patient took her restorative ride in the frigid air, and the nurse rubbed her cold hands to bring the blood back into them. Waldo waited for the snow to melt, promising another retreat to Philadelphia, Baltimore, points south. On February 8, just a few weeks after his sermon at the Second Church, Ellen died.

She had relied on opiates and a few verses from the Book of John, read aloud by her devastated husband, to get through her final hours. *In my Father's house are many mansions.* Ellen seemed to accept her death almost casually, as she had done from the beginning. "She saw no reason why her friends should be distressed," wrote Charles Emerson in a letter to Aunt Mary, seeing that "it was better she should go first, & prepare the way."

Waldo both accepted her death and did not. The part of him that accepted it was the devout Unitarian, now in even greater need of comfort and utterly convinced that Ellen had gone "to heaven to see, to know, to worship, to love, to intercede." To his journal he confided some doubts. He had none about her immortal soul. Yet he wondered about his ability to keep her memory alive in the corruptible kingdom of Chardon Street:

This miserable apathy, I know, may wear off. I almost fear when it will. Old duties will present themselves with no more repulsive face. I shall go again among my friends with a tranquil countenance. Again I shall be amused, I shall stoop again to little hopes and little fears and forget the graveyard.

Here is the modern, peculiar, self-interrogating Waldo, who is wracked by grief and already foresees his own dereliction of it. He, too, is a realist in the end. But he did not forget the graveyard in Roxbury, which he visited constantly and regarded as "pleasanter to me than the house."

Indeed, it was the part of him that could not and would not accept Ellen's death that led him, a little more than a year later, to pry open the coffin resting within the family vault. He noted this in a journal entry of March 29, 1832, without any further comment. Exactly what he saw we do not know. But a body in the cool confines of a wooden box is slow to decay. Ellen might have looked maddeningly like herself to Waldo— even as the empty vessel in its burial clothes would have confirmed for him the separate existence of her soul. In any case, he had already begun to toy with the notion that the material world was a kind of thin skin stretched over a deeper reality. What he called natural facts—objects, animals, a pebble or a persimmon or another person—were there to be *seen through*. Perhaps, mercifully, he saw through this one.

4

THE SHINING
APPARITION

I am writing these lines on a December afternoon, surrounded by tall, gray, columnar trees that have lost their lower limbs and resemble the masts of ships. Thanks to man-made global warming, still contested by one in three Americans, there is no snow. The millions of pine needles on the ground should be covered by now; instead, they look indecently exposed in the sunlight. Underfoot they are springy and bronze-colored, a pleasure to encounter. So is the warm air. I walk down the steep road to the lake, a New England beauty whose surface is unnaturally glassy, delivering high-resolution images of the blue sky and the conifers. Here and there, the rays of the low sun penetrate to the bottom. I'm almost disturbed to see the mossy, messy irregularity beneath the surface: another violation of privacy.

I set off around the lake. When I get to a spot where the sun is shining brightly through the trees and lighting up the green leaves—which should have fallen by now, but are hanging on in a state of deciduous confusion—I take a picture, confident it will capture nothing. I arrive at a small cataract. Here the adjacent lake drains into this one, making a gift of the boundless, boring water, and I find myself peering down into the channel.

Its rectangular shape reminds me of another opening: a grave. My father had died not long ago, and was buried in a Jewish cemetery in Queens, a leafy place largely tenanted by benevolent societies and schools of biblical instruction. His grave, as the funeral rites began, was just a hole in the ground. My father wasn't in it yet. He was still parked on a nearby gurney, in a poplar coffin. I looked into the hole and was curious to see the striated walls, the damp soil, a protruding root or two. It was a kind of experiment, a sounding of the depths. It struck me that my father, a scientist, would have enjoyed studying it as well. For a moment, that seemed the saddest thing—not that I would never see him again, but that he wasn't on hand to peer into the hole with me.

I continue my walk around the lake. Now the afternoon light is brilliant and selective, magnifying certain details while leaving others in the dark. It is golden, a little syrupy, it gilds the fallen leaves in their exhausted mounds on the shoreline. It is better than a photograph. The animals are on vacation, or hibernating in their burrows. The muskrat I've heard so much about is nowhere to be seen, nor are the ducks, who are supposed to be courting right around now.

All of which means that the path is empty. I have the lake and the light, which is beginning to disappear, to myself. I head back the way I came, feeling tranquility and desperation, emotions that seem partially borrowed from the landscape itself and are no doubt disguised forms of grief. No other emotion has the same genius for cryptic coloration. It can pretend to be anything, even happiness, even when the happy person is on the verge of tears.

. . .

Grief drove Waldo, too, into the woods. He had always loved nature, of course. Although a city-bred child, he relished his summers in Concord, with their berry-picking expeditions and frolics among the poplars and Balm-of-Gilead trees. But this was something different. Five years after Ellen's death, having renounced his pulpit, undergone what we might now call a nervous breakdown, and traveled to Europe and back, he felt a kind of life stirring in him again.

He had retreated to Concord, always a safe haven for the diminishing band of Emerson brothers. There he spent much time roving the wooded hills around Walden Pond, submerged in aqueous light that time of year.

On June 22, 1836, he recorded a paean to the natural world in his journal, a city boy's expression of ecstatic communion. "Truly in the fields I am not alone or unacknowledged," he wrote. "They nod to me & I to them. The waving of the boughs of trees in a storm is new to me & old. It takes me by surprise & yet is not unknown."

The ground had already been prepared. There was Waldo's earlier, Wordsworth-inflected verse, with its dutiful attention paid to the flowers, wind, and water. There was also his visit to the Muséum Nationale d'Histoire Naturelle in Paris, three years before.

Waldo had been underwhelmed by the Louvre and scandalized, perhaps pleasantly, by the city's loose sexual vibe. What really turned him on, though, was the museum's vast collection of birds, shells, minerals, insects. This cabinet of wonders, he wrote, "makes the visitor as calm and genial as a bridegroom." He was surrounded by schoolboys clutching their notebooks, and yet they hardly distracted him from the African gray parrot, the giant blocks of quartz, the crystalized gold.

In this diversity of forms he saw a mystical unity. He decided that nature itself, in all its freakish splendor, was shaped by man's perception of it. There was

> not a form so grotesque, so savage, nor so beautiful but is an expression of some property inherent in man the observer—an occult relation between the very scorpions and man. I feel the centipede in me—cayman, carp, eagle, and fox. I am moved by strange sympathies, I say continually, "I will be a naturalist."

Waldo seems to be suggesting here that nature was a projection of the mind. He was certainly familiar with such philosophical arguments, advanced as they were not only by Kant but by Berkeley. The latter had declared that the material world existed only in so far as we perceived it. Having anticipated the many wags who would laugh at the notion of the world blinking off every time we stopped looking at it, Berkeley further argued that the entire cosmos was perceived at every moment by a greater mind—i.e., by God.

Did Waldo subscribe to this form of Idealism? I think he was tantalized by it, intellectually and emotionally. It gave some abstract underpinning to his own sense of being alone in the world. Yet I think his understanding in the museum was somewhat metaphorical. He might not believe that the mind created matter, but he was confident that the two things emanated from a common source, and were joined by (in his beautiful phrase) strange sympathies.

Waldo didn't go on to a career as a naturalist. Still, his visit to the museum nudged him toward his mature view of nature—which, as with most things Emersonian, is many things at once. It is a balm, a teacher, a cupboard to be ransacked by human hands, and the begetter of language itself, which mankind insists on deploying in the most rudimentary ways. ("We are," he later wrote, "like travelers using the cinders of a volcano to roast their eggs.") And it is something else: a conduit of the spirit, emancipating our puny perceptions, connecting us to everything. It is *alive*, borrowing its energies from us and returning them as well.

There is an irony here: Waldo derived this vision of a universe in perpetual, palpitating flux from a collection of dead birds and insects. But it is less surprising from a man who, within a few years, would begin to the doubt the permanence of death itself.

. . .

There is nature, and there is *Nature*, which Waldo published in 1836. He had begun to contemplate the book at least three years earlier, while he was stuck in Liverpool, waiting for his ship to sail back to America. He was bored. It was too cold to go out. "There are no books in the house," he lamented in his journal, "I have digested the newspaper. I have no companion."

On September 3, 1833, a desperate Waldo went out to the Liverpool & Manchester Railroad depot. There he examined the locomotives, smoke-belching novelties with pet names: Rocket, Goliath, Pluto, Firefly (another one, which Waldo didn't see, was tautologically called Novelty). He recorded a few paragraphs about the steam engine in a notebook. Then Waldo started jotting down his ideas about natural history, producing a very skeletal outline of what would become his first book.

His vessel sailed, to his great relief, on September 5. The next day, off the Irish coast, he wrote in his journal: "I like my book about Nature, and wish I knew where and how I ought to live."

Where he would live, of course, was Concord. He flitted around in the months after his return, and spent several weeks with his brother William in New York City, which he viewed as a spiritual sinkhole. In the fall of 1834, he arranged for a wagon to cart his things over to Concord. He and his mother, who had been living with him in the wake of Ellen's death, would board with Ezra Ripley at the Old Manse. There Waldo holed up to write, in the small second-floor study with its smoke-blackened walls and forbidding portraits of Puritan divines, who would have had little use for the pantheistic bombshell he was preparing.

He occupied himself with many other things for the next two years. There was itinerant preaching, lectures on natural history, and (last but not least) a second marriage. But the composition of *Nature* became his great mission. On June 28, 1836, he wrote to William: "My little book is nearly done." Two months later, the little book was published in an anonymous edition of 1,500 copies.

Waldo immediately dispatched one to Thomas Carlyle, the dyspeptic essayist and historian he had met during his European travels. He described it in modest terms. "I send you the little book I have just now published," he wrote, "as an entering wedge, I hope, for something more worthy and significant."

Carlyle replied soon after. He allowed that the book was something of an opening salvo. Yet he affirmed its importance in the vigorous, shoulder-punching manner favored by the two correspondents:

> Your little azure-colored Nature gave me true satisfaction. I read it, and then lent it about to all my acquaintance that had a sense for such things; from whom a similar verdict always came back. You say it is the first chapter of something greater. I call it rather the Foundation and Ground-plan on which you may build whatsoever of great and true has been given you to build.

However measured his response, Carlyle was certainly cheering Waldo on. Some readers were less enthusiastic. One of these was Francis

Bowen, a Harvard philosophy professor who panned the book in *The Christian Examiner*. He disliked the author's preference for airy-fairy subjectivity over scientific rigor. He mocked Waldo's selection of Benjamin Franklin—rather than Plato!—as a philosophical poster child. "The reader feels as in a disturbed dream," he wrote, "in which shows of surpassing beauty are around him, and he is conversant with disembodied spirits, yet all the time he is harassed by an uneasy sort of consciousness, that the whole combination of phenomena is fantastic and unreal."

I quote Bowen not because his spitballs made any difference. *Nature* was quickly recognized as a Transcendentalist call-to-arms and cultural watershed, albeit one whose first printing *still* hadn't sold out almost eight years later. No, I quote him because he was *right*. The book is indeed dream-like and disembodied. It is also something of a kitchen-sink production, in which Waldo took on the nominal topic of nature but crammed in an assortment of tangents, many of which would preoccupy him for the rest of his life.

No matter. *Nature* is a marvel, whose aphoristic fireworks, so at odds with the argumentative edifice Waldo thought he was building, still take the reader by surprise. It feels like something new, something prophetic and personal at the same time.

. . .

Waldo's initial task is to sweep the table clean. This isn't merely the beginning of *Nature*—it's the beginning of American literature, in all its impatient, iconoclastic glory. Out with the old, in with the new, the author declares:

> Our age is retrospective. It builds the sepulchers of the fathers. It writes biographies, histories, and criticism. The foregoing generations beheld God and nature face to face; we, through their eyes. Why should we not also enjoy an original relation to the universe?

The blunt sentences with their mounting bravado are hard to resist. The last one, about approaching the universe on one's own terms, is Emerson in a nutshell. It's worth noting, however, just how much is packed into these lines. They are a theological argument, an ex-minister's assault on the very church he had abandoned in 1832. They are a rejection of the ancestor cult that had driven Waldo into the ministry to begin with. There is a suggestion, too, of the New World boosterism he would soon expand upon in "The American Scholar."

To make a new start, Waldo argues, we must come up with a theory of nature. "Let us interrogate the great apparition," he writes, "that shines so peacefully around us." The unwitting reader may now expect something systematic. Surely the author will erect some kind of philosophical structure, using the syllogistic nuts and bolts so favored by the great Puritan divines. No such luck. Instead, he leaps directly into subjective experience: the way we *react* to the natural world, its capacity to transform us.

It is not simply a matter of beauty—although Waldo was, like all of us, fond of a pretty sunset. It is a matter of awe, of receptivity. If we open ourselves to nature, it will flood us with the sort of ecstatic knowledge we crave, and can hardly bear. It will allow us to shed the ego, the self-castigating consciousness, that separates us from the cosmos. Hence his silly and sublime image:

> Standing on the bare ground—my head bathed by the blithe air, and uplifted into infinite space—all mean egotism vanishes. I become a transparent eye-ball. I am nothing. I see all. The currents of the Universal Being circulate through me; I am part or particle of God.

Now, this is rich stuff. To the contemporary ear, it may sound inflated. Indeed, it did to some of Waldo's contemporaries, including the artist Christopher Cranch, who produced a satirical image of the author as a top-hatted, spindle-legged, anxious-looking eyeball. But a genuinely ecstatic experience cannot be conveyed via understatement. It demands that we push language to its maximum capacity—to the point at which it starts to fail. And what Waldo is describing, or attempting to describe, is something many of us have felt.

Perhaps it is less frequent than it used to be. Perhaps it has been displaced by the din of social media, whose promise of universal connectivity is a kind of parody, or mechanical approximation, of what Waldo felt. But most of us will recognize something of his experience. We, too, have noted the flicker of heightened intensity, the rawness of perception. We may feel that we are being *addressed*, that some sort of superior intelligence is descending into us. "I conceive a man as always spoken to from behind," Waldo would later write, "and unable to turn his head and see the speaker." Or we may simply experience the oceanic feeling of being absorbed into something much bigger than ourselves.

Modern people, shriveled materialists (and that includes me), will protest that the oceanic feeling is an illusion. We are joined to nothing at those mystical moments. We are simply being fooled by our infinitely accommodating brains. After all, the chemicals in our heads can generate all sorts of mystical perceptions. Dopamine makes us hallucinate. Noradrenaline allows us to revisit the past in holographic detail.

Waldo, as we will see, actually takes up the question of whether it's all in his head. But for the moment, he defiantly reverses the current and argues that ecstasy is a two-way street—that our emotions flow back out into the material world and alter it. The emotion he has in mind is grief:

> Nature always wears the colors of the spirit. To a man laboring under a calamity, the heat of his own fire hath sadness in it. Then, there is a kind of contempt of the landscape felt by him who has just lost by death a dear friend. The sky is less grand as it shuts down over less worth in the population.

In the last stages of his work on *Nature*, Waldo had lost his brother Charles. The culprit, as it would be again and again, was tuberculosis. Writing in his journal on May 16, 1836, he noted: "The eye is closed that was to see nature for me, and give me leave to see." It's almost as if the act of perceiving had been delegated—had been fraternally *outsourced*— to this accomplished younger brother, now cut down by the family scourge.

Recording all of Charles's sterling qualities, Waldo goes on to say, "He sympathized wonderfully with all objects and natures, and, as by a spiritual ventriloquism, threw his mind into them." Spiritual ventriloquism, strange sympathies: they are all means of connection, making more bearable the old, uneasy solitude. But the death of a loved one reminds us of how alone we really are. In this sense, *Nature* is a memorial

Standing on the bare ground, my
head bathed by the blithe air, & uplifted
into infinite space. all mean egotism
vanishes. I become a transparent eyeball.
Nature p. 13.

FIGURE 3. Drawing of Emerson as transparent eyeball, an illustration for RWE's "Nature," by Christopher Pearse Cranch. Metropolitan Museum of Art, Gift of Whitney Dall Jr., in memory of Emily Dall, 1976.

to the departed Charles Emerson, who once casually noted to his fiancée his propensity to "lose my human nature and join myself to that which is without."

. . .

What we have read so far is a kind of overture. Now Waldo does get a little more systematic, discussing nature in terms of the gifts it renders to humankind: commodity, beauty, language, discipline. Commodity is the crudest of these benefits. It is the soil and rain, the fruits of the earth, which human beings reap with little notion of their great good luck in possessing them. We are, in other words, *spoiled*. "The misery of man appears like childish petulance," Waldo writes, "when we explore the steady and prodigal provision that has been made for his support and delight on this green ball that floats him through the heavens."

More exalted is beauty. It is prettiness, yes, but it is something more: a soul-expanding source of joy and relief. There is, the author notes, a certain utilitarian value to all this. At the end of the day, lawyers and shopkeepers can emerge from their airless, money-grubbing establishments and be refreshed. Beauty is, in this limited sense, "medicinal." Waldo then ventures onto more dubious ground, asserting that beauty is "the mark God sets upon virtue." This seems like a leftover from his days at the Second Church: sugary, pious, reheated. In our era, we have grown suspicious of the beauty-and-virtue equation. Even in his own, more innocent age, Waldo must have known better. Were the Greek corpses at Thermopylae, which he cites as an example, really more beautiful than the Persian ones?

My sense is that Waldo was aligning himself with a long philosophical tradition, going back as far as the fifth-century thinker Dionysius (or, confusingly, Pseudo-Dionysius), who declared that beauty and goodness were basically the same thing. Jonathan Edwards, the colossus of New England theology, came to a similar conclusion: since the natural world was an exfoliation of God's will, how could its beauty *not* encompass morality as well as aesthetics? It's not that Waldo disagreed with either of these men. He, too, turned to nature as a vast warehouse, a divine depository, of what was beautiful. Yet he also considered such beauty a means to an end—a "herald," as he put it, of something both inward and eternal.

If Waldo had concluded with that insight, he would have had a fine little essay. But here is where things get really interesting. Having sung the praises of nature as a physical reality—blooming, buzzing, impossibly fecund—he now dematerializes it! The vehicle for this magic trick is language. Or, more precisely, a theory of language derived from the opium-gobbling Samuel Taylor Coleridge and the mystical metallurgist Emanuel Swedenborg.

"Words are signs of natural facts," Waldo begins. The idea that language is a symbolic version of reality is nothing new. Most of us already take it for granted. No, it's the *next* step of this onion-skin syllogism that carries us into the ether. Natural facts, Waldo continues, are themselves signs of spiritual facts. The material world, then, is superficial, symbolic: not the real thing, but a thumbnail sketch of what lies behind it.

Of course he puts it more memorably than that. The point of *Nature* is not the watertight logic of its arguments, but the indelible idiom Waldo uses to express them. He sounds like nobody else. The pulpit manner, the prancing, periodic sentences in their Unitarian finery, are still there. But they are offset by something much more immediate: the sound of a man thinking. Many lines, and sometimes entire paragraphs, are transplanted straight from Waldo's journals. They tend to be more terse, apothegmatic, off-the-cuff. Often Waldo will follow up something in his more flowery vein with a couple of these jabs:

> There seems to be a necessity in spirit to manifest itself in material forms, and day and night, river and storm, beast and bird, acid and alkali, preexist in necessary Ideas in the mind of God, and are what they are by virtue of preceding affections, in the world of spirit. A Fact is the end or last issue of spirit. The visible creation is the terminus or circumference of the invisible world.

Now, having dispatched commodity, beauty, and language, Waldo moves on to discipline. This, I would guess, is the point at which many a contemporary reader will start to fidget. The fireworks display of the previous section—the argument that the material world is a stand-in, a stunt double, for the spiritual one—is a hard act to follow.

Indeed, one of the lessons of *Nature* for Waldo (who abandoned his initial plan to write a companion volume called *Spirit*) was that his own mind was better suited to shorter forms. He was an aphorist, forever seeking compression, economy, the minimalist blow to the head. Discussing the unity of nature in his book, he could easily have been describing his own methodology as a writer: "Each particle is a microcosm, and faithfully renders the likeness of the world."

. . .

There are still two sections left in *Nature*, and readers are urged to persist. Waldo regains much of his fire and grapples once again with the complexities of Idealism. His earlier remark about the physical world preexisting in the mind of God points directly back to Berkeley, whose entire philosophical system was erected on the idea that material substance (to use his phrase) was an illusion. "There is not any other substance than *spirit*," Berkeley argued, "or that which perceives." Kant, too, is in the mix, with his insistence that we can fully grasp the "the world as it appears to us," but not the reality behind that phenomenal façade. Last but not least, Waldo had begun dipping into Eastern philosophy while he was still at Harvard, reading such secondary sources as Charles Grant's *Restoration of Learning in the East* (1807), which suggested a clear overlap between Hindu belief and Berkeley's immaterialism. With all these thinkers swirling in his head, he quite naturally wanted to address their "noble doubt" as to "whether Nature outwardly exists."

It is, after all, a very germane topic here. The material world, in Waldo's argument, has arguably been downgraded. It is less reality than a description of reality: a kind of spiritual shorthand, pointing always to something more real than itself. Isn't Waldo just a hop, skip, and a jump from denying that it exists at all?

The answer, he quickly asserts, is No. "The frivolous make themselves merry with Ideal theory," Waldo writes, "as if its consequences were burlesque." For him, though, these were not joking matters. Nor could

"Ideal theory" neatly erase the material world. His reasoning is both theo-logical and intuitive. First: God, who still figures in Waldo's conception of the universe, is not in the business of whipping up cheap mirages for the masses. "God never jests with us," Waldo insists. In addition, Idealism strikes him as sterile and sad, trapping the human soul in the bell jar of its own consciousness:

> If it only deny the existence of matter, it does not satisfy the demands of the spirit. It leaves God out of me. It leaves me in the splendid laby-rinth of my perceptions, to wander without end. Then the heart re-sists it, because it baulks the affections in denying substantive being to men and women.

For that matter, we do not simply occupy nature as we would a stage set. Instead, God "puts it forth through us, as the life of the tree puts forth new branches and leaves through the pores of the old." If nature doesn't exist, neither do we. That would seem to settle the question—for the moment, anyway. Waldo would never truly abandon the Idealist stress on mind over matter, but he was willing to tilt the scales in one direction or the other, as the shrewd Yankee in him contended with the apostle of pure consciousness.

Next comes a fable. It goes like this. Once upon a time, man and nature were identical and overlapping entities. Then, due to spiritual shrinkage, man was gradually dwarfed by his natural surroundings. He is now a fraction of himself, worshipping what he once inhabited with such ease. "Yet sometimes," we read, "he starts in his slumber, and won-ders at himself and his house, and muses strangely at the resemblance betwixt him and it."

It's a beautiful image. You might call it a vision of the Fall with God engineered out of it—along with the apple, the serpent, and sin. Waldo's Adam doesn't stumble into the hornet's nest of consciousness. Instead his great mistake is to *retreat* from it: to settle for a pittance of what we can truly think, feel, perceive.

Then Waldo heads into the exhortatory home stretch. The long con-cluding paragraph is pure prophecy—in the good and bad senses of that word. The language sweeps us along, building on imagery that Waldo had introduced earlier and *almost* persuading us that *Nature* is a unified whole rather than a glorious cluster bomb. Now comes the part that moves me, that makes my skin prickle no matter how many times I read it. This is Waldo's vision of the individual as limitless, held back only by fear, stupidity, caution, custom, tribal deference.

I know quite well that I'm not limitless. My own triviality is, for me, an article of faith, not to mention a useful perspectival device when pondering the great world. But when Waldo argues to the contrary, I believe him:

> Every spirit builds itself a house; and beyond its house, a world; and beyond its world, a heaven. Know then, that the world exists for you. For you is the phenomenon perfect. What we are, that only can we see. All that Adam had, all that Caesar could, you have and can do.

Here is the mighty self, the individual-as-cosmos, the blessing and curse that Waldo bequeathed to America! Here is the thing to read when you feel powerless, helpless, or like an ant with an ant-like fealty to social arrangements, your antennae quivering with received wisdom! It will momentarily make you feel heroic, and not in a self-deluding way, but in terms of potential. Every human being deserves to feel this way. To grasp this fact, especially in a society organized around covenants and crowd behavior, was a stroke of genius.

Yet genius can be intoxicating—inebriating, really. Waldo, having inhaled his own vapors, felt empowered to go even further as he crossed the finish line. *Nature* ends with a prediction: there is to be a revolution in consciousness. In keeping with Waldo's earlier description of mind and matter as one and the same, this revolution will transform the physical world as well. All will be changed, changed utterly.

He sketches out this transformation, half of it resembling a visit from the exterminator, in impressive detail. "Swine, spiders, snakes, pests, mad-houses, prisons, enemies [will] vanish; they are temporary and shall be seen no more." There is, to be sure, a personal element to his prophecy. Man will enter into this new world "without more wonder than the blind man feels who is gradually restored to perfect sight."

Here, surely, is another allusion to Waldo's own earlier struggle with blindness, not to mention the lost brother whose death had deprived him of vision in every sense of the word.

Did he believe what he was saying? I suspect so, at least while the prose-making engine was running hot and the barrier between common sense and prophecy had dissolved. Still, I feel a strange itch to know whether Waldo meant these lines literally—whether he truly foresaw a transfigured nation—or was offering them as a metaphor. To put it another way: Did he write *Nature* in a mystical fever, or was he the cool and collected author who only *appeared* to have a direct line to eternity?

Perhaps his journal can give us a clue. If you look at the entries for the spring of 1836, when Waldo was finishing *Nature*, you see an awesome focus on the task at hand. He is working out the ideas, and much of the specific phrasing, that will go into final product.

In a sense, then, every waking moment is a dry run for the ecstasy of those final pages. On June 3, he writes: "Shall I not treat all men as gods?" On June 7, he writes: "Nature is a perpetual effect. It is the great shadow pointing to an unseen Sun." On June 4, however, neatly sandwiched between these visionary notations, is something else:

> The painters have driven me from my apartment. What a droll craft is theirs generally considered! There is certainly a ridiculous air over much of our life.

I was strangely relieved to encounter this dose of dailiness. Even an ecstatic gets kicked out of the house when the workmen arrive. What Waldo found so droll about their craft is not clear. Perhaps it was the Sisyphean task of concealment, covering up dirt and discoloration with the thinnest possible layer of paint. I do think it was the effort to appear immaculate that struck him as ridiculous.

Also delicious, also droll, is the faint echo of the exalted imagery of *Nature*. Just as man is expelled from his spiritual habitation, so is Waldo expelled from his new house on the Cambridge Turnpike—from his own little Eden with its ground-floor study. The expulsion never ends. We pass continually from one state to another and ultimately, wearily, recognize flux as our native condition or cross to bear or reason for being. Yet we also feel a nagging sense of incompletion. We yearn for more. I think that's what Waldo meant by the great blaze of language at the end of his book. The kingdom is not attainable but we will struggle forever to get there.

. . .

A few days after my walk around the lake, it was Christmas. The weather was still warm, with temperatures in the mid-sixties and an ongoing sense of seasonal bewilderment. We were supposed to be in the dark, dank, frigid portion of the year. The snow on the ground, the sparkling sheath of ice on the trees—we waited and waited for them. But instead it was perpetual spring. It was a gift, which we felt a little uneasy accepting. Did we actually deserve it?

Outside the sun was shining, the lake never froze, the cataract kept up its Heraclitan routine. The deer grew bolder and the geese crisscrossed the sky, sometimes flying in the wrong direction. Inside, a multitude of small brown bugs appeared. They landed on the pages of a book I was reading, flexing their jointed legs and looking confused. Some flew into the recesses of the floor lamp and stared, I thought, at the bulb.

These were marmorated stink bugs—scuttling, shield-shaped insects with exquisite patterns on their backs. They were not natives, but had snuck into the country via Pennsylvania in 1998. For that reason they struck me as real aliens: visitors from a parallel universe. I will not pretend that I developed a spiritual affinity or strange sympathy with them. I hate bugs. I squashed a couple and they gave off a sad postmortem perfume. Yet I was touched by their eagerness to escape. The warm weather had fooled them, too, and they sought the counterfeit spring outside the window, where they fully expected to be happy and, for all I know, to live forever. Bugs: believers in eternity! Waldo, of course, knew that such claims might fall on skeptical ears—even children were subject to doubt. In an essay called "Immortality," he recounts that one child, confronted with the idea of eternal life, quite reasonably responded: "It makes me feel so tired."

5

RUIN AND RESURRECTION

Wait a minute. Let's reverse course. Let's roll back the tape. You will have noticed that in *Nature*, God gets short shrift. It's not that He has vanished completely—in fact, Waldo suggests that our diluted perception of the deity is one of the great problems of the era. Still, God is a distant presence, sidelined by more urgent matters. How did the earnest pulpit performer of the early 1830s end up batting for the pantheists? To put it another way: Why had Waldo forsaken Him?

There is a simple answer. He quit. As I have noted before, Waldo renounced his ministry at the Second Church in October 1832. But this raises the more complicated question of *why* he stepped down.

He was, to begin with, wracked with grief. Ellen had died the previous year, and only a few months had passed since Waldo walked out to Roxbury and pried open her coffin. He had not stopped mourning her. He would never stop. Yet his official explanation to his parishioners, who had observed the ailing Ellen Emerson in the front pews during her truncated life, had nothing to do with grief.

No, Waldo quit the pulpit for a very specific reason: he could no longer celebrate the Lord's Supper. The ritual struck him as hollow, as *wrong*. He asked to be excused from this one ministerial duty. When his request was declined, he abandoned the Second Church—indeed, he abandoned the very notion of institutional Christianity, and struck out for the Transcendentalist hinterlands. You might say it was Christianity's loss. It seems strange, however, that the productive relationship between Waldo and his faith foundered on a bit of bread, a sip of wine.

Granted, this is the formulation of a nonbeliever. No doubt Waldo would have considered me a laughable literalist. But as it happens, the Lord's Supper has been a theological bone of contention for centuries. Waldo's motives for rejecting it—like his motives for doing almost anything—were crazily complex and more intimate than we might expect. His spiritual decisions were, always, personal decisions, made with an antinomian disregard for the rules of the game.

· · ·

The Lord's Supper is, of course, a reenactment of Christ's final meal with his disciples. Breaking up a loaf of bread and distributing it to his companions, he is supposed to have said, "This is my body, which is given for you: this do in remembrance of me." And so a ritual was born. By the ninth century, however, theologians were already bickering over whether the wafer and wine were literally transformed into the body and blood of Christ, or whether the ceremony was primarily a reenactment: a metaphor.

Most took a literalist tack, arguing for what was called "real presence." The case was hardly closed, though. Three centuries later, Thomas Aquinas was still swatting away objections to real presence in his *Summa Theologica* (1273). How, for example, could Christ's body be physically present in more than one church at a time? Aquinas, so hefty that a half-moon shape had to be cut out of his desk in order for him to sit down, and therefore not a man unmindful of physical dimensions, had a somewhat dodgy answer. "Christ's body is not in this sacrament in the same way as a body is in a place," he wrote, "its dimensions equal to the dimensions of the place it occupies. It is present in a special manner which only applies to the sacrament."

More than two centuries later, the theologians were still arguing. Luther himself, attending a crucial sit-down called the Colloquy of Marburg in 1529, vehemently dismissed the idea that the sacrament was no more than a symbolic act. Facing down a cadre of metaphor-minded reformers, he is supposed to have written his position in chalk on the table. HOC EST CORPUS MEUM: THIS IS MY BODY.

Waldo was certainly aware of these disputes. He opposed the sort of literalism that Luther had expressed so bluntly at Marburg. That is, he viewed the Lord's Supper as a metaphorical enterprise: a commemoration rather than a mystical reenactment. As such, it struck him as superfluous.

For a Unitarian to take this position was not unheard of. They tended to be rational-minded, reconciling faith with the latest scientific advances. As Waldo told his congregation in an 1832 sermon, "Religion will become purer and truer by the progress of science." That said, many Unitarians continued to argue for the authenticity of the supernatural episodes in the Bible—claiming, indeed, that such episodes were *empirical evidence* of the Christian faith. Here, again, they were following in the footsteps of John Locke, who had declared the miracles to be divine "credentials" issued by the Almighty Himself. Andrews Norton, the uber-Unitarian at the helm of the Harvard Divinity School, would soon assert with nostril-flaring vehemence that any denial of the scriptural miracles was a "denial of the existence of God."

Yet the bedrock of Norton's creed was the idea that there was just a single repository of divinity: God and only God. Jesus Christ was a great moral exemplar but also a human being, a creature of flesh and blood. If you believed that, then how could you endorse the transubstantiation that Aquinas had defended with such zeal?

Worrying the question was, in fact, an Emerson family tradition. Readers will recall that William Emerson, the eldest of the brothers, saw his faith crumble away while he was studying in Göttingen during the 1820s. But five years later, having shrugged off any obligation to wrestle with such issues, he was *still* jousting over the Lord's Supper with Ezra Ripley.

Word of this dispute, conducted on eggshells by the dutiful William, probably got around. Waldo was in any case appealing to his brother throughout this period for mischief-making material. He begged him to send along topics for provocative sermons. On one occasion, he urged William to flip though Eichhorn and the other Higher Critics and mark the passages that would most efficiently torpedo the authority of the New Testament.

For a practicing pastor, even one with an eroding sense of vocation, this seems like borderline perversity. But Waldo, like his older brother, was incapable of pretending. He took these matters too seriously to simply go through the motions, as Goethe had suggested to William years earlier. This struck him as a form of spiritual lip-synching, and a form of lying. For that matter, Waldo's doubts about his own suitability for the ministry went back to his days at divinity school. So in early June of 1832, he informed the Second Church that he could no longer administer the Lord's Supper. Then he waited for the explosion.

. . .

His journals, in the weeks leading up to this announcement, include the usual mix of quotations, data collection, and aphoristic woolgathering. Yet everything seems to point, in one way or another, to his impending break with the Second Church.

"Cold cold," he wrote on June 2. "Thermometer Says Temperate. Yet a week of moral excitement." The chill, one assumes, was metaphysical—a reaction to the wide open spaces of unbelief. On the same page, he reiterated his unhappiness at performing a job that struck him as essentially curatorial. The church was no more than a museum of clapped-out customs, and Waldo was tired of functioning as a glorified docent:

> I have sometimes thought that in order to be a good minister it was necessary to leave the ministry. The profession is antiquated. In an altered age, we worship in the dead forms of our forefathers. Were not a Socratic paganism better than an effete superannuated Christianity?

He had not, I should stress, stormed out the door. In his letter to the Proprietors of the Second Church, he simply asked to be excused from administering the Lord's Supper. The committee included not only his friends but a cousin, George B. Emerson, so Waldo hoped for a fair hearing. But the committee declined to give him the loophole he had requested. Now Waldo was faced with a choice. He could backpedal and hold his nose while administering the rite, or he could quit.

As it happened, there was a short intermission while the church closed for repairs. Waldo fled Chardon Street—with its magnet, its dumbbells, its Chickering piano that nobody played since Ellen's death—and sought the advice of Aunt Mary.

She was not, of course, in town. This remarkable eccentric, who liked to wear her own funeral shroud while doing errands, had no fixed abode. She bounced around New England, staying with relatives or at boarding houses, dispensing literary and theological barbs to all comers. At the moment, she had made landfall in Waterford, Maine. There she was living in a house she had purchased, then unwisely signed over to her brother-in-law, which made her an even more cantankerous guest.

Waldo wanted Aunt Mary's advice because she was the living embodiment of the family: an Emersonian avatar. That was why she had stumped so ardently for all the brothers to enter the ministry. The fulfillment of this ancestral mission meant everything to her—not least because her beloved brother and father had perished early in their own ecclesiastical careers, and because her own brilliance as a thinker and writer, which far outstripped theirs, had no such possible outlet. There was, in other words, a powerful vein of vicarious joy in seeing at least one nephew take to the pulpit.

He had already written, in early 1832, to share his doubts about the ministry. She did not take it well. The letter she sent in return began, with no salutation, by comparing him to a parricide—a killer of his own parents. It was a kind of double treachery he was contemplating: a simultaneous attack on family and faith. She decried the awful influence of materialist philosophy, not to mention the "withering Lucifer doctrine of pantheism." True, Aunt Mary's own vision of Christianity was anything but conventional. But in seeking her counsel as he prepared his exit strategy, Waldo was surely testing his own mettle. Perhaps he still hoped to be proven wrong.

His brother Charles, who had joined Edward in Puerto Rico for a consumption-fighting stay the previous year, had recently returned home. Waldo invited him on the trip to Waterford, and the two headed north on June 21. For a week they remained with Aunt Mary at Elm Vale, as the house was called.

It must have been a strange visit. Charles had assigned himself a bit of detective work. He intended to rummage through the land records and determine whether the house could be wrested back into Aunt Mary's hands. Also, their hosts had gone over to what most Emersons would regard as the dark side—i.e., Methodism—and spent much of their time at a four-day-long revival meeting. This outburst of religious enthusiasm probably put a damper on any discussion of Waldo's apostasy. One imagines both brother and aunt applying gentle pressure throughout the long spring days, since Charles too believed that Waldo should remain at the Second Church and "administer the ordinance as nearly as he conscientiously can."

Aunt Mary then accompanied her nephews to Fryeburg, Maine, where Waldo had a preaching engagement. Now the three travelers separated. Charles went back to Boston, and Waldo crossed over into the White Mountains of New Hampshire, where Aunt Mary would soon join him under the "brow and shaggy lid" of the Presidential Range.

Given the propensity of these people to document every moment of their lives, there is an intriguing silence that surrounds this interval in the wilderness. It feels like a press blackout, or one of those ominous drops in air pressure that precedes a big storm. Waldo and Mary rode north toward Crawford Notch on July 13. This was steep and forbidding terrain, especially for a woman in her late fifties. When Thomas Cole painted Crawford Notch seven years later, the place *still* looked rugged, with a couple of modest dwellings in sight and some nasty clouds looming over the flank of Mount Washington.

Up the rough mountain trails they went, before stopping at Ethan Allen Crawford's public house. It is fascinating to ponder their conversation that day. These were two cerebral people. The temptation is to envision them as cognitive clouds, or transparent eyeballs, or anything but the physical beings they were. Waldo at the time was tall, pale, gangly, with dark hair and sideburns disappearing under his chin. Him we can just about picture.

But there are only two surviving images of Aunt Mary. One is a silhouette made when she was a young woman—a confident, long-lashed apparition that she called her "pilgrim profile." The other is a posthu-

FIGURE 4. Posthumous tintype of Mary Moody Emerson,
1863. Courtesy of Houghton Library, Harvard University.

mous tintype, which is to say, a photo of her corpse, hands neatly
crossed, bonnet tied. Neither gives much sense of the living, breathing,
furiously *thinking* personality. In a way that would have pained but not
surprised her, she has disappeared—at least her likeness has. Yet this
blurry figure doubtless interrogated her nephew throughout the afternoon.

Then she hurried back to Fryeburg, leaving behind a hasty, equivocal note.

Her note was surprisingly close to a blessing. Of course she wished Waldo to retreat from his pantheistic ways and recognize the divinity of Jesus. Yet she bowed to the demands of his conscience, just as she had with William, a few years earlier. "My solitude opens far distant views," she wrote, "& would see you climbing the h[e]ights of salvation thro' the lonely roads of what appears to you truth & duty."

This grudging approval must have cheered Waldo. Yet it hardly settled the question. The next day, insisting there was nothing to write in his journal, he wrote in it nonetheless:

> There is nothing to be said. Why take the pencil? I believe something will occur. A slight momentum would send the planet to roll forever. And the laws of thought are not unlike. A thought I said is a country wide enough for an active mind.

Cleary he was waiting for a sign—a divine wink, nudge, or nod. "The good of going into the mountains is that life is reconsidered," he wrote the next day. But he was still arguing with himself. Shouldn't he be able to tolerate the tiny dose of cynicism that Goethe had urged on his brother all those years ago?

Waldo recognized that his objections might be regarded as nitpicking. "I know very well that it is a bad sign in man to be too conscientious," he wrote, "& to stick at gnats." Yet he simply could not abide that particle of bad faith. The problem, in a sense, was that he took the ritual more seriously than the communicants themselves.

. . .

It was almost over. Waldo returned to Boston a few days later, determined to avoid the Lord's Supper. But if he was done with the pantomime of bodily consumption, the pantomime was not done with him. What I'm saying is that the body, too, is a kind of literalist. Now Waldo's was determined to punish him, and he came down with a terrible bout of diarrhea. The illness is simply too apt not to be viewed as psychosomatic payback, at least in part. When he refused to eat the flesh and blood of Christ, his intestine staged an unbearable mutiny, which went on for weeks.

There is a certain low comedy here. Yet Waldo was in pain, both physical and psychic. He tried to comfort himself with the doctrine of compensation. With his body in a state of collapse, he wrote, "I will remember that after the ruin the resurrection is sure." Meanwhile, he refused to budge on the decision he had made up at Crawford Notch.

His separation from the Second Church was almost complete. With repairs on the building finished, Waldo preached to the congregation on September 9. Pointedly, he chose Romans 14:17 for his text: "For the kingdom of God is not meat and drink; but righteousness, and peace, and joy in the Holy Ghost." The sermon was a lengthy, logical, and rather scholarly debunking of the Lord's Supper as a spiritual necessity.

Waldo knew he had already lost the debate. He simply wanted to make his case. The historical evidence for the compulsory rite was flimsy, he told his parishioners. More to the point, what he valued in Christianity was its "reality, its boundless charity, its deep interior life," all of which seemed at odds with the encrustation of old customs.

It made no difference. According to Charles, who attended Waldo's last-ditch defense, the packed house seemed moved by what he described as a "noble sermon." But it was the Society of Proprietors—the wealthy and conservative steering committee—that held the reins. They debated among themselves for weeks, allowing Waldo to deliver one last sermon on October 21. Then, a week later, they voted to fire him.

His career in the ministry was over. The societal blowback was extreme in some quarters. His friend Frederic Henry Hedge later recalled: "The sensation caused by this step was prodigious. Even friends were shocked by it. Hints of insanity were not wanting."

More disturbing to Waldo, one assumes, was the disappointment of his own family. Not only had he shucked off the ministerial mantle that his forebears had worn for generations—he had also plunged the entire clan into financial uncertainty. The Second Church agreed to pay his salary through the end of December. After that, he and his dependents would be on their own.

Weary, depressed, still stricken with stomach problems, Waldo allowed his mother to break up the Chardon Street household. Most of the furnishings were auctioned off. Then, on December 24, Waldo set sail for an alternate universe: Europe. He would return almost a year later, in ruddy good health and with a sketch of *Nature* in his pocket. As he had foreseen, ruin was followed by resurrection, and Waldo never regretted his conscience-stricken wrangle with the Lord's Supper.

Many an Emersonian heavyweight has argued that the ritual itself was almost irrelevant. In this view, Waldo had been pondering his break with institutional Christianity for a long time. The Lord's Supper was simply his excuse.

This is some truth to this. He had been tiptoeing away from God for years, if we take God to mean the domesticated deity that he and his peers encountered every Sunday in a thousand New England churches. Sometimes he seems to approach God and flee from Him at the same time. The effect, spiritually speaking, is like watching somebody run in place, as fast as possible.

For that matter, there is a strange circularity to Waldo's consciousness, especially as we experience it in his journals. His thoughts, impulses, dreams, and schemes never proceed in a straight line. They double back on themselves, pick up thematic threads first introduced years before, eerily anticipate what is to come. Things do not happen *in order*. There is a floating, omnidirectional sense to the way his life unfolds, which conforms to what Waldo called the "great principle of Undulation in nature."

So you might say that he left the church before he left it. Choosing the Lord's Supper as the last straw—the pernicious gnat he couldn't help but swipe at—might have been an arbitrary decision.

But I'm going to argue otherwise. Let's say you had recently suffered through the decline of the person you loved most in the world, whose frailty and youth seemed to put extraordinary pressure on every minute of her life. Let's say that person had died of a wasting disease whose most visible symptom was the coughing up of blood. The red wheezers, the clots in her handkerchief—all of these clinched the association between her death and those bright premonitory smears. Now let's say you were obliged to perform, every single Sunday, a ritual in which a cup of Madeira wine was supposedly transubstantiated into blood. You drank the blood, tasted its acidity and sacramental sweetness on your tongue. Wouldn't you recoil at a certain point? Wouldn't it break your heart to pretend?

. . .

A postscript: what Waldo began by leaving the Second Church, he completed with his Divinity School Address. This speech, delivered at Harvard in July 1838, was a homecoming—he had been a lukewarm graduate of that very school just twelve years earlier. Now the students had invited him back. Waldo, whose ideas about a more intuitive form of worship had been steadily germinating since he left the fold, was eager to take the battle to the very heartland of his abandoned faith. Perhaps he could enlighten these ministers-to-be before they went out the door.

He still functioned, at least intermittently, as a minister himself. That is, he mounted the pulpit on a freelance basis, pinch-hitting for absent pastors throughout New England. But now he was ready to stop—to transform himself into a secular minister of sorts. Perhaps the Divinity School Address was a half-conscious attempt to bar the door against any future backsliding.

In any case, he began his sneak attack with a song of praise to the natural world. "In this refulgent summer it has been a luxury to draw the breath of life," he wrote. "The grass grows, the buds burst, the meadow is spotted with fire and gold in the tint of flowers."

There is an argument to be made that he was already goading the audience. Behind such a word as "luxury," the theologically-minded crowd might well detect the lurking presence of *luxuria*, which meant "lust"—one of the seven deadly sins, no less. Still, some of his listeners may have been fooled into relaxing. One imagines them slouching slightly in their seats, grateful to be out of the sun and relieved that Waldo wasn't on the atheistic warpath.

He soon cut his bucolic vision down to size. He reminded his listeners that such astonishments were paltry compared to the all-encompassing entity of human consciousness. What he really wants to convey is that the greatest truths are embedded in the "foolish details," in the thorny facticity of everyday life. Every minister must be a phenomenologist, attuned to what is directly before our eyes:

> The child amidst his baubles, is learning the action of light, motion, gravity, muscular force; and in the game of human life, love, fear, justice, appetite, man, and God, interact. These laws refuse to be adequately stated. They will not by us or for us be written out on paper, or spoken by the tongue. They elude, evade our persevering thought, and yet we read them hourly in each other's faces, in each other's actions, in our own remorse.

The remorse, I think, was his own—possibly at the shafts he was about to fire. In any case, Waldo now began to round on his former colleagues. First he put in a pitch for intuition as the taproot of spiritual life, rather than scriptural learning. Such knowledge "cannot be received at second hand," he argues. "Truly speaking, it is not instruction, but provocation, that I can receive from another soul."

At this point, the divinity students might have been scratching their heads a bit. But worse was to come, especially if you subscribed to Andrews Norton's view of the Biblical miracles—i.e., their reality. "The very word Miracle," Waldo intoned, "as pronounced by Christian churches, gives a false impression; it is Monster. It is not one with the blowing clover and the falling rain." Miracles, he suggested, were not only false, not only unnatural, but sinister. (In a surreal use of the same word just the year before, he lamented that "the state of society is one in which the members have suffered amputation from the trunk, and strut about so many walking monsters.")

This was an unmistakable assault. So too was Waldo's strafing of an unnamed minister who "sorely tempted me to say, I would go to church no more." His failure, in Waldo's view, was to respect the desiccated forms of worship more than the spirit itself, with its dizzying admixture of the inner and outer life. In this sense, the minister had turned his back on experience. He was ignoring the things of this world, which were not the tinfoil vanities condemned by the Calvinists but *what we were here for*.

I think it's worth quoting the passage at length. Let's linger on the theatrical juxtaposition of the snow (usually an emblem of erasure, but here a granulated form of élan vital) and the pastor, who starts to dematerialize before our eyes:

> A snowstorm was falling around us. The snowstorm was real; the preacher merely spectral; and the eye felt the sad contrast in looking at him, and then out of the window behind him, into the beautiful meteor of the snow. He had lived in vain. He had no one word intimating that he had laughed or wept, was married or in love, had been commended, or cheated, or chagrined. If he had ever lived and acted, we were none the wiser for it. The capital secret of his profession, namely, to convert life into truth, he had not learned.

The conversion of life into truth! That would be Waldo's profession henceforth. Meanwhile, he had dynamited what was left of his connection to the church. His speech, which he decided to print and distribute in August over the objections of his friends, prompted an eruption of angry broadsides from the Unitarian brass.

Norton himself struck back with a pamphlet entitled *A Discourse on the Latest Form of Infidelity* (1839). In it, he runs through a rogue's gallery of atheistic enablers—including Baruch Spinoza, the philosopher and Sephardic Jew whose own synagogue had excommunicated him for his "abominable heresies," and the German theologian Friedrich Schleiermacher, whose emphasis on religious feeling rather than practice struck Norton as both dangerous and dishonest. (He even assails the shifty Schleiermacher for his *name*, whose meaning in English is "veil-maker.") Waldo he never mentions. But Norton makes it clear that a plague is threatening American Christianity. He insists that miracles are real. In fact, he enlists geology and a kind of proto-Darwinism to demonstrate that since our knuckle-dragging forebears materialized out of a void (or so he argues), their very existence is miraculous.

No less pernicious, in Norton's opinion, is the fancy prose used to advance these blasphemous arguments. Again, there is no mention of Waldo, but the target of his wrath would have been clear to Norton's readers. "A man of talents has only to be obscure in his style and meaning," he declares, "in order to be regarded by a large proportion of the world, and among them not a few recently fledged literati, as very profound."

Waldo would not respond, at least in print. Norton, unable to contain his rage, took to the pages of Boston's *Daily Advertiser* and urged all concerned citizens "to whip that naughty heretic." But in his journal, Waldo reminded himself to avoid the "vulgar mistake of dreaming that I am persecuted whenever I am contradicted." Again, he declined to strike back.

It should be noted that the graduating class of 1838 numbered just seven students, one of whom missed Waldo's address. There were, then, just six fledgling ministers and a scattering of family members and faculty taking shelter from the hot sun during his appearance. Waldo's clarion cry, his insertion of the ecstatic self into American religion, was hardly heard by anybody. Even the printed version was limited to a small number of copies.

I doubt that Waldo was concerned, though. Questions of scale mattered very little if you envisioned the entire universe as a vast flux, its energies pouring in and out of the brain. A tiny, perspiring audience would upload his words to the Over-Soul—that Emersonian cloud of consciousness, shared by every single human being—as rapidly as a gigantic throng. "The ocean is a large drop; a drop is a small ocean." He was nothing if not patient.

. . .

A postscript to the postscript. I see that I have loaded the dice against Andrews Norton. This turns out to be a bad habit of New England historians, starting with the brilliant Perry Miller. Of course the temptation is great. We have Waldo and his scintillating cohort in one corner, and in the other, a crabby old man in spectacles defending the status quo.

But Norton was once a young hothead himself, with perfect hair and what appear to be, in a contemporary engraving, large fire-emitting eyeballs. In his youth, he fought the good fight against the gloom and doom of Calvinism. Only later did he turn into the stuffed shirt and Emerson-baiter that we love to mock: the man who, according to a campus joke at Harvard, would have entered sniffily into Heaven with the comment, "It is a *very* miscellaneous crowd."

Another reason not to dismiss Norton for his pro-miracle stance is that he *won*. That is, although we might like to think of the United States as a product of the Enlightenment—a materialist wonderland presided over by Benjamin Franklin, Thomas Edison, and Steve Jobs—we have never stopped believing in miracles. According to a 2021 survey, two out of three Americans believe that Jesus Christ had risen from the dead. A similar number believe that He will return to the earth to judge all the human beings who have ever lived, and that nonbelievers are in for a very rough time indeed.

This isn't because Norton's Unitarianism spread over the republic like kudzu. For a brief shining moment, in fact, that seemed like a possible outcome. In 1822, so astute an observer as Thomas Jefferson remarked that the "present generation will see Unitarianism become the general religion of the United States." Achille Murat, Waldo's atheist pal, felt the same way. Unitarianism, he argued a decade later, was spreading "from one end of the Union to the other."

But as I have already mentioned, the evangelicals—particularly Methodists and Baptists—were already swamping the older creeds. Just one glance at the scorecard should be sufficient. Between 1770 and 1860, the total number of Congregational churches in the country rose from 625 to 2,234—a respectable rate of growth, you might think. But during the same period, the number of Methodist churches rose from 20 to 19,883. The Baptists grew at a similar rate. Even a smaller sect like the Disciples of Christ, which didn't even exist until 1803, boasted 2,100 churches just five decades later. The evangelicals, whose outbursts of enthusiasm and anti-institutional zeal were regarded with such distaste by the buttoned-up Unitarians of Boston, carried the day.

Where does this leave Waldo? It's complicated. He was clearly no evangelical, and I mentioned earlier his puzzlement at what he called the "monstrous absurdities of the Methodists at their Camp Meetings." (In the relevant journal entry, he tellingly erased the word *enthusiasts* and substituted *fanatics*.) This was not only a theological choice but a temperamental one. Nobody was more ill-suited to the garment-rending theatrics of revivalism than Waldo. *His* ecstasies were internal. When he declared in "The American Scholar" that the current era "was bewailed as the age of Introversion," he didn't actually have a problem with that. Indeed, the interior of a person was precisely where the action was, as far as Waldo was concerned.

Yet one of his guiding influences was Edward Thompson Taylor, the evangelical pastor of the Seamen's Bethel Church in Boston and a self-described "Unitarian graft on the Methodist stock." Father Taylor treated his sermons as performances. He jammed them with maritime slang, anecdotes, and vivid, user-friendly metaphors. No wonder Waldo described them in terms that would one day be applied to his own lectures: "A string of rockets all night." So there was, early on, a slow drip of Methodist ardor into his veins.

More to the point, his insistence on a personal relationship with God aligned him more closely with the evangelicals than he might have imagined. His God was not theirs, of course. In Waldo's hands, He had been effectively rebranded as the Over-Soul, or nature, or consciousness itself. But you approached Him, always, on your own terms. You didn't need a mediator in a cassock. You didn't need an *expert*. Indeed, for some of the evangelicals, serious immersion in the theological curriculum made a minister that much more useless.

"I have seen so many educated preachers who forcibly remind me of lettuce growing under the shade of a peach-tree, or like a gosling that had got the straddles by wading in the dew, that I turn away sick and faint." That was Peter Cartwright, one of the great circuit-riding Methodists of the nineteenth century. "Any preacher who is a real preacher will tell you that: 'Don't follow me, follow Christ.'" That was Bob Dylan, during his evangelical interlude of the late seventies, which shows exactly how little had changed since Waldo's day. Dylan, too, ended up with a more elastic notion of God, which caused him to drift away from the gospel before too long. But any time Americans start regarding the minister as a drag, a hurdle, an impediment to grace, Waldo and his Divinity School Address will creep into the conversation, consciously or not. He was the one who told us to ignore the sermon in favor of the snowstorm—sound advice for believers and nonbelievers alike.

. . .

And where does this leave me? I'm a nonbeliever, a secular Jew, with a strange penchant for watching Joel Osteen's sermons on TV. This perpetually smiling man presides over the largest evangelical congregation in America, housed in a converted sports arena where the Houston Rockets used to play. At beginning of his Sunday program, the airborne camera glides over the 16,800 congregants—it is, I believe, God's POV—and the flashing lights and whiz-bang visuals certainly would have gladdened the heart of Father Taylor.

Osteen always opens with a joke. Sometimes it's funny. Then he delivers his sermon, which is always the same sermon, about getting over your selfishness and bad attitude by cultivating a relationship with Jesus. There is also relentless uplift, more than a dash of the prosperity gospel, and the occasional plug for the pastor's books. (One of them, published in 2015, has a rather Emersonian title: *The Power of I Am*.)

The congregants look very, very happy, and I watch them with incredulity and envy. It's not easy being a materialist. You're forced to make up meaning on the fly, and the moment you stop, panting with ontological fatigue, you are lost. It's as if some homemade contraption, a bamboo bicycle from *Gilligan's Island*, was all that kept you from plunging to the bottom of things. You're exhausted. You need a miracle. I'm joking, but the unease I'm talking about is deeply sad and unsettling.

Also, it is worse in the wake of great loss. Everything is ruptured: emotions, relationships, the million Lilliputian filaments that we mistake for tethers but are actually securing us, keeping us in place. What is gone is more palpable, more *real*, than what is here. What is here means so little. That's when we realize that our customary, heedless sense of significance is propped up by nothing more than our own belief, like a fiat currency. What are we doing here? Why are we doing it, if not for some carrot-and-stick arrangement in the world beyond, the world of light and astonishment and wholeness whose very plausibility

I have doubted every second of my adult life? *Help me,* is where you end up. *Help me in my unbelief.*

It is, oddly, Waldo who has come to the rescue. His solution to the problem of nihilism is simple and elegant, the product of a Yankee tinkerer with intangible materials. Seeking the meaning of life turns out to *be* the meaning of life. "A strange process too, this, by which experience is converted into thought," he writes, "as a mulberry leaf is converted into satin. This manufacture goes forward at all hours."

The silkworm may have its own agonies, but the metaphor works. So does Waldo's system of secular transcendence. By making God another name for nature, or the soul, or some variety of consciousness that is both universal and spiritually bespoke, he gave me a seat at the table. Sure, I'm sometimes put off by the residue of piety in his prose. Yet he invites the reader into a nondenominational communion that may require no more than extreme attention to the things of this world, a form of curiosity that borders on tenderness or even love. That is real presence enough for me.

6

A CONJUNCTION
OF TWO PLANETS

There are first marriages and there are second marriages. The first is an exercise, always, in blind faith. This isn't a bad thing: faith is blind by definition, it's a wager on something you feel so intensely that evidence is beside the point. Two young people agree to take a leap into the void. They understand neither themselves nor the other person. This lack of understanding, this delicious opacity, is what makes the leap possible in the first place. Call it innocence. The void, meanwhile, is not empty but stuffed to capacity with tenderness, awe, sex, companionship, dirty diapers, acrimony and irritation, the million small discoveries that make every marriage a kind of endless road to Damascus.

Time passes. You decide whether the wager was a good one or a bad one. You wonder whether such judgments really have anything to do with the inflatable lifeboat in which you and your spouse have been drifting for so many years. You are still, after all, afloat—unless you are not.

Which brings us to the second marriage. Experience, also delicious, has replaced innocence. Both parties are more fully formed, some of the gaps in consciousness have closed up like fontanels. You know what you want, or think you do. So the second marriage may resemble a mutual-aid society, or a Warsaw Pact between consenting adults. The joy is there, and the comfort, and the invigorating strangeness of another person. But you are no longer playing house, no longer rehearsing. This is the real deal, the long march, with plenty of time for love to turn into something else—affection, maybe, or tolerance—and then magically reconstitute itself like a dinosaur from a microscopic dab of DNA. The *duration* of love, its weirdly irreducible quality, is the whole point of the second marriage. You expect less, and if you're lucky, you get more.

Waldo, in the wake of Ellen's death, seemed unlikely to remarry. "There is one birth & one baptism & one first love," he wrote in his journal just a few days after she died. These are the words of a man in a defensive crouch, fending off any hopes of future happiness. Better to expect nothing—to hibernate out in Concord and pour his grief and occasional gladness into the pages of *Nature*.

Yet his life, as I mentioned earlier, has an omnidirectional flavor to it. Things happen, but not in the expected order. So it was that his future wife wandered into Boston's Twelfth Congregational Church in 1829 or so, and was struck by the curving, swan-like neck of the man in the pulpit. As her daughter Ellen later recounted, "She didn't know a human being could have a neck so long." Transfixed by what the minister had to say, she hardly moved throughout the entirety of the sermon and felt some muscle aches when it was over.

Here was Waldo's first intersection with Lydia Jackson. He was already engaged to Ellen Tucker, or perhaps the two were married by then. Lydia recalled seeing him again soon after, on a Sunday morning, as he walked to church with his vestments flapping in the breeze. Five years passed. Waldo lost his wife, his calling, his congregation. Then, in 1834, he came several times to lecture in Plymouth, Massachusetts, where Lydia was living with her aunt.

She attended his lecture, said nothing further about his neck, and deliberately avoided meeting him. That must have taken some effort, since Waldo's old friend George Bradford, who had set up the lecture, was Lydia's German teacher. At this point, a whiff of romantic comedy enters the picture, a sense that the single woman and the eloquent pulpit performer will end up together. Of course such stories are largely retrospective. Their function is to make the second marriage seem fated, perhaps the correction of an earlier mistake. We don't want to believe that love is arbitrary. We persist in this belief even if the first marriage should have taught us otherwise, which is no surprise, since love— which Waldo once compared to a "divine rage and enthusiasm"—is incidentally what we are all living for.

There was, in fact, a genuine convergence here. Lydia was a devout Christian with a do-it-yourself streak—which is to say, a willingness to borrow from several different traditions. She admired Isaac Watts, for example, whose Calvinist verses were the beating heart of the New England hymnal, but also Swedenborg's mysticism and the sunlit serenity of the Unitarians.

Officially, Christ came into her life nine years before her marriage. "It seemed," she later recalled, "as though a curtain were drawn aside." But her piety was on display much earlier than that. At age fifteen or sixteen, she was tormented by metaphysical doubts and already suspected that the Congregational Church would be no help whatsoever. She was comforted instead by a slender volume called *Hymns for Infant Minds*, the work of the English poet Jane Taylor, whose religious output has long since been eclipsed by her best known composition: "Twinkle, Twinkle, Little Star." Indeed, Lydia dreamed of meeting Taylor in Heaven and bursting into tears.

A few years later, she found an even more unlikely avatar: Napoleon. Learning of the tiny dictator's penchant for sleeping no more than four hours per night, she used it as the basis for a self-purifying regimen. She spent those extra, groggy, freezing hours reading religious tracts, starving herself, jumping rope, and leaping over a wooden footstool.

It was this ardent anchorite who now crossed paths with Waldo. As I have already said, their collision course made a certain amount of sense. Waldo had quit the Second Church three years earlier, and his increasingly elastic Unitarianism dovetailed with his future bride's anti-institutional approach to belief. The thing is, they were converging from opposite directions, and would soon shoot right past each other. Lydia's faith would settle into a more conventionally Christian groove, while Waldo wandered further and further afield until Christianity struck him as just another cul-de-sac, an impediment to seeing the world as it was.

. . .

But she didn't know that yet. It was 1834. She had been attending the young clergyman's lectures and sermons, and had been teased about their affinities. Now she had a waking dream. As she climbed the stairs at home, Lydia had a vision of herself descending the same stairs with Waldo, dressed in a wedding gown. She was shocked by the image, briefly examined her conscience on the staircase, and said aloud, "I have not deserved this!" There is something both vague and punitive about the comment. Was it her momentary mortification that she didn't deserve, or the actual prize of the young clergyman? In any case, she stuffed the whole matter back into her subconscious.

Waldo, meanwhile, returned to Plymouth to lecture on January 21, 1835. Clearly some stealth courtship had gotten underway during the preceding months. It's odd that Waldo said so little in his journal or letters about something this momentous. It makes you wonder whether *his* side of the courtship wasn't also a subconscious affair, conducted at a smiling distance by a man still afraid to betray the memory of his first wife. Perhaps he couldn't acknowledge his attraction to this intense woman with gray eyes and a taste for theological speculation that nearly matched his own.

Two days later, back in Concord, Waldo made a note in his journal. "Home again from Plymouth," he wrote, "with most agreeable recollections." The same evening, Lydia had another spectral encounter with him. He seemed to be standing over her, his face very close, gazing at her. The next day, while lolling on the sofa in an uncharacteristically relaxed vein, she was brought a letter. It contained a proposal of marriage from Waldo.

This is a peculiar document. It is written by a man not exactly in love—a man trying to fan the flames of what he calls "deep and tender respect" into something more combustible. He alludes to Coleridge, always the way to a woman's heart. He begs to be the recipient of *her*

love, which might be the real thing or simply a matter of shared interests: "I am persuaded that I address one so in love with what I love." He
is affectionate, he is ardent, but mostly he is trying to will something
into being.

Vision or no vision, the proposal took Lydia by surprise. She invited
Waldo to Plymouth to discuss it with her. They sat in the parlor and
talked, and out of shyness or embarrassment she closed her eyes (since
we seldom go into marriage with our eyes open) and wondered whether
she was up to the labor-intensive job of being his wife.

Also, she was clearly intimidated. He was a pure product of Boston
intellectual life; she was a small-town autodidact who jumped over
footstools. Yet he put her at ease on this question in a lovely exchange,
recorded decades later by her daughter: "She was telling him something and was afraid it was uninteresting, and asked him. He answered,
'Uninteresting! It is heaven!' and his eyes seemed to her to be like two
blue flames."

That did it. They were engaged. He gave her the diamond from Ellen
Tucker's wedding ring—an ominous sign, perhaps, or maybe just Yankee thrift again—and they agreed to have it set as a pin, which the jeweler promptly screwed up. That, too, begs to be read as a portent. So
does Waldo's description of his engagement to his brother William as a
"very sober joy." So does the tone of the letters he sent Lydia during the
next few weeks, the first of which concludes with the terribly romantic
hope that "the winds of heaven blow away your dyspepsia."

No matter. The engagement went forward. Waldo peppered his fiancée with letters. Lydia upgraded her wardrobe in an Emersonian manner, including a lilac silk dress that, in the words of one friend, made her
look "externally as well as internally *transcendental*." She was discreetly
inspected by a number of Waldo's intimates. His brother Charles denied
that she was beautiful, but considered her a "sort of Sybil for wisdom."
The writer and educational reformer Elizabeth Peabody noted a certain
fragility, as if "her mind wore out her body." Sarah Freeman Clarke, a
Transcendentalist fellow traveler and painter who would later illustrate
Margaret Fuller's travelogue *Summer on the Lakes*, called Lydia a "beam-
ing soul."

All of this smacks of special pleading, as if Lydia's looks were just barely rescued by the quality of her inner being. Yet the surviving photographs show a perfectly attractive woman. She had a strong nose, lustrous hair drawn back from a part in the middle (she seldom cut it), and striking, deep-set eyes, which were often lowered in a gesture of repose or self-abnegation. The only problem with her appearance, I suspect, is that she trailed behind her girlish predecessor. But that would be a problem, or at least a predicament, for the rest of her life.

The wedding was set for September 14. The day before, Waldo headed up to Plymouth in a chaise. Concerned that onlookers might find the bright yellow reins too festive, too anti-Puritanical—they might think, he later wrote, that he had "been weaving them of golden-rod"—he discarded them for a more sober green set. He reached his destination the next afternoon, and promptly derailed the nuptial logistics by talking to his beloved for three straight hours on the sofa in the parlor.

At some point somebody must have alerted Lydia to the problem. She hustled upstairs to change into her wedding dress, an eleven-year-old white muslin affair to which fashionably puffy sleeves had been added. She also wore some curly hair extensions, which her scandalized daughter, writing decades later, called "immoral as painting"—i.e., makeup. No doubt all this adornment took time. The minister, who would perform the service in the parlor, was slated to arrive by 7:30. At length, the exasperated groom mounted the stairs to ask what was going on. The two met on the landing and descended together: that is, they fulfilled Lydia's first vision of her life with the man she would call, to her dying days, Mister Emerson. Then they spoke their vows, and stood before the fireplace to receive their sole wedding gift, a dual inkstand.

. . .

It wasn't only theology that drew together the couple while simultaneously pushing them apart. They both had very specific ideas about marriage, which did not always overlap. Lydia sketched out her ideas in a letter to Elizabeth Peabody, just weeks before she recited her vows. She began with a lengthy Swedenborgian preamble. Not a hardcore follower of the

Swedish mystic, Lydia was nonetheless persuaded by his picture of the universe as a great duality, in which every element of the visible world had its equivalent in the invisible one. "Every society of Heaven," she quoted, "is also in perfect correspondence with the human form."

Here she was nicely aligned with her future husband, who shared this layer-cake conception of the cosmos. She also subscribed to Waldo's idea that nature and human life were, on the deepest level, analogous. The notion of a family tree, for example, was no glib metaphor but an essential truth: we *were* made of roots and branches. (In a comic aside, she added that some families "represent the entire plant even to its thorns.")

Lydia believed that couples, however, were composed of opposites. Such people were meant to be together—not because they were similar, but because they were different. Over time, they would smooth out each other's kinks and behavioral curlicues. Of course a good attitude and a high tolerance for irritation was necessary for this undertaking. Otherwise it could fail badly. If husband and wife declined their mission, Lydia explained, and instead "clash and make discord, out of what were given as the very elements of harmony—it is their own fault."

This machinery of mutual correction, she added, did not allow for middling outcomes. Marriage was "no half way condition, but one of great happiness or misery." She was, again, writing all this before she was actually married. No doubt the forty-seven years she spent as Waldo's wife led to a more nuanced view—to a sense that happiness and misery might mingle in unpredictable ways, not canceling each other out but producing a kind of emotional chiaroscuro.

Waldo, on the other hand, had been married for some time when he wrote his own conjugal manifesto. This was "Love," published in *Essays: First Series* in 1841. He begins with some of his friskiest, sweetest prose about human feelings. At the ancient age of thirty-eight, he was first of all determined to knock down the old slander that love is reserved for the young—for those in the "heyday of the blood." Instead, he argued, it was a miniature incendiary device that took decades to set the consciousness ablaze. Love, we read, is "a fire that, kindling its first embers in the narrow nook of a private bosom, caught from a wandering spark out of another private heart, glows and enlarges until it warms and beams upon multitudes of men and women, upon the universal heart of all, and so lights up the whole world and all nature with its generous flames."

A tall order, you might say—lighting up the whole world with what we conceive as a private emotion. It is made easier by the contagious nature of those feelings. "All mankind love a lover," Waldo writes. It is such a surprising phrase from this lofty man. But love, for him, was very much an affair of the intellect. It began, he knew, in the physical world, with small gestures: a glance, a word, a touch. But its true flourishing was in the imagination. "In the actual world—the painful kingdom of time and place—dwell care, and canker, and fear," he declares. "With thought, with the ideal, is immortal hilarity, the rose of joy."

There is an awful lot of rapture here. One wonders whether Waldo isn't being evasive: talking about love as simply one more escape from the actual. It's a relief, then, to see how astute he can be about it. He recognizes that the rose of joy is hedged about by anxiety and even despair. "In the noon and the afternoon of life," he writes, "we still throb at the recollection of days when happiness was not happy enough, but must be drugged with the relish of pain and fear." The recollection is clearly his own. The language suggests the torment of Waldo's first marriage—the way in which Ellen, slowly and then quickly consumed by her illness, was lost to him almost from the moment he found her. This is a particular man describing a particular emotion.

Not for long, though. Love, he now argues, transforms not only the lover but just about everything else. Once more Waldo invokes the feedback loop of the individual soul and the natural world. Passion, he writes,

> makes all things alive and significant. Nature grows conscious. Every bird on the boughs of the trees sings now to [the lover's] heart and soul. The notes are almost articulate. The clouds have faces as he looks on them.

Love, then, makes Transcendentalists of us all. The perceptual scales fall from our eyes. We are as nearly attuned to nature as—well, the author of *Nature*. But having made this equivalency, Waldo seems to retreat from the boldness of his earlier assertions. The warmth goes out of his argument. Loving another person becomes, annoyingly, a path to spiritual purification. Who that person *is* matters less, which is where Waldo and Freud unhappily intersect. "Thus even love," he declares, "which is the deification of persons, must become more impersonal every day."

Would Lydia be satisfied with that? Perhaps not. But she must have relished her husband's endorsement of marriage as a means of mutual improvement. In the company of his wife, Waldo writes, a man "attains a clearer sight of any spot, any taint, which her beauty has contracted from this world, and is able to point it out, and this with mutual joy that they are now able, without offense, to indicate blemishes and hindrances in each other, and give to each all help and comfort in curing the same."

Granted, the burden of perfection here seems to weigh more heavily on the wife. She is to remain spot-free, taint-free, while one vaguely wonders how many of a man's flaws can be chalked up to simple wear and tear. Still, I think Waldo was sincere in his desire for a two-way relationship. He recognized many dents in his spiritual comportment and suspected that Lydia was the woman to help pound them out.

. . .

So who improved whom, and how? Just a week after their engagement, Waldo took the strange step of changing his fiancée's name. He began addressing her as Lidian, which had an exotic flavor and preemptively dodged (or so he argued) a quirk of New England pronunciation. Doubters, such as his cousin Sarah Ripley, were simply informed that the bride's parents had bungled matters at her baptism and chosen the wrong name.

What Lidian (as I will now call her) thought of this is not recorded. The name stuck. Waldo meanwhile urged her to address him more informally: "I hope you will be able to find a more affectionate name than Mr E." She, too, refused to budge. There is something comical about this Battle of the Names, with each party struggling to define the other.

Meanwhile a secondary skirmish was waged, regarding where the newlyweds would live. Lidian favored Plymouth, where she had grown up, while Waldo lobbied for Concord. Having made his case to Lidian, Waldo promptly denied having any real power to persuade her: "For me to measure my influence would be to deal with infinitesimal quantities & I might commit suicide." He was influential enough, however. In July, he paid $3,500 for an L-shaped house overlooking the Cambridge Turnpike in Concord, where the couple would live for the rest of their lives.

Of course it would be Lidian's job to get Bush, as they dubbed the house, up and running. Her letters of the time, many of them to her sister Lucy Jackson Brown, are jammed with domestic detail. They suggest that Lidian, who had considered herself a prospective spinster and never run a household before, was a quick study. There is much talk about nailing down the parlor carpet, about the chimney draft and the brass plates on the doors. There is the burning issue of bells: "Mr E. thinks we must not deny ourselves bells—the want of which we feel much." She asks her sister how to mend an old coat, since Waldo sometimes went about in what she considered rags.

None of this struck as her drudgery. She had, after all, lived with a sequence of relatives after the early deaths of her parents, and must have felt her third-wheel status in many of those households. Now she was able to run one of her own, and clearly found it a bracing experience. Her joy at living with Waldo (and, temporarily, his brother Charles) seems inextricable from her domestic learning curve:

> Sometimes it comes over me as *so* strange that I should be housed with these two wonderful beings—turning out coffee for them and helping them to pie! Consulting also about the keeping of pigs & hens—and telling Waldo to be sure to stop at the grocers in his morning expedition, and ask him to send home some eggs & ginger—and to inquire the price of mollasses & rinsing-tubs.

And so it went. Lidian, we should remember, was a woman whose intellectual and spiritual curiosity was very much on par with her husband's. One Plymouth resident had gone so far as to call their impending marriage a "conjunction of the two planets." Yet she would spend much of her life reckoning with kitchen chores. This strikes the modern eye as a kind of defeat. Had yet another female consciousness been steamrolled out of existence by an alpha-dog male? Or to put in another way: Was the model of mutual improvement simply a ruse?

I think not. Lidian's influence, which she saw no need to ironically disclaim, was enormous. She jogged Waldo out of his accustomed orbit in ways that almost nobody else could. She was devoted to the great causes of the age: abolition, female suffrage, and animal rights, among others. Waldo's initial attitude toward these reform movements was one of gentle ridicule. In "New England Reformers," a lecture he delivered in 1844, he wrote: "One apostle thought all men should go to farming; and another, that no man should buy or sell: that the use of money was the cardinal evil; another, that the mischief was in our diet, that we eat and drink damnation. These made unleavened bread, and were foes to the death to fermentation."

To be fair, some of these reformers *were* nutcases with wild eyes and bare feet, their matted beards dotted with vegetarian crumbs. They knocked at all hours on Waldo's door in Concord. They presented their schemes for global improvement, and chomped on Lidian's bread and butter while questioning the moral purity of what they were swallowing. He was right to be wary of the crazies.

Lidian was not a crazy. But her reformist impulses were sometimes extreme. Her passion for animal rights—not a universal sentiment during the 1840s—reached some particularly zany heights. She was protective of flies, wasps, spiders. When a rat occupied the chimney in Waldo's study, the rest of the family was eager to catch it, while Lidian thoughtfully placed two pieces of toast and half a donut up in the flue. She was no less solicitous on behalf of the chickens. As her daughter later recounted, the "miseries of her hens were ever present to Mother's mind," and during the winter months, she was tormented by the thought of their cold feet. To remedy this, she went outside and wrapped the entire roost in bits of woolen fabric. Alas, when the spring came and the hens were free to roam, they tore up the garden and had to be confined once again. This, too, made Lidian miserable: "If she was a hen she should feel it a flagrant act of injustice and tyranny." (It was the Emersons' friend and neighbor Henry David Thoreau who ultimately mitigated the problem by sewing tiny cowhide shoes for the hens.)

I bring all this up only to suggest that Emerson might have viewed some of Lidian's passions with affectionate amusement. Abolition was another matter. While Waldo had always regarded slavery as a moral stain, he had little fondness, at least in his younger days, for actual abolitionists. As he wrote in his journal, "They are a bitter, sterile people, whom I flee from."

Some of his response was temperamental. An instinctive solitary, Waldo shrank from the contact sport of politics. Yet this also feels like an out, a dodge, a failure. No theory of moral compensation would destroy the custom of human chattel. Waldo would, in time, figure this out. His transformation from cloistered metaphysician to antislavery agitator is something I will return to later, and at length. For the moment, I want to stress that Lidian got there first.

She was the one who helped to found the Concord Female Anti-Slavery Society in 1837. She was the one who invited such prominent abolitionists as Wendell Phillips and George Luther Stearns to the Emerson home for what her daughter called "pow-wows refreshing to her very soul." For Lidian, abolitionism was no mere expression of abstract principle but a call to engage, to *act*. She made this clear in an 1837 letter to her niece Sophia, when she recounted a visit by Sarah and Angelina Grimké, a pair of crusading sisters who broke with their slave-owning family in South Carolina to become ardent activists:

> They dined & took tea with [me] one day and it was a pleasure to entertain such angel strangers—pure & benevolent spirits are they. I think I shall not turn away my attention from the abolition cause till I have found whether there is not something for me personally to do and bear to forward it.

Her objections to slavery, one senses, were Christian but also rooted in an absolute inability to tolerate pain—not hers so much as anybody else's. "She was always more sensitive to suffering than to happiness," her daughter recalled.

Would Waldo's subsequent career as an activist have been possible without Lidian's encouragement and example? I think not. There is no doubt that Waldo venerated his wife's depth of feeling. When he wasn't calling her Lidian, he called her Asia, an affectionate (if Orientalist) nod to her hidden reserves of emotion and thought. Over the course of a long marriage, they *did* exert a gravitational tug on each other—the Plymouth neighbor who described them as two planets got it right. So I will insist that the improvement was mutual.

In fact, I will go further and say that Lidian represented the reality principle for her deeply cerebral husband. She kept him anchored to the world of molasses and rinsing tubs and ordinary pain. It was her own hypersensitivity—her tendency to absorb the woe of others like a parabolic dish—that shielded her from Transcendental solipsism. It allowed her to serve as a check on Waldo's infinity-addled impulses, which he dearly needed.

. . .

There were, of course, some complexities. During the first five years of their marriage, Waldo seems to have muted his increasingly skeptical view of Christianity. There were communal prayers every morning before breakfast with the family and servants, and another round of prayers before bed. Indeed, when it appeared that her sister Lucy Jackson Brown might join the household, Lidian assured her that these prayers would "be a chief comfort and blessing to you, as to me. These seasons are my very *happiest*—blessed be God!" She added that her husband was devoted to that same God "in a degree beyond my hopes," which is a real testament to Waldo's kind-hearted Christian camouflage.

Again, I should stress that Lidian's notion of Christianity was hardly conventional, nor rooted in the mild-mannered Unitarianism that had driven her husband from the pulpit. In an 1839 letter, she sketches out what she calls her "serene theosophy," suggesting a faith more reliant on ecstatic or direct intuition. This seems in line with Waldo's beliefs, while her description of unbelief as a nervous disorder—the body betraying the soul—is all her own. "All despondency is founded on delusion," she writes. In her own case, she adds, such nihilism "originates in bodily disease—or fatigue at least. It is in the nerves,—the soul disowns it."

Around 1840, though, something happened. Perhaps Waldo had finally recoiled from the ritual of prayer, just as he had recoiled from the rite of Holy Communion. In any case, he put a stop to the morning and evening worship sessions. (Lidian and Waldo's mother, Ruth Haskins Emerson, who lived at Bush, resisted this atheistic initiative by reading the Bible and reciting hymns together in private.) More to the point, Lidian came to recognize that her husband "was not a Christian in her sense of the word, and it was a most bitter discovery."

The damage went beyond her intimacy with Waldo. Having lost a vital connection to the man she adored, she also worried that his dwindling sense of Christian belief had weakened her own. By 1841 Lidian was in the midst of a spiritual crisis. She had lost "that blessed nearness to God in which she had lived so long." She never regained it, and always imagined a kind of deficit at the core of her being.

Waldo, meanwhile, brought his own problems into the marriage. The departed Ellen would always cast a long shadow. Lidian, who gamely named their second child Ellen Tucker Emerson, must have frequently felt eclipsed. The comparison was unfair from the start. Waldo's first marriage was too brief and too full of dread for him to fully settle into it. In an 1840 journal entry, Waldo seemed to compare his freewheeling past with Ellen to his current domesticity with Lidian. "Once I was in love and whenever I thought of what should happen to me & the maiden, we were always traveling," he wrote. "I could not think of her otherwise. Again I was in love, and I always painted this maiden at home."

Granted, this is a poetic formulation, not a session at the marriage counselor's. For that matter, his life at Bush was often blissfully happy. Still, it was right about this time that he began to express doubts about the institution of marriage itself. It struck him, rather suddenly, as artificial. In a better world, he insisted, we would enjoy "brave ties of affection not petrified by law, not dated or ordained by law to last for one year, for five years, or for life." He was, in a sense, comparing his rarified ideas of intimacy with the dailiness of an actual partnership. Predictably enough, the soft-boiled egg and the perambulator came up short.

Over the next year or so, his complaints about the institution grew more bitter. First he concluded that literary men in particular were poor candidates for domesticity. "The writer ought not to be married, ought not to have a family," he declared in his journal. "I think the Roman Church with its celibate clergy & its monastic cells was right." Man and wife might be beautifully matched at the start—that much Waldo conceded. But the meeting of souls was unlikely to last. After that, being "married & chained through the eternity of Ages, [was] frightful beyond the binding of dead & living together."

Conjugal life, in other words, was little better than being shackled to a corpse. Not a pretty picture, is it? Yet the ferocity is hardly definitive. What I mean is that Waldo's feelings about matrimony were mixed and mercurial, as they were about so many things. A human being who had constructed an entire belief system around solitude—who had only just declared that his ultimate subject was the "infinitude of the private man"—was unlikely to relish every moment of the joint operation that is marriage. Yet he basked, much of the time, in the quotidian delights of family life. How might he square these contradictory impulses? It was an ongoing argument with himself, which would go on for decades.

This argument reared its head most memorably in a "droll dream, whereat I ghastly laughed," as he noted in an 1840 journal entry. In it, a congregation had assembled to "debate the Institution of Marriage," and the first few speakers had been scathing in their criticism.

> One speaker at last rose & began to reply to the arguments, but suddenly he extended his hand & turned on the audience the spout of an engine which was copiously supplied from within the wall with water & whisking it vigorously about, up, down, right, & left, he drove all the company in crowds hither & thither & out of the house. Whilst I stood watching astonished & amused at the malice & vigor of the orator, I saw the spout lengthened by a supply of hose behind, & the man suddenly brought it round a corner & drenched me as I gazed. I woke up relieved to find myself quite dry, and well convinced that the Institution of Marriage was safe for tonight.

I hardly know where to start. The orator, who *is* Waldo as surely as the audience member who narrates the dream, is a defender of marriage, literally hosing down his opponents with the vehemence of his words.

He drives them into the street, and while Waldo calls this behavior malicious, there is something antic about the whole scene. It's like a parliamentary debate at a frat house. It's also a sexual metaphor—a bulletin from the interior on Waldo's erotic life, although its meaning is hardly cut-and-dried. Is sex the great enabler of a functioning marriage, or is it the other way around? The orator's lengthening, well, spout seems to deliver joy and chaos alike. In any case, Waldo is drenched at the end, feels the shock as he awakens, and is relieved find himself dry in his bed.

Even Joel Porte, a great Emerson scholar not inclined to take the low road, was willing to call this a wet dream. It is certainly climactic. Yet it resolved nothing—the gentle war of attrition that was the Emerson marriage went on for many more years.

. . .

To be more precise, the Emersons still had four decades of conjugal life before them. They shared a good many joys, including the raising of four children: Waldo was born in 1836, Ellen in 1839, Edith in 1841, and Edward in 1844. They shared, too, the terrible grief that attends the loss of a child, when Waldo died of scarlet fever in 1842, at the age of five. I will return to this topic later. For now, I just want to note that such a loss can unite husband and wife or drive them apart—or, more likely, both things at once.

For Lidian, the grief probably merged with her sense of being spiritually marooned in the household, and destroyed forever some of her capacity for happiness. "For the next thirty years," her daughter recalled, "sadness was the ground-colour of her life." Feeling cut off from her husband, she sometimes took to her bed, that great Victorian balm for psychological starvation. There she experimented with various remedies ("poppy and oatmeal," in Waldo's phrase), read both the Bible and a stack of medical textbooks, and persistently stumped the doctors who were summoned to her bedside, since they could find nothing wrong with her.

Waldo, no less devastated by his son's death, took the opposite tack: denial. He threw himself into writing, lecturing, traveling, all the while

FIGURE 5. Lidian Emerson with young Edward Emerson, 1847.
Courtesy of the Concord Free Public Library.

flaying himself for his lack of grief, which he had very specifically stuffed
into the deepest recesses of his heart. He wrote a long elegiac poem for
the boy and then delayed publication for four years and dismissed what
he had written as nothing special.

Lidian knew better. "How intensely his heart yearns over every memento of his boy I cannot express to you," she wrote her sister Lucy
Jackson Brown just weeks after Waldo's death. "Never was a greater

hope disappointed—a more devoted love bereaved." And *he* knew that the lost child would unite them always. Sharing their parental memories, he understood, would torture and comfort them in equal measure—it would, as he put it, "magnify our lost treasure to extort if we can the sweetest wormwood of the grief."

What bond could be deeper than this one? Yet Waldo remained Waldo, a man wary of personal entanglements even while he engaged in chaste flirtations with a couple of female admirers. He needed to keep his distance. On one occasion, he actually apologized to Lidian for his lack of husbandly heat. "A photometer," he lamented to her, "cannot be a stove," suggesting that he was better at storing erotic and emotional energy than dispensing it.

And still, these people *needed* each other. Waldo provided stability, solvency, and a model of spiritual (if not exactly Christian) aspiration. Lidian ran the household, raised the children, agitated for the great causes of the day, and reliably popped the balloon of her husband's pretensions. "Save me from magnificent souls," she told him. "I like a small common-sized one."

In case he didn't get the message, she also handed over something she called the Transcendental Bible. This brief parody, scribbled in pencil on a sheet or two of paper, *almost* sounds like the real thing—the very best sort of parody. "Loathe and shun the sick," went one typical injunction. "They are in bad taste, and may untune us for writing the poem floating through our mind." Another, lengthier section lampooned Waldo's philosophy with a series of snarky parentheticals:

> If you ask not a wise Providence over the earth in which you live (although wishing a wise manager of the house in which you live) if you care not that a benign Divinity shapes your ends (though you seek a good tailor to shape your coat) if you scorn to believe your affliction cometh not from the dust (though bowed to the dust by it) then, if there is such a thing as duty, you have done your whole duty to your noble self-sustained, impeccable, infallible Self.

This satiric production was brought out at regular intervals and read to the household. Waldo would laugh at the very thought of it, and on one occasion, he appreciatively told his daughter, "Yes, it was a good squib of your Mammy's."

Good squibs, with their gentle dose of mockery, were what he needed—it's a pity Lidian didn't write more of them. But even in her endless tug-of-war with Waldo over Christian belief, she ended up with many of the best lines. In one letter, she summed up their differing views of Jesus. He was her Master, while Waldo took the deflationary tack of regarding Him as a "most excellent Jewish youth." In another, written when Waldo was touring Egypt and maintaining an exhausted radio silence, Lidian teased him for traveling not only with their daughter Ellen but with a cohort of missionaries and Sunday school teachers. The company, she wrote, would be "very charming of course to such as St. Ellen and your narrow minded wife; but intolerable bores to the enlightened philosopher."

This is acerbic, no doubt. She was stuck in Concord, after all, while the elderly Waldo swanned up and down the Nile. Yet the long marriage allowed much room for equivocation, and for love to rise once again from the ashes of ambivalence. On that count, Lidian was wrong: married life is not a zero-sum choice between mirth and misery. It is instead a constant navigation between one or the other, with a million course corrections along the way. Or a halfway house, in the older sense of the phrase—a midpoint between two known locations—in which both parties only imagine themselves to be confined, and by choice.

7

THE AGE OF THE FIRST PERSON SINGULAR

No story can be told in isolation. Instead, every tale is flanked by its fellows, and experience itself is a buzz of competing narratives, a babel of what happened. So while Waldo conducted his slow-motion courtship of Lydia Jackson, and married her, and built a life within the thin walls of the house they came to call Bush, he was also writing essays.

These were not incidental creations. That alone is a fact worth noting: the essay was still a sketchy item in Anglo-American letters, mostly written and read on the fly, not regarded as a top-drawer literary genre.

Of course there was the shining example of Michel de Montaigne, one of Waldo's heroes, who had retreated to his circular tower in 1571 and emerged a decade later with a sheaf of brilliant, mirror-like investigations of the self. There was Francis Bacon, arguably Montaigne's opposite number in England, who nonetheless regarded his essays as "recreation to my other studies"—i.e., a left-handed hobby. There were Richard Steele and Joseph Addison, whose Augustan elegance was much in vogue among the Unitarians. Last but not least, there was the coruscating William Hazlitt, who had died in obscurity right around the time Waldo began coming into his own as an essayist.

But Montaigne was a French import. Bacon was an Elizabethan relic. Steele, who more or less invented the literary magazine with *The Tatler* (1709), leaned heavily on coffeehouse gossip and moral instruction, as did Addison, whom the eighteen-year-old Waldo praised in his journal for "unfolding, in pleasing forms, the excellence of Virtue." As for Ha-zlitt, he had come out of the rough-and-tumble world of British journal-ism and pamphleteering, and there was something slightly raffish about him. Indeed, the essay itself seemed a little disreputable, a little indul-gent. With its mussy tone and casual warmth—with its air of *dishabille*—the essay seemed always to have just rolled out of bed.

Yet it was perfectly suited to Waldo. He was a man who lived and died by the sentence. He was happy to read certain long-form narratives: Mil-ton, Carlyle, *Faust*, wrist-wrenching stuff like William Robertson's *The History of the Reign of the Emperor Charles V* (in three volumes) or Henry Ellis's *Journal of the Proceedings of the Late Embassy to China* (a relative bantamweight at 526 pages). But as a writer, he had almost zero interest in telling such protracted tales, or tales of any length whatsoever. This wasn't a matter of attention span. It was a metaphysical preference. He saw the world—perceived it and processed it—in small doses. This didn't necessarily make him a miniaturist, since the smallest things were simply metaphoric versions of the biggest things, and vice-versa. An epic could be jotted on a thumbnail, an aperçu inscribed on the very cosmos. But the way to do it was by the sentence.

Waldo had no qualms about this. He was, perhaps, a touch apologetic in a letter to Carlyle: "Here I sit and read and write with very little sys-tem and as far as regards composition with the most fragmentary result: paragraphs incompressible [and] each sentence an infinitely repellent particle." But elsewhere he made his preference for the killer sentence a kind of credo. "I am a rocket manufacturer," he declared in his journal. He rolled out linguistic projectiles of all calibers—from firecrackers to cruise missiles—and thought of each one as his last word on the subject at hand. Until, that is, it was time to write another sentence.

These he assembled into essays. Why? The form was, for starters, a first cousin of the sermon. It was compact, persuasive, veined with pro-verbial phrases that either came from the Old Testament or sounded like they should have. The sermon was, for Waldo, primarily a poetic genre. ("The preacher should be a poet," he told a bunch of Harvard Divinity School students in 1838, not long before he delivered his bunker-busting address there.) The essay was a natural alternative—a secular sermon. Also, its formlessness, its lack of any road map aside from the author's intuition, must have appealed mightily to Waldo. It mimics the way we think, the mumbling, rumbling, roundabout workings of consciousness and what Cynthia Ozick (herself an essayist and Emersonian-by-default) once called "the hum of perpetual noticing." Thoughts, like stories, are manifold and associative. In both cases, the ramifications—the forking fireworks—are what give them the chaotic quality of animate things. Which explains the *vividness* of the best essays: they duplicate our habits of consciousness. They are, quite literally, like life.

Yet Waldo's methodology was a little weird, and explains a lot about the flavor of his essays. Most of what he wrote had its inception in his journals. These were his laboratory, his parts bin, his cabinet of wonders. They enabled him to take his wildest thoughts for a test drive, and to fuss and fidget in the privacy of his own home—which is to say, his own mind.

He understood early on that he would be cannibalizing his journals for his published work. To that end, he began indexing them by topic. That is, if he wrote a pungent paragraph about friendship, or pine trees, or the many defects of Unitarianism, he made note of the page and volume in a separate notebook. He did this year in and year out—a massive effort that paid major dividends once he set to work as an essayist. Whenever Waldo settled on a topic, he simply consulted his index, pulled all the relevant sentences and paragraphs, and spliced them together.

His great friend Bronson Alcott once described this procedure, which we might call composition-by-database, in detail. Alcott acknowledged that some of Waldo's readers were thrown by his creations, with their meager sense of forward motion. "It makes no difference, they say, whether you begin at the last paragraph and read backwards, or begin at what he meant for the beginning," Alcott wrote. "There is some principle in that."

In other words, guilty as charged. But there was also, Alcott argued, an underlying logic to Waldo's methods—"a thread on which he strings all his pearls." Each essay, Alcott suggested, was preceded by years of thought. Each was a fantastical work of compression, producing diamonds from the pure carbon of the commonplace. The labor, in other words, was ongoing and subliminal. The cut-and-paste job was merely a final consummation, during which the author assembled whatever he had

> written, perhaps during the last twenty or forty years, touching the question. He copies [the passages] off; sees in what order they can be strung together; perhaps spreads them before him. I remember hearing of an instance when a neighbor went in to see him, and there was the philosopher and poet leaning over his papers spread out on the floor before him, singling out paragraphs, perhaps, or trying what would be best for the introduction.

Not every reader was persuaded. In a famously tart assessment, the author and pioneering feminist Margaret Fuller compared the essays to "a string of mosaics or a house built of medals." She was one of Waldo's biggest fans, it should be noted—the ideal audience for his Roman candles. She recognized the sublime quality of the individual sentences while quibbling with the somewhat random relationship of one to the next. What she really wanted was what many of us want from an essay: an orderly progression of thoughts. Whereas for Waldo, this would consign his sentences to a kind of servitude, as if they were chained at the ankles. He preferred to move in seven-league boots, in any direction he pleased, with the horizon (as he once wrote) in perpetual retreat.

. . .

Let's zoom in on "Self-Reliance," the second item in *Essays: First Series* (1841) and still his most famous work. It is one long plea on behalf of the inner life, the intuitive life, the blaze of understanding that so outshines the low-wattage wisdom of the tribe. It is a rampaging assault on the herd mentality. Hasn't Waldo done this before, you ask, in both *Nature* and the Divinity School Address?

There is continuity here, to be sure. But in *Nature*, Waldo directed his rhetorical barbs at the past—at the sheer ballast of human history. In the Divinity School Address, it was the fossilized forms of institutional worship that drew most of his fire. Here, he is simply urging readers to separate themselves from the stultifying pack. This, he argued, was the imperative faced by every American in the midst of what Waldo else-where called the "age of the first person singular."

"To believe your own thought," he writes in the very first paragraph, "to believe that what is true for you in your private heart, is true for all men—that is genius." His belief in intuition was absolute. Back in the early 1830s, he was already smuggling such arguments into his sermons, insisting that the subjective self was the "voice of God himself which speaks to you and to all mankind without an interpreter."

Perhaps his parishioners, drowsing in their pews on Sunday morning, took little note of this theological dynamite. Perhaps they didn't notice that Waldo was removing his own job from the equation. Yet his argument in that 1832 sermon was essentially antiscriptural. By the time he took up the cudgels in "Self-Reliance," it was all of society that he was denouncing as a Procrustean bed of conformity.

He knew how hard it was to break free. He knew that belief in the self was infinitely more difficult than belief in God, which was like the force of gravity—you could fall without really trying. The altar of the self was different, and demanding. We doubt ourselves. We are *designed* to doubt ourselves, since consciousness is a heightened form of self-scrutiny, and we are anxious to shout down that inner voice, having written it off as the most unreliable of narrators.

This, Waldo insists, is a terrible mistake. "In every work of genius," he writes, "we recognize our own rejected thoughts: they come back to us with a certain alienated majesty." The line is a famous one. It has that epigrammatic ring to it, and in the second clause, one of Waldo's cherished rhythms. Note those rock-skipping monosyllables followed by something fancier, more Latinate, which slows the reader down and makes those final words sound, well, majestic.

He follows up with many more zingers: "There is a time in every man's education when he arrives at the conviction that envy is ignorance; that imitation is suicide." (*Not* the sincerest form of flattery, as per Oscar Wilde.) "Trust thyself: every heart vibrates to that iron string." We are approaching refrigerator-magnet territory here, but that is not Waldo's fault: he simply said it as succinctly as it could ever be said. Then he begins unloading his ordnance by the paragraph, to devastating effect:

Society everywhere is in conspiracy against the manhood of every one of its members. Society is a joint-stock company in which the members agree for the better securing of his bread to each share-holder, to surrender the liberty and culture of the eater.

I shun father and mother and wife and brother, when my genius calls me. I would write on the lintels of the door-post, *Whim*. I hope it is somewhat better than whim at last, but we cannot spend the day in explanation.

This second paragraph sounds a little churlish, doesn't it? Waldo would respond that he is on solid theological ground, since Jesus him-self (in Matthew 19:29) praised every follower who had abandoned "brethren, or sisters, or father, or mother, or wife, or children, or lands, for my name's sake." A true believer must spurn the entire family—not to mention real estate.

But Waldo also launches a collateral attack on philanthropy, which sounds less attractive to the modern ear. He is repelled by the *performance* of generosity. He regards it as a feint, a way of concealing your miserly sympathies for the creatures living under your very nose. It's the kind of behavior that Charles Dickens would ridicule, just a decade later, in *Bleak House*, when he described the "telescopic philan-thropy" of Mrs. Jellyby. She has no interest in helping the indigents right down the block. No, what excites her is the prospect of teaching African "natives to turn piano-forte legs and establish an export trade." This would have tickled Waldo. It was goodness shouted from the rooftops, goodness as window dressing—what we now call virtue signaling.

The problem was that he swung too far in the opposite direction. He poured his scorn upon every form of charitable relief, presenting himself as a Transcendentalist Scrooge. "Are they *my* poor?" he asks. "I tell thee, thou foolish philanthropist, that I grudge the dollar, the dime, the cent I give to such men as do not belong to me and to whom I do not belong." This is ugly. In some way he knew it, since he admits to donating the "wicked dollar" with some frequency. Yet he immediately doubled down on the connection between his cheapskate behavior and his spiritual scruples. Do-gooders, he argues, perform their philanthropic dance as an "apology or extenuation of their living in the world—as invalids and the insane pay a high board." This is brilliant rhetoric and *still* ugly.

Reader, I wish it were otherwise. I wish Waldo hadn't found the activists of his age so comical that he devoted much of "New England Reformers" to mocking them. They were, to him, irresistible targets, well-meaning cartoons. As I have already noted, many of these aspiring saviors of the world turned up on his doorstep. Others attended such reformist gatherings as the Chardon Street Convention, held in Boston in 1840.

Waldo wrote an article about Chardon Street for the *Dial*, in which he noted the long-winded diversity of the crowd: "Madmen, madwomen, men with beards, Dunkers, Muggletonians, Come-outers, Groaners, Agrarians, Seventh-day Baptists, Quakers, Abolitionists, Calvinists, Unitarians and Philosophers—all came successively to the top, and seized their moment, if not their hour, wherein to chide, or pray, or preach, or protest." I suppose I can bear Waldo making light of the Muggletonians, a splinter sect founded in 1651 by two London tailors who believed themselves to be biblical prophets. Less comprehensible is his attack on the Calvinists and Unitarians. That sounds like Thanksgiving dinner at the Emerson household, to be honest, with a pitched battle about predestination over the cranberry sauce.

But where he really went wrong, in the remarks above and in "Self-Reliance," is his disdain for the abolitionists. I have already mentioned Waldo's foot-dragging progress on this topic. At this point, he considered the abolitionists, too, guilty of long-distance beneficence—of fine feelings directed as loudly as possible at people who were far, far away. This was a foolish conclusion. It's a blemish on a great essay. The damage would be much worse if Waldo hadn't matured into a fiery opponent of slavery himself, who recognized that the moral universe extended far beyond his own backyard. We can somehow, by squinting, project the better man onto his less evolved predecessor.

. . .

Luckily, Waldo soon steers back into the main argument, which is the sovereignty of the self. "For nonconformity," he writes, "the world whips you with its displeasure." Church, tribe, state, community, virtually any group numbering more than two people—they are machines for ironing out the spiky irregularities of who you are. But we are no less in thrall, Waldo continues, to the past: to what we have already done, said, regretted.

We simply cannot stop hauling our previous existence into the dock, there to be judged by what he calls the "thousand-eyed present." The underlying terror is that we will prove to be different people at different times—that the continuity we so covet is a kind of fraud. But that doesn't bother Waldo, not in the least. "Why drag about this corpse of your memory, lest you contradict somewhat you have stated in this or that public place?" he demands. "Suppose you should contradict yourself; what then?"

He actually *loves* the idea that we are perpetual works in progress. We reconstitute ourselves with each passing second. Any notion of fealty to what we were ten minutes or ten years ago is a trap, an absurdity. Which brings us to another of Waldo's tentpole assertions:

A foolish consistency is the hobgoblin of little minds, adored by little statesmen and philosophers and divines. With consistency a great soul has simply nothing to do. He may as well concern himself with his shadow on the wall.

Consistency, in other words, is simply another kind of conformity. It is the past taming the present with a whip and chair, cowing it into submission. Yet the implications go deeper. They suggest a certain prescience about neuroscience, of which Waldo and his contemporaries knew nothing. I think he would have smiled and nodded at having anticipated the truly fragmented self—consciousness caught on a narrative treadmill, making itself up as it goes along.

Still other discoveries would have stirred him to knowing laughter. Every time we move our eyes, for example, a process called saccadic suppression shuts down the bulk of visual data until our gaze has alighted on a new target. In other words, we are essentially blind for about two hours each day. This is Waldo's kind of thing: the pure poetry of natural facts. It also aligns nicely with his belief that we *are* blind for much of our lives, groping our way through a Potemkin village version of the real. Even worse, this blindness is largely voluntary. Most men have "bound their eyes with one handkerchief or another," he writes, because blindness is a form of communal belonging. We fear reality, with its stupefying brightness, as we fear staring into the sun.

At this point in "Self-Reliance," however, Waldo does something odd. Having established that the self is no more than a bundle of cognitive fragments, he declares the very opposite. There is something, it turns out, called *character*. It is unchanging and inescapable. "A character is like an acrostic or Alexandrian stanza—read it forward, backward, or across, it still spells the same thing." We may sometimes veer away from who we truly are. Indeed, we may dedicate our entire lives to escaping from the straitjacket of the self, like so many hapless Houdinis. But in Waldo's view, these efforts are pointless, a kind of statistical jitter. No matter how various or vigorous our deviations, a single "tendency unites them all. The voyage of the best ship is a zigzag line of a hundred tacks. See the line from a sufficient distance, and it straightens itself to the average tendency."

Okay. But isn't a baked-in self at odds with the notion of consciousness that Waldo sketched out in the preceding paragraphs? I thought we were creatures of flux. I thought we lived in a perpetual present, without (as he writes) "prospect or retrospect." Doesn't that put the kibosh on any real continuity of character?

Not if you believe, as Waldo did, that fate and freedom were two sides of the same coin. Fate was what you were given. It was character, it was history, it was the core of a human being. Freedom was the ability to jettison those things. Freedom let you cut loose the metaphysical millstone around your neck. It gave you a new way of connecting to your past, and forced you to quarry a new self from the debris of the old one.

It must be repeated, though, that Waldo thrived on contradiction. It was a feature, not a bug, of the way he saw the world. To lash yourself too tightly to a single position meant that you would never explore the others, which might be no less clarifying. Thinking meant *changing your mind*, in every sense of that phrase. How could it be otherwise, given Waldo's hearty disdain for consistency? He would not travel down the familiar ruts of logic, linearity, precedent. Instead he advances over the stepping stones of his individual sentences and trusts his gut to make them hang together: musically, emotionally, spiritually.

So let's put the hobgoblin behind us and see where Waldo goes next. There is a brief paean to the self-reliant man, who makes not only himself but the external world in his image. This sounds a bit like the feedback loop between humanity and the material universe that Waldo floated in *Nature*. But here the stress is on the magnificent potentiality of each and every human being, and Waldo scales up his voice to match the largeness of his assertion. "Every true man is a cause, a country, and an age," he writes. Such a being "requires infinite spaces and numbers and time fully to accomplish his design—and posterity seems to follow his steps as a train of clients."

We are on visionary turf again. It is one thing to rage against the imbecility, the knee-jerk timorousness, of the tribe. It is another to propose an alternative: to suggest that the ordinary man or woman is also extraordinary, that reality is little more than raw material for the imagination. "An institution," he writes, "is the lengthened shadow of one man." He goes on to insist that "all history resolves itself very easily into the biography of a few stout and earnest persons." This is not, I should say, the Great Man theory at work. Waldo has his pantheon, as do we all, but the thrust of his argument is that *all* men are Great Men, not merely a select few in period costume.

Then Waldo latches, rather strangely, onto a new target: travel. The notion of the Grand Tour—which, let's recall, he himself had undertaken just a few years before—unleashes some indelible sentences:

> At home I dream that at Naples, at Rome, I can be intoxicated with beauty, and lose my sadness. I pack my trunk, embrace my friends, embark on the sea, and at last wake up in Naples, and there beside me is the stern Fact, the sad self, unrelenting, identical, that I fled from. I seek the Vatican, and the palaces. I affect to be intoxicated with sights and suggestions, but I am not intoxicated. My giant goes with me wherever I go.

What, you may wonder, has prompted this tirade against good old-fashioned tourism? Especially given that Waldo's own sojourn in

Europe, back in 1833, had been so restorative? To some extent, I think, it's the quotidian kicking in. He has just spent thousands of words extolling the self, decreeing that its powers are virtually unlimited. Reality, he insists, is at our beck and call—if we can only shut out the white noise of conformity and heed our inner promptings.

But the man writing these words was, like the rest of us, only occasionally a god. He was more often a shy, skeptical, pained human being, very much aware of his own flaws. He knew that half the time, the self is not a direct line to divinity but a burden. It was something we dearly wish to escape. Yet we cannot, nor could Waldo. Wherever he went, his giant went with him. The phrase is beautifully apt, an admission that if the self is vast, so are the deflationary powers of consciousness. So is (in a word) sadness.

. . .

I will not try to unpack the entire essay. That would require a chapter many times longer than this one, even if I simply copied out the best bits—which is actually my ideal prescription for reading Waldo's essays. He challenges us, really, to reverse-engineer a production like "Self-Reliance." He assembles an anthology of his best thoughts on the subject, from which the reader carves out another, smaller anthology. He strings together far-flung sentences from his journals, and we take them apart again.

Once you accept that your role as reader is to winnow the aphoristic wheat from the chaff, Waldo's essays suddenly seem less forbidding. Take what you need, he seems to say, and no more. This was how he read, after all, sifting through world literature for the golden utterances. As a writer, I would argue, he meant to be read in the same way. He *designed* his essays to be disassembled.

Chatting with a college student named Charles Woodbury during the 1860s, Waldo dismissed the very idea of attaching one sentence too securely to the next. "The moment you putty and plaster your expressions to make them hang together," he said, "you have begun a weakening process." He wanted his sentences to be portable, and easily plundered by the discriminating reader, whose joint property they instantly became.

Two additional points should be made. The first is about "Self-Reliance," whose central argument has long since become American gospel. We might assume that this nation's love affair with individualism was already underway when Waldo wrote his essay. That is not quite the case. The word *individualism* had hardly entered the language when he was writing "Self-Reliance." It was coined, in fact, by Alexis de Tocqueville, and made its first recorded appearance in *Democracy in America* (1835), where the author dwelled on its sheer novelty. Nowhere else, he suggested, did human beings congregate in such small numbers, or recoil from any sort of company at all. Individualism caused "each member of the community to sever himself from the mass of his fellows and to draw apart with his family and his friends, so that after he has thus formed a little circle of his own, he willingly leaves society at large to itself."

De Tocqueville, readers will recall, had also noted the tendency of Americans to form associations, fellowships, guilds. He was, in other words, as tolerant of contradiction as Waldo was—or willing to recognize that these two phenomena, solitude and community, might have a symbiotic relationship. In any case, he did insist that individualism was a hallmark of the new nation, and also a dangerous tendency. He disapproved of its atomizing effects, its whittling away of community, its treacherous conception of freedom. Individualism would eventually destroy civic life, he argued. It was to the private sphere what democracy was to the public sphere: inspiring yet corrosive, and likely to imprison the average citizen "entirely within the solitude of his own heart." Waldo read De Tocqueville's masterpiece in 1841, and would have noted the author's very mixed feelings about the infinitude of the private man.

But individualism—not just the word but the actual concept—was more generally in a bad odor. This Waldo knew. In an 1842 journal entry, he wearily conceded that many of his contemporaries thought that "the vice of the age is to exaggerate individualism." The term was even more unpopular abroad. In France, for example, it connoted either a violent rending of the social fabric or a kind of moony, adolescent focus on the inner life: a caricature of Romanticism.

All of which is to say that Waldo's fiery endorsement of the self did not always fall upon friendly ears. It was denounced as selfish, egotistical, anarchic. Some critics considered it downright blasphemous, since it conveyed the sort of antinomian disdain for established religion that had gotten Anne Hutchinson kicked out of the Massachusetts Bay Colony a mere two centuries earlier. It was denounced as *silly*. Yet Waldo stood his ground, and lived to see his ideas become part of the cultural oxygen.

But not right away. That was the other point I wanted to make. The work collected in *Essays: First Series* was literally world-changing. It enchanted Henry David Thoreau and Walt Whitman, Emily Dickinson and Leo Tolstoy, Mahatma Gandhi and Friedrich Nietzsche. (It was Nietzsche who remarked, "Never have I felt so much at home in a book.") Yet relatively few people read Waldo's second book when it was first published.

Of course, *Nature* hadn't flown off the shelves, either. The small edition printed in 1836 sold so slowly that no reprint was required until 1849—and *that* edition also took years to sell out. But *Essays* fared little better, at least in this country.

To some extent, the problem was with Waldo's publisher, the Boston-based James Munroe and Company. The industry itself had changed in recent decades. Boston retained a certain cachet as the nation's intellectual powerhouse. Yet it had been rapidly outstripped as a publishing hub by New York City and Philadelphia, both of which had much better access to the Midwestern market (via, respectively, the Erie Canal and the Susquehanna River). It's amazing, really, to ponder how much the trajectory of early American publishing was shaped by such geographical factors. Rivers, for example, tended to freeze by early January and remained impassable until March. This encouraged publishers to bring out their most promising titles in the autumn and spring—a custom that continues to this day.

By the 1840s, then, Boston publishers already seemed a little musty and provincial. Their contracts were seldom favorable to the author. Waldo's arrangement with Munroe was perilously close to what we would now call vanity publishing. He paid up front for the typesetting and printing costs. (Later on, he would also pay for the manufacture of stereotype plates, which would allow a given book to go back to press without resetting all the type.) Copies of *Essays* were then sold for a dollar, with Munroe pocketing twenty-nine cents on each sale. Waldo wasn't kidding when he told one correspondent, "I print them at my own risk."

To make matters worse, Munroe was running two businesses at once: a publishing house and a bookstore at 134 Washington Street. This was an obvious conflict of interest. Munroe was much more eager to sell copies at his own store than ship them out to the Ohio Valley, where he would have to split his commission with the local bookseller. Waldo recognized the problem in an 1846 letter, noting that his publisher would "not press the sale of the book at a distance which he prefers to sell at his own counter." In another discussion of Munroe's operation, he put it even more succinctly: booksellers, he grumbled, were "a vanity & vexation."

It wasn't only Waldo, by the way, who complained about Munroe's strictly local conception of publishing. Lydia Huntley Sigourney, whose poetry and self-help books had a sizable audience, was astonished to learn that the stuff she published with Munroe was unavailable not only in Ohio, but in her hometown of Hartford, Connecticut.

Even locally, however, it's hard to feel that Munroe was beating the drum very hard on Waldo's behalf. In 1848, the publisher purchased an ad in the *Stranger's Guide* to Boston. To prospective customers, Munroe bragged that he kept "constantly on hand all *standard books*, etc. in every variety of binding." But only after listing various editions of the classics does he move on to "miscellaneous publications." This category includes Waldo, who is fourth in the roster, right behind Charles Follen (the German-born abolitionist and gymnastics fiend who might have introduced the Christmas tree to America) and George Washington Burnap (a Unitarian stalwart whose voluminous output has long since vanished into the mist). So much for the hard sell!

It took at least three years, then, to unload all 1,500 copies of *Essays*. Is that a little or a lot? The literacy rate in the United States at the time was close to 90 percent. Yet the country was still a relative stripling, with a total population in 1840 of seventeen million and a correspondingly small pool of readers. The mass media, too, was in its infancy, at least in New England. Many publishers were essentially job printers, who turned out circulars, newspapers, invoices, and announcements alongside their loftier fare—or even hobbyists, producing small-batch product for the neighborhood. (Of the 1,573 printing offices counted in the 1840 census, two-thirds were located in rural villages.)

On the other hand, some of Waldo's peers, including those in the publishing backwater of Boston, had much bigger audiences. Henry Wadsworth Longfellow, for example, claimed to have sold more than 300,000 books by 1857. He was also more richly remunerated than Waldo ever was: in 1874, a New York newspaper paid him the latter-day equivalent of $80,000 for a *single poem*. Yet Longfellow, who declared that the first volume of Waldo's essays was jammed with "magnificent absurdities," had consciously aimed for populist success. These efforts made him a celebrity, a national bard, both at home and abroad.

Waldo may have envied him, to judge from the slyly dismissive remark he addressed to Longfellow after tackling *The Song of Hiawatha*: "I have always one foremost satisfaction in reading your books—that I am safe." But in his own books, Waldo had something else in mind: not safety, but prophecy. And as he learned, so much of prophecy is talking to oneself. So much of literature, too.

8

BEAUTIFUL ENEMIES

Waldo wrote the first volume of *Essays* (and just about everything else) in a single room. That would be his study, in the house at 28 Cambridge Turnpike, now accessed via a dainty turnstile in the white picket fence, upon whose lower rail Waldo used to deposit his cigar butts. The study is on the right when you enter. Every time I have visited, I am over-whelmed by the fact of being there.

The reason is simple. We all know that authors sit in actual rooms when they write. But Waldo more than most had aimed for a demateri-alizing effect: he wanted to peer right through the threadbare surface of the actual into the realm of the spirit. Surely such magic should take place in a glittery virtual-reality chamber, not in a normal room with burgundy rugs and a slight air of mustiness. You enter, and everything is still. All the twelve-over-twelve windows with their runny panes are sealed shut. There is a low blue sofa. There is a small, round table in the middle, with a rocking chair pulled up beside it—Waldo often rested his writing pad on his knees. There is the author's Aeolian harp on the windowsill, a suitable emblem for a man who was always eager for the natural world to stir him into speech.

What strikes me about the room (which is an exact replica, the origi-nal having been torn out and installed in the nearby Concord Museum in 1930) is its atmosphere of seclusion. With its dim light and sluggish ventilation and dark portraits on the walls, it seems like a hermit's cave. It was a place to think, and a kind of receptacle for thoughts. It was a place to be alone, and we might assume that Waldo never left it.

Wrong again. His study may have been his shrine, his laboratory of the self, but Waldo was not quite so solitary as he claimed. He was in fact surrounded by friends, intimates, acquaintances, admirers. The urge to flee this madding crowd was strong. Yet Waldo never built himself a modest Fortress of Solitude (he left that to Thoreau). Indeed, he was a social animal, who was touchingly eager to compensate for his own aloofness. His extraplanetary affect—which caused Margaret Fuller to remark that he always seemed to be on stilts—made him unhappy. He wished to defeat it.

To that end, he became a philosopher, or at least a theoretician, of friendship. That his theories simply validated his discomfort with emotional intimacy should surprise nobody. What is philosophy for, if not to turn our worst anxieties into general principles? And what is writing for, if not to put our words in the reader's mouth, our thoughts in the reader's head, our pain and perplexity in the warm cavity of the reader's heart? The simultaneous urge to draw near and to run away brought Waldo to an interesting impasse in "Friendship," which also appeared in *Essays: First Series.*

He begins the essay by suggesting that there is actually a surplus of affection blanketing the world. "We have a great deal more kindness than is ever spoken," Waldo declares. In fact, "the whole human family is bathed with an element of love like a fine ether." This warm-hearted assessment echoes "Love," which happens to be the preceding essay in the collection. Yet almost immediately, he begins backpedaling. Friendship, he says, is so intoxicating a prospect that it must always fall short. "A new person is to me a great event, and hinders me from sleep," Waldo reports. "I have often had fine fancies about persons which have given me delicious hours; but the joy ends in the day; it yields no fruit."

So the caffeinated pleasures of friendship almost instantly turn into the opposite: disillusion, disappointment, sterility. There is even a suggestion that friendship *must* be abandoned, that an emotional apostasy is the only conceivable exit. Perhaps our affection for others is a false faith, little different from the one that Waldo had already left behind. "Friendship, like the immortality of the soul, is too good to be believed," we read. Truly, these were fighting words for a defrocked minister.

This naysaying continues for much of the essay. Perhaps, Waldo suggests, friendship is like any other organic process, which is to say, transient and cyclical. "Is it not that the soul puts forth friends as the tree puts forth leaves, and presently, by the germination of new buds, extrudes the old leaf?" The sentence, with its cunning use of natural metaphor, is a beauty. Yet its conclusion is bleak. To some extent, Waldo blames himself (and by implication, the reader). We are simply not worthy of what friendship has to offer. We latch onto its superficial comforts—we satisfy ourselves with backslapping cordiality—and forget what we are missing, which is an actual communion of souls. For Waldo, anything less was a sham.

This is setting the bar very high. It leaves little room for kindness, courtesy, small talk. It allows Waldo, at least for a while, to treat friends as one more variant on his favorite punching bag: society. Friends are *other people*, friends are the death of solitude. They park themselves on your blue sofa. They keep interrupting your ecstatic state to ask for a glass of water. "Every man alone is sincere," we read. "At the entrance of a second person, hypocrisy begins."

Waldo does have some shrewd things to say about actual friendship. He argues that true friendship requires a mixture of affinity and antagonism. We are drawn to people like ourselves, but not *too much* like ourselves—they must offer a kind of springy resistance to our affections, and keep us an at an amicable distance. What we cannot tolerate, Waldo says, is a "mush of concession" from the other party. This makes sense. No friction, no sparks. Or as Waldo puts it: "Better be a nettle in the side of your friend than his echo."

In fact, he argues, the defining characteristic of "high friendship" is our ability to do without it. A true friend, he suggests, should drive you sufficiently crazy that you cross the street to avoid him. At the same time, a true friend is a divine companion. This being the case, Waldo suggests that you never visit your friend's house or meet his family. That would simply profane and cheapen your rapport with your "beautiful enemy," who should be playing by the same set of rules. Has anyone ever jotted down a more effective recipe for driving away the human race?

It's clear that Waldo's self-hobbling vision of friendship flows directly from his old tendency to view other human beings as not quite real. This was, of course, a philosophical position: a Kantian insistence that we are confined to surfaces, that we acquaint ourselves with the phenomenal exterior of other people but never get at the noumenal nut, the essence, inside them. Yet it went deeper with Waldo. It was an *emotional* position, a deep sense of isolation that prompted Fuller's crack about him being on stilts. He felt this way very early on. In a journal entry of May 28, 1826, when he was twenty-three years old, he wrote:

> Friendship is something very delicious to my understanding. Yet the friends that occupy my thoughts are not men but certain phantoms clothed in the form & face & apparel of men by whom they were suggested & to whom they bear a resemblance. The gods gave life to Prometheus's ivory statue and the revolution of events may one day give me the men for the prototypes.

This is loneliness of an extreme kind. Waldo's awareness of what he is missing—the communion with others, as visceral as a taste on the tongue—makes the situation even more poignant. He flees from others and craves their warmth. So of course his unified field theory of friendship is bound to be ambivalent.

"We walk alone in the world," he writes in his essay. "Friends, such as we desire, are dreams and fables." He was desperate to encounter friends on a higher spiritual plane. Yet he was equally determined to avoid the pain that is so often the price of admission to any real rapport. His last-ditch hope was that "elsewhere, in other regions of the universal power, souls are now acting, enduring, and daring, which can love us, and which we can love." The location of these souls was unclear—they might be across the street, or in Timbuktu, or (quite possibly) in the afterlife. The main point was that they were inaccessible to Waldo. But perhaps other souls might make themselves present in *this* life, given half a chance.

. . .

The essay, then, was theory. What about practice? Let's take a look at two of Waldo's warmest and most sublime friendships, with personali-

FIGURE 6. Henry David Thoreau, 1856. Courtesy of the Concord
Free Public Library.

ties as convoluted as his own. For starters, there is Henry David Thoreau. Fourteen years Waldo's junior, he worshipped him from afar at
first, repeatedly checking out *Nature* from the Harvard library. His idol
had already made some effort on Thoreau's behalf, pressuring the
school's president, Josiah Quincy, to grant him a twenty-five-dollar prize
at graduation. Waldo knew about his young admirer, a scholarship student frequently teased for his green homespun coat—and Thoreau,
who had grown up in Concord, certainly knew about the town's
Unitarian-baiting celebrity.

It's not clear exactly when they met. It would be nice to know the date, the better to imagine the tall, elegant, slope-shouldered Waldo and the stumpy, tongue-tied Thoreau shaking hands for the first time. What is obvious is that Thoreau was immediately drawn into the older man's orbit. On October 22, 1837, the recent college graduate commenced his journal—a project that would run to millions of words and supply the raw material for his books. As much as *Walden*, the journal was Thoreau's bright book of life. And it began, tellingly, with a stray comment of Waldo's:

> "What are you doing now?" he asked. "Do you keep a journal?" So I make my first entry to-day.

That Waldo would urge his friend to run off and start a journal is no surprise. Keeping a journal was not an adjunct to *his* daily life, either, but the heart of it—a way of living through language. What is striking is how quickly Thoreau threw himself into the role of disciple. He wanted to walk like Waldo, talk like Waldo, denounce society in Waldo-like tones. This was pleasing to his idol. I don't mean that it simply appealed to Waldo's vanity. No, he sensed a kindred spirit and responded to it, with a warmth quite foreign to his own theories of friendship. On February 17, 1838, just a few months after ushering Thoreau into his circle, he described him in nearly infatuated terms:

> My good Henry Thoreau made this else solitary afternoon sunny with his simplicity & clear perception. How comic is simplicity in this doubledealing quacking world. Every thing that boy says makes merry with society though nothing can be graver than his meaning.

Yet Thoreau is a *boy*, whose needling jabs at society are most effective for their simplicity—for their childish insistence that the emperor is, after all, stark naked. Waldo's delight in him was obvious, and earnest. Still, he conceived of their relationship as a master-and-disciple affair. That worked just fine as long as Thoreau bought into the same arrangement, which he did for the next few years.

Thoreau copied Waldo in every way he could. This elicited some mirth from the poet, critic, and diplomat James Russell Lowell, who noted in an 1838 letter: "I met Thoreau last night, and it is exquisitely amusing to see how he imitates Emerson's tone and manner. With my eyes shut, I shouldn't know them apart."

Such behavior would seem to violate Waldo's dictum about friends needing to maintain their differences. But Thoreau *was* different, in ways that Waldo surely recognized. He was rustic where Waldo was cosmopolitan, a young bachelor to Waldo's family man. He was a relative newcomer to Concord, while his mentor's roots went back many generations. He was also an Aristotelian to Waldo's Platonist.

What I mean is that Thoreau was practical in a way that Waldo was not—he was comfortable with the materiality of things, and fascinated by their every detail. Nature for him was not merely a perceptual skin and symbolic system but an incomparable richness on its own terms. He studied it, sniffed it, touched it, tasted it in ways that were off limits to the older man. He had little of Waldo's fastidiousness. What he had instead were five extraordinary senses and a perpetual cash-flow problem, which Waldo sometimes helped to alleviate. Also, he liked to dance.

Some of these differences were slow to emerge. Thoreau was a youth, after all. One imagines him gallivanting through the woods with Waldo, very much a sidekick or puppy in human form, exclaiming over the pond lilies or the spicy scent of the hickory buds. As a writer, he was still in the process of assimilating Waldo's style. One of his earliest journal entries is simply a list of paradoxes, clearly modeled on his mentor's self-detonating sentences. "The highest condition of art is artlessness." "By sufferance you may escape suffering." The level of mimicry is touching. In time, Thoreau would take this taste for paradox to new and pugnacious heights. For the moment, though, these were little more than finger exercises, ways to sound like Waldo.

For the next few years, this Mutt-and-Jeff team was inseparable. The older man lectured and labored on the essays that would make up his first collection. The younger washed out as a schoolteacher (for his reluctance to beat the pupils), worked on and off in the family's pencil factory, and honed his craft as a writer.

Waldo went to great lengths to assist him. He loaned him money on many occasions. He spoke to publishing bigwigs on Thoreau's behalf, including Margaret Fuller—whose magazine, the *Dial*, happened to have been founded by Waldo. She printed Thoreau's verse but batted back his early essays. "The thoughts seem to me so out of their natural order, that I cannot read it through again without pain," she declared, which suggests that Thoreau had been all too dutiful in his imitation of Waldo.

But Waldo's embrace of his new friend went far beyond professional matters. He clearly loved Thoreau. There may have been a homoerotic element to his attachment—both men had been powerfully drawn to other men, and had further benefited from the era's blurry sense of male intimacy. A man could share a bed, or frequent professions of love, without being labeled homosexual. He was simply a creature of feeling. I am not suggesting that Waldo and his young charge got up to some sort of sexual mischief on the shores of Walden Pond (although anything is possible). Yet they shared the sort of exalted communion that Waldo described in "Friendship." They demonstrated that such a thing was possible, despite what Waldo elsewhere called "the porcupine impossibility of contact" with other people.

Waldo went further. He made Thoreau part of his family, in every way he could. In 1841, he invited him to join the Emerson household. To some degree, this was part of an experiment in communal living—an idea very much in the air at the time. Waldo recognized that he wouldn't last twenty-four hours at Brook Farm, the utopian collective founded that same year by his friends George Ripley and Nathaniel Hawthorne (who didn't last too long there himself). His nervous system was not designed for communal bowls of porridge and clog-dancing before the fire. But he could embrace the concept on his own terms, by inviting his beloved friend to live in the white house on Cambridge Turnpike.

Thoreau moved in. He occupied a room at the top of the stairs. His role in the household was hard to define: some combination of kid brother, babysitter, personal trainer, administrative assistant, handyman, and apprentice. Waldo's delight in his presence was clear. In a June 1841 letter to his brother William, he wrote: "I work with him as I should not without him, and expect now to be suddenly well & strong though I have been a skeleton all the spring until I am ashamed. Thoreau is a scholar & a poet & as full of buds of promise as a young apple tree."

He regarded Thoreau as a junior partner in the relationship. But he was aware, too, of his disciple's burgeoning talent, if confused as to exactly what kind of talent it was. Waldo still saw Thoreau primarily as a poet—a compliment of sorts, since that is how he saw himself. In September 1841, he noted in a letter to Margaret Fuller that his houseguest was "full of noble madness lately, and I hope more highly of him than ever." This suggests a High Romantic, flouncing around in scarves and eating the verdigris off pennies (as the young Flaubert did) in the hopes of an easeful death.

But Thoreau was nothing of the kind. His flintiness, his sardonic view of society, his dab hand with a hammer and chisel—all of this made him a rational and recognizable product of New England. He was much too sane to flirt with madness, although he sought out ecstasy as earnestly as his landlord. Nor was he much of a poet. Like Waldo, he required the wide open spaces of prose: an approximation of the infinite, unlike the recurrent gait of verse, which gave him something like muscle cramps.

. . .

Again, this was not a run-of-the-mill friendship. It was more akin to a romance—in its intensity, and in the way it allowed the two parties to inflict pain on each other. There was little pain at first. Indeed, the two men drew even closer during the catastrophic year of 1842, when Emerson lost his son Waldo and Thoreau his brother John. The next year, Thoreau ended his long residency at Bush and struck out on his own. He intended to find literary employment in New York City—a place that Waldo regarded as the hellish antipode of Concord. Still, Waldo kept him inside the familial tent, arranging for his protégé to work as a tutor for his nephew in Staten Island.

That very year, however, Waldo confided some doubts to Margaret Fuller. Thoreau's failure to bear literary fruit made him think that "our American subsoil must be lead or chalk or whatever represents in geology the phlegmatic." A year later, he confessed that the younger man's incessant paradox-making gave him migraines. He could no longer tolerate Thoreau's "old fault of unlimited contradiction. The trick of his rhetoric is soon learned: it consists in substituting for the obvious word and thought its diametrical antagonist." That Thoreau had developed this tic in flagrant imitation of his idol gave Waldo little comfort. No, it made him "nervous and wretched" to read much of Thoreau's prose.

By 1845, when Thoreau began his hermetic retreat at Walden Pond, the friendship had cooled. There are numerous ironies here, starting with the fact that Waldo, who considered his disciple's withdrawal to a tiny house a kind of stunt, also owned the land on which it was built. Perhaps, too, he was less than pleased by Thoreau's literalism. It was one thing to worship nature and write an entire book about that sacred discipline. It was another to actually *move there*—to leave behind the creature comforts and hunker down in the dirt. Was Thoreau trivializing Waldo's ideas, or was he actually beating him at his own game?

Either answer would have been disagreeable to Waldo. I suspect, too, that his disappointment in Thoreau had grown deeper. His protégé had not panned out as a great American poet. (Instead Waldo would have to settle for Walt Whitman, the wildest of all consolation prizes.) Thoreau had published little. His disdain for getting and spending, which had delighted Waldo when they first met, may now have struck him as the posing of a sulky adolescent. In any case, he gave Thoreau a wider berth during his encampment at Walden. He seldom visited, even though he and Thoreau had frequently walked the two miles between his house and the pond.

His absence had to be noted by his younger friend. Indeed, the scholar and biographer Robert D. Richardson points out that Waldo is cited precisely once in *Walden*, in what he calls the book's saddest sentence: "There was one other with whom I had 'solid seasons,' long to be remembered, at his house in the village, and who looked in upon me from time to time; but I had no more society there." The elegiac note, and the pain, are hard to miss.

From there, it would get worse—much worse. To an extent, the rift between the two men was papered over during Waldo's second sojourn in Europe, which began in October 1847 and lasted nearly ten months. Despite his mixed feelings about Thoreau, he once again summoned him to his household, leaving him in charge of Lidian and the three children.

In other words, he was willing to treat Thoreau as his domestic proxy. It was a great compliment. But there was also a psychological undertow. If Waldo believed that the younger man had been playing house out at Walden Pond, he now invited him to up the ante—to manage a *real* household, with the additional role of paterfamilias. Perhaps he expected him to fail in these duties, as he had failed to fulfill Waldo's earlier dreams and expectations.

If so, he was sorely disappointed. Thoreau was the father Waldo had never been, doling out popcorn and piggyback rides to the children. He doubtless relaxed some of his mentor's more rigid rules, such as his ban on "boisterous laughing" and card games ("Never in the daylight!"). I'm not suggesting that Waldo was a nutty disciplinarian—the Great Santini of Greater Concord. He was, however, a starchier figure than Thoreau, whom the children adored.

The younger man surely noted the difference. In his letters to Waldo, he seems to be goading his mentor in a way that couldn't have done wonders for their relationship. After assuring Waldo that he and Lidian "make very good housekeepers," he dilates on his rapport with young Edward Emerson, who was then nearly three:

> He very seriously asked me, the other day, "Mr. Thoreau, will you be my father?" I am occasionally Mr. Rough-and-tumble with him that I may not miss him, and lest he should miss you too much. So you must come back soon, or you will be superseded.

Waldo did not take the bait. In his next letter to Thoreau, he merely thanked the younger man for his "thoughts and tidings," and for his paternal pinch-hitting over the previous months. "It is one of the best things connected with my coming hither," he writes, "that you could and would keep the homestead; that fireplace shines all the brighter, and has a certain permanent glimmer therefor." His gratitude sounds genuine. And why not? Waldo, so wary of intimacy at close quarters, found it much easier to love people at a distance.

Yet after his return, the relationship kept unwinding. Even when Waldo attempted to boost his former protégé's career, he made matters worse. He suggested, for example, that Thoreau publish his first book,

A Week on the Concord and Merrimack Rivers, with the famously sales-quashing James Munroe. This not only ensured a commercial bellyflop but meant that Thoreau incurred considerable debt, which he would spend the next few years repaying. What Thoreau most resented, meanwhile, was Waldo's fatal withholding of useful criticism until it was too late. "While my friend was my friend he flattered me," he confided to his journal in the summer of 1849, "and I never heard the truth from him, but when he became my enemy he shot it to me on a poisoned arrow."

Waldo was now little fonder of his old sidekick. The previous year, he had suggested that he was not quite human: "As for taking Thoreau's arm, I should as soon take the arm of an elm tree." So it went throughout the last decade of Thoreau's life. The old friends were too tightly meshed to cut each other loose. Yet they got on each other's nerves, especially now that Thoreau had fully digested Waldo's influence and made himself into a freestanding, sometimes ornery genius.

The master-and-disciple arrangement had broken down and the two men had nothing to replace it—nothing but goodwill and emotional momentum. In a town the size of Concord, they regularly crossed paths. There were strolls, conversations, politesse. Still, they must have sensed their differing trajectories. Waldo's greatest work was mostly done, and within a decade or so he would stop writing altogether, whereas Thoreau had commenced a lengthy siege in the attic of his family's boarding house, refining the masterpiece that was *Walden*. The old leaf of their friendship, in Waldo's formulation, had long since been extruded.

Or had it? In the spring of 1862, Thoreau was dying of tuberculosis. Waldo visited him on his sickbed, bringing him bulletins about the natural world that his feeble disciple could no longer gather for himself. On April 1 and again on April 18, Waldo reported that the ice on Walden Pond was still thick enough to support a man. There is a wonderful poignance here: Waldo has temporarily made himself a kind of operative for Thoreau, and also testified to the springy, surprising solidity of his friend's great project.

And then, on May 6, after the failing Thoreau eagerly sniffed a bunch of hyacinths a visitor had brought, he was gone. It was Waldo who demanded that the funeral ceremony be held in the First Parish Church, the casket heaped with spring blossoms and wild boughs. It was Waldo who gave the longest funeral address: a sermon, really, delivered in what his future biographer Franklin Sanborn called a "broken, tender voice." He would later refine it into an article for *The Atlantic*—part essay, part eulogy, part lamentation—in which all of his love for Thoreau and some of his impatience were unmistakable.

The deceased was, he noted, a "born protestant." By this he meant an instinctive defier of accepted wisdom—which is to say, an Emersonian. He celebrated his old friend's independence, his integrity, his almost perverse gift for renunciation. But then he tiptoed into the minefield of Thoreau's conversational style, his love of paradox, his exhausting (to Waldo, anyway) tendency to turn every proposition on its head. Suddenly one hears the sound of fatigue:

> This habit, of course, is a little chilling to the social affections; and though the companion would in the end acquit him of any malice or untruth, yet it mars conversation. Hence, no equal companion stood in affectionate relationship with one so pure and guileless. "I love Henry," said one of his friends, "but I cannot like him; and as for taking his arm, I should as soon think of taking the arm of an elm-tree."

This was a low blow, especially as part of a funeral elegy. The discerning reader will note that Waldo has ascribed his own comment about Thoreau's wooden personality to another person (the first remark, about loving but not liking him, had been made by Elizabeth Hoar, a close family friend who had been engaged to Waldo's brother Charles prior to his sudden death). I find the whole business—the shaft of hostility, and the careful mussing of the trail—as sad as it is revealing. The elegy feels like an X-ray, in which all of Waldo's affections and antagonisms are revealed in mortifying detail.

The love, it should be said, is what prevails. He discusses at great length the dead man's solicitous attention to nature, his role as the custodian of the Concord River and the "attorney of the indigenous plants," as if reporting on a particularly glorious specimen himself. Indeed, the careful portraiture is nothing if not Thoreauvian. Waldo recalls his companion's straw hat, his gray trousers, his spyglass and pocket diary and length of twine, exactly as his old friend would have described the particulars of, say, the soapwort gentian. The elegy, then, is an act of *submission*, which Waldo begrudged while Thoreau was alive but gladly conceded once he was gone. If that's not a lesson in the fluid mechanics of friendship, and in the self-defeating nature of emotional thrift, nothing is.

The ill will returns in the home stretch of the elegy. It is here that Waldo faults Thoreau, incorrectly, for his lack of ambition. "Instead of engineering for all America," we read, "he was the captain of a huckleberry party." Waldo simply could not let go of his idea that his protégé had made implicit promises and failed to carry them out. Young men like Thoreau, he had noted many years before in his journal, "owe us a new world." Precisely what that meant is hard to say—the fulfillment, perhaps, of his own fantasies about the American-poet-as-Prometheus—but in Waldo's eyes, Thoreau had cruelly defaulted on *some* kind of debt. Waldo felt cheated. His attachment to Thoreau was, in his own words, too good to be believed.

He believed it anyway, in the concluding paragraphs of the elegy. He quotes a sentence or two of Thoreau's that might as well be an epitaph for their long, loving skirmish, in which each party refused to be subsumed by the other: "I ask to be melted. You can only ask of metals that they be tender to the fire that melts them." Like it or not, Waldo was effectively fused to the younger man. At the end of his life, with his memory almost gone, he would turn to Lidian and ask, "What was the name of my best friend?" She would answer, "Henry Thoreau." And Waldo, peering back through the mist of their beautiful entanglement, would say, "Oh, yes, Henry Thoreau."

. . .

Waldo's friendship with Thoreau had, as I have already suggested, all the elements of a great romance. It was missing only the gelignite of physical attraction. Granted, both men now seem a little bit queer, Waldo having squelched his teenage attraction to Martin Gay and Thoreau sublimating his own desires in his approximately closet-sized dwelling at Walden Pond. Yet that seemed to factor very little into their relationship. For

FIGURE 7. Margaret Fuller, 1846. Daguerreotype by Albert Sands Southworth. Public domain via Wikimedia Commons.

that matter, Waldo is probably the least erotic of all the great American writers. Which doesn't mean that his friendships were devoid of the mosquito buzz and delicious distortions of sexual curiosity. Case in point: Margaret Fuller.

Waldo first met Fuller in 1835. Seven years his junior, she was already regarded by many as the smartest woman in New England. At the beginning, she owed her ferocious erudition to her father, who had wanted a boy for his firstborn child. Presented with Margaret instead, Timothy

Fuller was determined to raise a prodigy: by the time she was six, she was translating passages of Virgil, and soon Greek and advanced mathematics would be added to the mix. Early and late, Fuller had a formidable mind, and by the time she met Waldo, she had also taught herself Italian and German and was preparing to write a biography of Goethe, then a very sexy commodity in Transcendentalist circles.

In other words, she and Waldo were fellow travelers when it came to the intellect. As personalities, however, they couldn't have been more different. Fuller was known as a spellbinding talker—she was an extrovert with a highly developed sardonic register and a taste for gossip. "She made me laugh more than I liked," the stuffier Waldo recalled of their early encounters.

But it wasn't only her carpet-bombing conversational style that put him off during her first visit to Concord in 1836. It was her physical being. Fuller herself had long since "made up [her] mind to be bright and ugly," and initially, Waldo concurred. Worse, her mannerisms seem to strike him as moral defects: "Her extreme plainness—a trick of incessantly opening and shutting her eyelids—the nasal tone of her voice—all repelled; and I said to myself, we shall never get far."

Yet she won him over. She was simply too brainy, too informed, too funny, and too eager to make inroads with the man she already regarded as the most powerful "of any American mind." She studied the family and its foibles and swiftly learned them by heart, the way she might master a language. She listened, rapt, as Waldo read aloud to her from the manuscript of *Nature*. No doubt Fuller felt she had been admitted to the inner sanctum. As for Waldo, only a couple of weeks after her first visit, he described his "extraordinary" new friend in glowing terms to his brother William:

> It is always a great refreshment to see a very intelligent person. It is like being set in a large place. You stretch your limbs & dilate to your utmost size.

This was no casual statement for Waldo. Only a select company was capable of such a soul-expanding effect. Indeed, that was practically a requirement for any sort of real intimacy with him. Even then, most friends ran afoul of the rules he set out in his essay, asking for too little or too much.

Fuller would eventually find herself in the second category. At first, however, she was on solid ground, having won not only Waldo's heart but Lidian's. "She loves you very much," Waldo assured Fuller in a letter.

She was also drawn more deeply into his circle after encountering Bronson Alcott during her initial visit to the Emerson household. Alcott needed a teacher to help him run his already scandal-mired Temple School in Boston. Fuller needed a job. Soon she was teaching French, German, and Italian to Alcott's dwindling pool of students, exercising what she proudly called her "magnetic power over young women." The gig lasted for only eight months—just long enough for Fuller to figure out that she would never be paid. Still, it had the advantage of cementing her connection to Waldo's bloviating wingman, whose every absurdity he promptly forgave.

Waldo begged Fuller to visit Concord, or to move there for good. "Will you commission me to find you a boudoir; or, much better, will you defy my awkwardness & come & sit down in our castle, summon the village before you & find an abode at your leisure?" he wrote her in October 1838. The idea, he insisted, was that she spend at least a year in the village, which he hoped to transform into a bucolic Athens. This was Waldo at his most effusive. In the very same letter, however, he aired some of his skepticism about human relationships, as if in a spirit of full disclosure. "We are armed all over with these subtle antagonisms which as soon as we meet begin to play, & translate all poetry into such stale prose!" he declared. "It seems to me that almost all people *descend* somewhat into society."

With these caveats echoing in her head, it's not really surprising that Fuller declined to move to Concord. Yet she become steadily more entangled with Waldo. First he invited her to join the Transcendental Club, a loose-knit group whose mansplaining members included Alcott, Hedge, Brownson, Parker, Thoreau, and various other restless Unitarians. She then took on the editorship of the Transcendental house organ, the *Dial*—whose contents, in Alcott's phrase, were supposed to express "views more in accordance with the Soul." This was setting the bar pretty high for a mere magazine. Fuller threw herself into the task, was never paid (again), but nonetheless cherished her role in the trenches with Waldo, whom she had come to love.

. . .

Loving Waldo, she would discover, was even more difficult than liking him. It was in her nature to want more. She already had a history of infatuations with men and women alike, all of whom were entranced by her mind but drew the line at a romantic relationship.

It was in *his* nature, of course, to want less. The situation was further complicated by Waldo's status as a married man, who happened to be experiencing a seven-year itch about two years early. I have already mentioned his chaste interactions with a set of young, smart, ambitious women. (As it happens, two of these women—Caroline Sturgis and Anna Barker—entered his life courtesy of Fuller, who was also infatuated with Barker and would be traumatized by her marriage in 1840.) These flirtations had taken a toll on the uncomplaining Lidian, who had no desire for an open marriage, not even in the Platonic sense.

During her visits to Concord, Fuller observed the fraying state of Waldo's conjugal life. The emotional distance between the Emersons did not make her eager to audition for the role of Waldo's wife. On the contrary, she saw how matrimony had left Lidian spiritually starved and confined half the time to her bed. But Fuller dearly wanted to be Waldo's soulmate, and she was not shy about pressing her case.

In November 1839, for example, she chided him for his lack of warmth. In his journal, he did not protest—he conceded her point. "It is even so," he wrote. "Most of the persons whom I see in my own house I see across a gulf. I cannot go to them nor they come to me." He indicated as much to Fuller, and added that he desired to break free of his "old arctic habits."

His honesty must have encouraged her. Surely a man so attuned to his own chilliness, and so frank about its destructive effects on his life, must wish to overcome it. And who better than Fuller to assist him, with her intellectual ardor and blowtorch personality?

Yet they still came at the prospect of intimacy from very different directions. Fuller wanted to be seen, understood, embraced. "I need to be recognized," she wrote him—a poignant request from an ugly duckling who was just beginning to suspect she might be a swan after all. "I am yours & yours shall be," she declared. As for Waldo, he preferred an exalted communion that seemed almost impersonal, winnowing away all those human particulars that Fuller was so eager to share. In his journal, he insisted that "spirits can meet in their pure upper sky without the help of organs."

No organs, huh? This was not merely Platonic but puritanical—a desire to wish away the body and all its bothersome complications. Again, it was not precisely romance that Fuller wanted from Waldo. It was a merger of souls, which sounds like his cup of tea, except that she wanted him to love her for *herself*, in all her blinking, big-nosed, brilliant, eruptive glory. And since she was a woman and he was a man, that inevitably introduced the question of sex into the equation. Waldo was not attracted to Fuller in any conventional way, but he was undeniably entranced by her. He viewed her as a magical creature, somehow sui generis. (So did Edgar Allan Poe, who famously remarked: "Humanity can be divided into three classes: men, women, and Margaret Fuller.") Yet even Waldo, responding to her outpouring of energy and charisma, had to recognize from time to time that she was indeed a woman.

Certainly his journal entry of September 26, 1840, was such an occasion. He had replied the previous day to one of Fuller's importuning letters. Hers is lost, his is full of flowery compliments but also some ominous storm warnings. They are, he reminds her, distinct beings, who "meet & treat like foreign states, one maritime, one island, whose trade & laws are essentially unlike." This must have been dreary news for Fuller, who dreamed of a joyful encapsulation with Waldo. Yet she was lucky not to read the more agitated outburst he scribbled in his journal the next day:

> You would have me love you. What shall I love? Your body? The supposition disgusts you. What you have thought & said? Well, whilst you were thinking & saying them, but not now. I see no possibility of

loving any thing but what now is, & is becoming; your courage, your enterprise, your budding affection, your opening thought, your prayer, I can love—but what else?

The last couple of sentences are more or less a face-saving recipe for Transcendental friendship. But it's the opening salvo that grabs the reader's attention, alluding as it does to the idea that two adults might actually have sex with each other. Whose supposition was it, exactly? We'll never know. Clearly, however, what Waldo later described as his "strange, cold-warm, attractive-repelling conversations with Margaret" were not completely devoid of erotic electricity.

. . .

Lidian could tell. After swallowing the bitter pill of Waldo's anticlericalism, she now had another indignity to deal with. Her husband had developed a swoony fixation on another woman. No matter that Lidian initially liked her; no matter that the woman's bluestocking vibe and stooping posture made her an unlikely rival. Fuller had some kind of grip on Waldo, and Lidian's default position was retreat—to her room, her Bible, her concoctions of poppy and paregorics.

The situation came to a boil in September 1842. Fuller had arrived to spend a couple of weeks at Bush. For the first three days, she saw nothing of Lidian, who had barricaded herself in her room with what was reported to be a "slow fever." Not wishing to be rude, Fuller finally knocked on the door to say hello. As she recorded in her diary:

> When I did go in, [Lidian] burst into tears, at sight of me, but laid the blame on her nerves, having taken opium &c. I felt embarrassed, & did not know whether I ought to stay or go. Presently she said something which made me suppose she thought W. passed the evenings talking with me.

In fact, Waldo had been spending the evenings in his study, most likely scrabbling together material for the next issue of the *Dial*, since Fuller had thrown off the editorial fetters a few months earlier. Lidian's immediate fears were unfounded. But the next day, she joined the group for supper and asked Fuller to take a walk with her afterward—something of an olive branch. Fuller replied that she already had plans "to walk with Mr. E." Lidian burst into tears, the embarrassed diners stared down at their plates, and Waldo, in Fuller's recollection, "looked on the ground, but soft & serene as ever." One can only imagine the tooth-sucking, the napkin-crumpling, the silence.

"My dear Lidian," Fuller said, "certainly I will go with you." The female antagonists took a short stroll, during which Lidian shared a fading hope that her luftmensch of a husband might yet "be capable of an intimate union."

By now, Fuller knew better. She took her walks with Waldo, too, in the coming days. According to Fuller, they talked, "as we almost always do, on Man and Woman, and Marriage." But these had finally turned into the sort of abstractions so relished by Waldo, rather than cryptic communiques about their own relationship. Fuller had already informed him that all the marriages she had ever encountered were a "mutual degradation." She would soon expand on these thoughts in "The Great Lawsuit," a *Dial* essay that was itself a dry run for her feminist manifesto *Woman in the Nineteenth Century*.

Waldo published no manifesto on the heels of these conversations with Fuller. Yet he seemed to deliver a kind of postmortem in "Étienne de La Boéce," a poem he tinkered with for years and finally completed in 1846:

> I serve you not, if you I follow,
> Shadowlike, o'er hill and hollow,
> And bend my fancy to your leading,
> All too nimble for my treading.
> When the pilgrimage is done,
> And we've the landscape overrun,
> I am bitter, vacant, thwarted,
> And your heart is unsupported.

No, these lines were not explicitly addressed to Fuller. Their nominal subject is the relationship between Michel de Montaigne and Étienne de La Boétie, which the French essayist memorialized in *his* meditation on friendship. But they capture the flavor of Waldo's rapport with Fuller: its advances and retreats, its nettling assertions of autonomy, its melancholy endgame.

When Fuller died, in 1850, he wrote an elegy for her. It was, like the one he wrote for Thoreau, a feat of sweet-and-sour portraiture. "Her attachments, one might say, were chemical," he recalled. Which is to say, almost involuntary. The suggestion was that he and Fuller had been inexorably drawn together by what their mutual idol Goethe called elective affinities. They were, to use another phrase he had borrowed directly from Goethe for his essay, beautiful enemies.

To put it yet another way: Waldo could not love Fuller, and he could not *not* love her—as good a theory of friendship as any. Despite his insistence on the transience of these relationships, his feelings for such friends survived everything, including death. They were, as he wrote of Fuller's quick-germinating intimacies, "new and permanent covenants." He did not walk alone in the world after all.

9

THE COSTLY PRICE OF
SONS AND LOVERS

Not long before their first child was delivered, Lidian advised Waldo to go see the newborn baby at a friend's house. He dutifully carried out this mission, and when he returned home, she asked him what he thought. "It was nothing at all!" he told her. "It had neither hair nor teeth!"

Yet the birth of his own child, on October 30, 1836, elicited a more complicated reaction. Waldo registered a strange sequence of emotions in his journal, from joy to alienation to pride to a kind of spectator status.

"Blessed child!" he first exclaimed. But studying the baby more closely, he added: "I see nothing in it of mine; I am no conscious party to any feature, any function, any perfection I behold in it." He might as well have been describing a laser printer. Yet further down the very same page, he seemed to recognize his role as life-giving progenitor: "Now I am Pygmalion." At the very bottom, he jotted down an endearing snapshot of Lidian and the newborn in their closed circuit of contentment, from which he was incidentally excluded:

What is most beautiful is to see the babe & mother together, the contrast of size makes the little nestler appear so *cunning*, & its tiny beseeching weakness is compensated so perfectly by the happy patronizing look of the mother, who is a sort of high reposing Providence toward it—that they make a perfect group.

There was some jostling over the baby boy's name. Several friends and family members lobbied for Charles, in commemoration of Waldo's brother, who had died just five months earlier. But Waldo held out for, well, Waldo. As he explained to his brother William: "I call him so because it is his natural name; then because it is an old family name; and lastly because it is a convenient & somewhat rare name."

I'm not sure the argument for convenience really holds water. More likely Waldo was simply being drawn into the fog of adoration and identification that enfolds so many new parents. The baby is so transparently yourself and somebody else, a tiny proxy and a visitor from a parallel universe.

Now there were two Waldos. The elder of the pair was soon transfixed by the younger. Writing to William again in early January, he proudly declared his son "the most thrifty of babies: he can suck cry laugh coo warble & jump." About a month later, there were new skills to brag about—again, to William, whose own son and namesake had already jumped through some of the same hoops. He wrote: "Waldo struggles, leaps; studies manipulation & palmistry, and optics, to prepare himself for an interview with his cousin Willie."

There was none of the cosmic detachment he brought to his closest friendships. He adored the child and feared losing him. In April, young Waldo got a bad cold and his father's immediate panic was palpable in his journal entry: "Ah! my darling boy, so lately received out of heaven leave me not now!"

It was not only the child's father who considered him a heavenly ambassador. When Ezra Ripley came to meet his great-grandson-by-marriage, he laid the baby on his stomach and tugged down the back of his nightshirt. Asked what he was doing, he replied: "I've been told that the child of this couple would probably have wings, and I'm looking to ascertain whether they have sprouted." There would, of course, be other children in the Emerson household: Ellen, Edith, and Edward. But for the duration of his short life, Waldo was a princely presence, treated as a vessel of wisdom by friends and family alike.

This is sometimes the first child's cross to bear. It is part and parcel, too, of the Victorian cult of childhood, which held that adults were mostly the ruined vestiges of their infant selves, smudged and spattered by experience. How much nicer to never grow old—an idea that was literalized in a great many works of the period, from Charles Kingsley's *Water Babies* to Lewis Carroll's maturity-evading *Alice's Adventures in Wonderland*. I suppose it doesn't matter whether Waldo was truly as good or wise or precocious as his parents imagined. Why should he be? He was just a toddler, laughing and crying and accumulating nouns and learning to pick up the period equivalent of Cheerios with his thumb and forefinger. An average child (does such a thing exist?) is more than miraculous enough.

There is just a single portrait of Waldo, taken in October 1841, when a traveling daguerreotypist passed through Concord. The process required that the subject hold still for a prolonged length of time—a nightmare for a five-year-old. Neither Lidian nor Henry Thoreau could persuade Waldo to look at the camera and freeze, but Henry's brother John somehow managed the trick. The mirror-like plate was exposed, a cloud of mercury vapor coaxed forth the latent image, and there was Waldo.

His hair was neatly parted. He wore a dark smock with a frilly white collar and a very serious expression, cute but imperious, like a Plantagenet toddler. Many years later, his brother Edward, noticing that the portrait looked dusty, lifted the glass lid and wiped the silvery plate with a soft cloth. The image vanished at once—an outcome that must have horrified the entire family. (Luckily, they had already obtained a couple of second-generation copies, less vivid but still serviceable as consolation prizes.)

He seems, in any case, to have been a delightful child. The facts are few. He crawled on the floor and blackened his tiny hands exploring the fireplace tongs. He wore a velvet cap, which his father disliked, viewing it as too fancy for a small town like Concord. At the age of two, he committed what his mother regarded as his first sin: ordered to put a lump of sugar on the table, he waited until Lidian's back was turned and took a bite. She heard "the crash of the dear little teeth on the sugar," whirled around, and asked him if he had eaten the forbidden lump. He lied and was overcome with shame. To Lidian, it was "as if she beheld the fall of angels." Whether Waldo, too, now believed that he had eaten of the

FIGURE 8. Waldo Emerson at age five, just a few months before his death. Courtesy of the Houghton Library, Harvard University, MS Am 1280.235 (Box 63: 706.17).

saccharine tree of knowledge is anybody's guess. He cried when his potato and squash overlapped on his dinner plate. At the circus, he watched the clown for a few minutes and then told his father, "Papa, the funny man makes me want to go home." When he was taken to view the body of Ezra Ripley—the man who had inspected him for angelic wings—he circled the corpse a couple of times and asked, "Why don't they keep him for a statue?" He promised to build his sister a spacious home, complete with what he referred to as an "interspiglion" and a "coridaga." (Nobody knew what these words meant, but I like to imagine the former was a pneumatic-tube system for communicating with the spirit world.) He also planned to build a special clock for her, whose chimes "would be heard all over the house, all over the yard, all over the world." In this ambition, he was certainly his father's son. He seemed, too, to share his father's habit of intense regard, observation, sizing up. Lidian later recalled his way of studying an object, gazing at it and blinking, "and by and by a slow smile would come."

There is his life in a paragraph—a brief life. Of course there was much more to it. A child's days are infinite in a way that an adult's are not. They are governed by a mythological clock, the very impulses in their brains travel at a relative crawl, the passage of time is encoded shakily or not at all. They are *beginners*, in every sense of the word. Their parents are not— and yet they, too, get a whiff of this eternality, like secondhand smoke. Meanwhile the newborn, the wrinkled passenger, the Proteus in diapers, keeps changing before their eyes. The umbilical cord falls off, and a century seems to have passed. How to measure it? "The pith of each man's genius," the boy's father famously remarked, "contracts itself to a very few hours." His son walked the earth for thousands of hours, for tens of thousands of hours, and yet they were still not enough.

For Waldo's life was brief indeed. On January 24, 1842, the boy came down with scarlet fever. Nowadays we would treat the illness, which mostly afflicts children, with antibiotics. Back then, the telltale signs— sandpapery rash, swollen tongue—were a source of terror for parents, who could do nothing to alter the outcome.

Ellen, still a baby, was infected as well, but she managed to recover. Waldo was not so lucky. For two days he sat in his trundle bed—when he was offered castor oil, he refused to swallow it. On the third day, he was delirious and no longer recognized Lidian, even when he called for her. The next morning, his father made a terse entry in his journal: "Yesterday night at 15 minutes after eight my little Waldo ended his life." When a family friend, Judge Rockwood Hoar, showed up to view the body, Waldo could say nothing in response to his questions but, "Oh, that boy!"

. . .

Few things stunned Waldo like the death of his son. He had already absorbed so much grief, lost his beloved first wife and two brothers. But those were losses he had been able to anticipate, to some degree— tuberculosis had put up its red flags early and often. His son's death came out of nowhere. The world of nature seemed to share his sense of grief and dislocation:

The morning of Friday I woke at 3 o'clock, & every cock in every barnyard was shrilling with the most unnecessary noise. The sun went up in the morning sky with all his light, but the landscape was dishonored by this loss. For this boy in whose remembrance I have both slept & awaked so oft, decorated for me the morning star, & the evening cloud.

He went on, in his journal, to list the particulars: the things that Waldo had touched, the coal and firewood, the hammer and pincers and file, the microscope and magnet and "every trinket & instrument in the study." The boy had played on the gravel piles in the meadow, had poked his head in the doghouse and the barn. He had entertained himself, too, with the English language, putting his childish stamp on it just as his father did: "For every thing he had his own name & way of thinking[,] his own pronunciation & manner. And every word came mended from that tongue." Again, the identification between father and son is heartbreaking. So is the invocation of mending, fixing, as if this gigantic tear in the fabric of Waldo's existence could somehow be stitched up.

"Sorrow makes us all children again," he lamented. In its wake, "the wisest knows nothing." The brief notes he wrote to family and friends on the very evening of little Waldo's death attest to this overwhelming emptiness. "What shall I say of the Boy?" was the question he posed to his brother William. To Aunt Mary, he was slightly more expansive: "My darling & the world's wonderful child, for never in my own or another family have I seen any thing comparable, has fled out of my arms like a dream." Even more desolate were the words he jotted to Elizabeth Hoar the next morning, after the surreal shrilling of the neighborhood roosters: "Everything wakes this morning but my darling Boy."

He was lucky, perhaps, to have some distractions on hand. His recent series of lectures in Boston had generated less income than in previous years, so the cash-strapped Waldo agreed to deliver five talks in Providence, beginning on February 10. These, too, failed to fetch a large crowd. Next he agreed to lecture in New York City in early March. For these appearances, he came to the city a few days early, in order to spend time with William on Staten Island and to meet such rising literary stars as Horace Greeley and Albert Brisbane. These two dragged him to a vegetarian restaurant and turned the full force of their Transcendentalist ardor on him. Waldo found them starry-eyed in the extreme and yet so intent on political activism that he felt himself "of no more use in their New York than a rainbow or firefly."

The lectures in New York City were more successful. One reviewer, assessing the final evening on March 15, predicted a bright future for the speaker: "We should not be surprised if he made a good many converts in Gotham." (The reviewer was Walt Whitman, and he surely tucked away one of Waldo's assertions that night: "We say of man that he is grass.") He also met Henry James Senior, a wealthy Swedenborgian who he liked more than any other New Yorker. Waldo described him to Lidian as "the best apple on the tree thus far." Yet his encounter with James must have been a trial, too, since this new friend promptly brought him upstairs during a visit to his Washington Square household to meet and greet his two-month-old son, the future philosopher William James. Waldo's host may not have known that he had just lost his own son a few weeks earlier. We can only imagine Waldo's sadness at regarding the child in his crib, and the effort it took to suppress it.

He had, for a little while, continued to jot down notes about little Waldo in his journal. "If I go down to the bottom of the garden," he wrote, "it seems as if some one had fallen into the brook." Nature, formerly his great solace and reservoir of transcendence, now spoke of nothing but death. It was a confirmation, of course, of his own earlier line about the natural world wearing the colors of the spirit, reflecting back sorrow like a physical sensation, like heat on the skin. He also recorded another of the boy's grandiose projects, a tragic variant on the bell that would be heard the world over. "It will sound like some great glass thing," little Waldo had promised, "which falls down & breaks all to pieces."

There is elegy here, and self-portraiture, too. It may have been more than Waldo could bear. That probably explains why he tore out the next couple of pages in the journal, left several more blank, and put the actual notebook aside for many weeks. In a different notebook, he began to jot down some thoughts about grief—more accurately, about the way grief was eluding him, sliding out of his grasp. For the most part, though, he reverted to his usual subjects. There were meditations on character, spirit, Hell versus Heaven, the fate of the *Dial* (which Margaret Fuller was just now abandoning). A reader might almost believe that Waldo had absorbed the blow and moved on.

But he had a genius for compartmentalizing. There was yet another notebook, a tiny volume he often used to log the books and articles he had read, and carried around in his pocket. It was there that he began to write "Threnody," an elegy to his departed son, which he would not publish for another four years. The first section he committed to paper described a gaggle of small children headed off to school each day, with Waldo—the "little chieftain"—marching protectively beside them. The boy's role as guardian is wrenching to contemplate. Nobody, certainly not his parents, was able to protect *him* from destruction.

The very next page includes a garbled passage of prose, which may be a remembrance of little Waldo's death ("I comforted him & he said Don't grieve for me") and another couplet from the poem. The defiantly grieving father covered the next few pages with other sections of "Threnody," often in language very close to the published version, which begins:

> The South-wind brings
> Life, sunshine, and desire,
> And on every mount and meadow
> Breathes aromatic fire,
> But over the dead he has no power,
> The lost, the lost he cannot restore,
> And, looking over the hills, I mourn
> The darling who shall not return.

Again, there is the invocation of nature, faintly echoing the opening lines of the Divinity School Address. But now its glorious refulgence falls short. It cannot breathe life back into the dead—into the "lost," a word whose helpless reiteration tells us all we need to know. Yet we have just scratched the surface: "Threnody" goes on for another 281 lines. More than half of the poem is an agonized attempt to fix the boy in memory. Waldo catalogues his haunts, his habits, the objects he left behind: "The painted sled stands where it stood, / The kennel by the corded wood, / The gathered sticks to stanch the wall / Of the snow-tower, when snow should fall."

This is all enormously touching. Less so is the perhaps inevitable idealizing of the departed Waldo, who is "Nature's sweet marvel undefiled." You don't miss your son because he was perfect. The suggestion, surely unintended, is that you would miss him less if he were imperfect. But perhaps it was easier to mourn, or to let go of, an abstraction of childhood rather than the actual boy whose voice was still ringing in your ears. It was *that* loss that was killing Waldo, who described his own "slow but sure reclining / Star by star his world resigning."

The final section of the poem ratchets up to an even higher level of abstraction. The poet is addressed by his "deep Heart," which tells him to look beyond the transience of his son's short life: "My servant Death with solving rite / Pours finite into infinite." This just doesn't cut it—not as consolation, and not as poetry, since the best lines are surrounded by gobs of Transcendental gossamer. Waldo was desperate: he was using his own rhetoric as a form of analgesic. "Silent rushes the swift Lord, / Through ruined systems still restored." It's a good line, fast and cryptic. But it's less true than the opening lines, in which Waldo has already acknowledged that what matters most will never be restored.

"Threnody" has enjoyed a curiously mixed reputation. Two years after the boy's death, when Margaret Fuller asked to see the unpublished poem, Waldo rather dismissively promised to send along a copy of his "rude dirges to my Darling." In our own era, the Emerson scholar and biographer Gay Wilson Allen called it "one of the great elegies in the English language." More recently, the poet Dan Chiasson argued that "the poem quickly stifles its desperation in the prescribed comforts of noble sentiment and regular music." For me, "Threnody" works best when it remains simple, direct, despairing. There is more tragedy in "I see my empty house, / I see my trees repair their boughs," than in all the philosophical footwork of the conclusion.

I suspect that Louisa May Alcott, the daughter of Bronson Alcott and author of *Little Women*, felt the same way. Discussing the boy's death forty years after the fact, she recalled his wretched father uttering to her the words, "Child, he is dead." The evident anguish on his face, and in his voice, she said, "gave those few words more pathos than the sweet lamentation of the Threnody."

. . .

I noted earlier that Waldo indexed all of his journals, assigning keywords to almost every page so that he could locate sentences for subsequent use in lectures or essays. When he was writing down his first scattered notes on his son's death, he indexed one of those pages—which he would later tear out and discard—with two words: *Grief* and *Experience*.

Those two things had become identical. To be alive was to feel, acutely and at every moment, what he had lost. Waldo understood that there was no real relief from these feelings. When we lose a loved one, we are often immobilized, empty, unwilling to go through the motions of ordinary living. This suspension of all activity is a homage to the dead, which cannot be kept up indefinitely—it is like holding your breath. Then one resumes eating, drinking, sleeping, reading, walking, talking, laughing. These activities filled Waldo with shame. They suggested that all of his pain and shock and disbelief had been neatly metabolized away, that he was a whole person again. But the loss was still there: a white noise, a black hole, a reprimand. He was *not* a whole person, and would never again be one, and the question was how to keep living in such a partial state.

This was what he struggled with in "Experience," one of the highlights of *Essays: Second Series*, which came out in late 1844. Waldo had sent a rudimentary version of the book to James Munroe at the beginning of the year. Six months later, he was still revising and expanding it. "I am really trying to end my old endless chapters that they may decently appear in the world," he lamented to Margaret Fuller, "but the stream of my thought too closely resembles our Concord River which is narrow & slow & shallow."

Eventually the current picked up again, and Waldo handed over the manuscript to his publisher. He was doubtless pleased to bring another book into existence. Yet it was a sadder, wearier, more chastened production than its predecessor—and nowhere more so than in "Experience," which begins by plunging the reader into a bad dream:

> Where do we find ourselves? In a series, of which we do not know the extremes, and believe that it has none. We wake and find ourselves on a stair: there are stairs below us, which we seem to have ascended; there are stairs above us, many a one, which go upward and out of sight. But the Genius which, according to the old belief, stands at the door by which we enter, and gives us lethe to drink, that we may tell no tales, mixed the cup too strongly, and we cannot shake off the lethargy now at noonday. Sleep lingers all our lifetime about our eyes, as night hovers all day in the boughs of the fir-tree.

Recall that "Self-Reliance," the tentpole essay in Waldo's previous book, had opened with a trumpet blast of affirmation. "Speak your latent conviction and it shall be the universal sense," the author promised, as if addressing an auditorium of superheroes-in-training. Now we are in a different world. Now we are in a state of confusion and fatigue: we are sleepwalkers who can never quite awaken.

Anybody who has ever struggled with depression will recognize the somnambulistic tone. Waldo was crushed, deflated, and scared (not merely intrigued) by his frictionless progress through the world. "All things swim and glimmer," he wrote. "Our life is not so much threatened as our perception. Ghostlike we glide through nature, and should not know our place again."

The last sentence is lovely and desperate, joining the living to the dead. But the sentence before that is just as crucial. Waldo's grief has deepened his sense of isolation, which was pretty formidable to begin with. And so his investigation of experience is not only emotional but perceptual, which is to say, philosophical. Yet unlike the abstractions that scuttled the second half of "Threnody," this is philosophy with teeth (mostly sharp) and heart (mostly broken).

Initially, though, the melancholic funk is pervasive. Waldo replays some of the travel-hating riffs from "Self-Reliance," which sound even more hopeless in this context: "Every ship is a romantic object, except that we sail in." In the earlier essay, at least, travel was a proxy for the past—for the Old World—which Waldo was so intent on condemning. Here his jabs merely suggest that nihilism is inescapable. "Our life looks trivial," he concedes, "and we shun to record it." We've come a long way from the dreaming Waldo who was offered the world like an apple and ate it whole.

But it is grief—the annihilating nub of experience—that is driving the essay. So Waldo returns to it, and to the sense, already expressed in his more intimate writings, that grief itself has slipped out of his grasp. "What opium is instilled into all disaster!" Catastrophic events deliver their own sort of anesthesia; they make us numb to our own sufferings. You would think that Waldo would welcome this respite from pain. But he vastly preferred reality to a narcotized stupor, and pursued its "sharp peaks and edges of truth," only to find that they, too, were chimerical. He simply could not touch them.

Here was his horrible confession. He could not feel what he was supposed to feel. "The only thing grief has taught me, is to know how shallow it is," he continues. "That, like all the rest, plays about the surface, and never introduces me into the reality, for contact with which, we would even pay the costly price of sons and lovers." That last phrase has a proverbial ring—no wonder D. H. Lawrence pinched it for his title. But it was, for Waldo, terribly literal. He had lost a son, a beloved wife, and even that was insufficient to give him a real purchase on experience.

Perhaps it was the same for everybody? Perhaps all human beings were as isolated as he was? A voracious reader of the latest scientific theories, Waldo cites Roger Boscovich, a Croatian polymath who proposed that the particles making up physical reality never touched. From a distance, Boscovich argued, particle called out to particle: there was a force of attraction. But once the particles drew near, they grew antagonistic, then mutually repellent.

Waldo simply scales up this theory, assuming that atoms and individuals behave in the same way. "Souls never touch their objects," he says. "An innavigable sea washes with silent waves between us and the things we aim at and converse with." Then he continues with some truly shocking sentences:

In the death of my son, now more than two years ago, I seem to have lost a beautiful estate,—no more. I cannot get it nearer to me. If tomorrow I should be informed of the bankruptcy of my principal debtors, the loss of my property would be a great inconvenience to me, perhaps, for many years; but it would leave me as it found me,— neither better nor worse. So it is with this calamity: it does not touch me; something which I fancied was part of me, which could not be torn away without tearing me, nor enlarged without enriching me, falls off from me, and leaves no scar. It was caducous. I grieve that grief can teach me nothing, nor carry me one step into real nature.

The suggestion that the loss of his son was no more troubling than a financial setback has puzzled and appalled readers for generations. Could Waldo possibly have been that cold? Of course not. We already know, from what he wrote in his journal and told his friends, that his son's death caused him unbearable pain. No, what he is expressing here is a kind of survivor's guilt.

The word *estate* is a clue. Waldo would have associated it first and foremost with Ellen's estate, the object of much legal wrangling. On the surface, he viewed his wife's bequest as a "work of mercy"—a postmortem act of kindness toward his entire cash-strapped clan. Yet it took six years to settle the counterclaims made by her family, in the course of which his own attorney dropped dead just a few days after presenting Waldo's case to the Massachusetts Supreme Court.

Meanwhile, as the litigation crept forward, he heard unpleasant rumors about his own behavior. The word was that "Mr. E. had refused all compromise," he told his brother William. Worse still, he could see why people viewed it that way. Is it any wonder, then, that Waldo saw the estate as a mixed blessing, an embodiment of his uneasy negotiation with the dead? It paid for his house in Concord, and indeed underpinned his finances for the rest of his life. But it had come at the costly price of his beloved wife, and nothing could quite erase the brutality of that transaction.

I would go a step further, and suggest that the older sense of *estate* lingered behind the newer, more transactional one. Derived from the

Latin *status*, the word could mean, simply, a state of being. Waldo used it in this sense on several other occasions. Viewed through these etymological spectacles, his lost estate is no mere parcel of property but an entire existence—his, and little Waldo's. (Note that the estate, like the dead boy, is beautiful.)

Another word worth heeding is the rather recondite *caducous*. It is a piece of botanical jargon: it means something easily detached and shed at an early stage. We've already seen that Waldo was fond of botanical metaphors to describe emotional predicaments. In "Friendship," you will recall, he compared the blossoming of new intimacies and the extinction of old ones to a tree dropping its wizened leaves. In that case, he seemed to be suggesting a zero-sum situation, in which your gains compensated for your losses.

Here, there is no such thing. There is no wound, no scar, no evidence that the boy had ever existed—just a drowsy sense of wonder and shame at having survived him. "Nothing is left to us now but death," Waldo writes. "We look to that with a grim satisfaction, saying, there at least is reality that will not dodge us."

I could parse every single word in this remarkable passage and *still* not really explain how its profession of numbness is shot through with the rawest grief. Waldo may have meant to outrage the reader, or himself. He certainly meant to flagellate himself, in the most public manner possible, for not feeling the pain that had actually made him numb in the first place. How right he was about opium and disaster! The body manufactures its own opioids—this occurs in the pituitary gland, which we might as well call Little Pharma. So, too, does the spirit. But Waldo *wanted* the pain, which he correctly identified with reality, and so he set himself up to fail either way. Also: I know he felt that grief because I can feel it myself.

· · ·

Yet Waldo is just warming up. He begins with his own sorrow—and his sense of being walled off from reality—and then makes it a general principle for everybody else. "Dream delivers us to dream," he writes, "and there is no end to illusion." As if that weren't damning enough, he adds that we are prisoners, too, of temperament: of our null, dull, quintessential selves. It's similar to his evocation of character in "Self-Reliance," a reminder that our vaunted freedom is always boxed in, at least to some degree, by fate.

We may *think* we are creatures of free will (which, in Vladimir Nabokov's beautiful phrase, "snaps its rainbow fingers in the face of smug causality"). Instead we are good-natured automatons. We believe in the role of impulse, at least in the moment. Yet in the long run, Waldo warns us, what we hear are not the beautiful improvisations of everyday life but "a certain uniform tune which the revolving barrel of the music-box must play."

This is a dreary conclusion. It is immediately complicated by the author's assertion that we are dependent on constant change. Our moods, our goals, our affections—they must remain in flux. Otherwise we are scarcely alive. Otherwise we prevent the deepest part of ourselves—the approximately God-shaped core of our being—from rising to the surface. "Like a bird that alights nowhere," Waldo writes, "but hops perpetually from bough to bough, is the Power which abides in no man and in no woman, but for a moment speaks from this one, and for another moment from that one."

Wait a minute! That sounds like the old Waldo, the emancipator of the self! But as soon as this Yankee demiurge rears his head, he is driven back into his burrow by his infinitely sadder successor. "What help from these fineries or pedantries?" we read. "What help from thought?" When Waldo, of all people, expresses his disdain for thinking, you know that something has gone terribly wrong. As he is quick to confirm, both he and the entire nation find themselves in a monstrous cul-de-sac:

A political orator wittily compared our party promises to western roads, which opened stately enough, with planted trees on either side, to tempt the traveler, but soon became narrow and narrower, and ended in a squirrel-track, and ran up a tree. So does culture with us; it ends in headache. Unspeakably sad and barren does life look to those, who a few months ago were dazzled with the splendor of the promise of the times.

Having bottomed out here, Waldo pirouettes once more. Or, more accurately, he splits the difference between two positions: Transcendentalist euphoria and cruel depression. This is a signal event in his thinking. Its rarity is on par with the unicorn, the black opal, the melanistic fox. What we see Waldo doing, in full view of the reader, is *compromising*.

This involves some backpedaling. So Waldo, the great spelunker of the hidden world beneath our own, declares: "We live amid surfaces, and the true art of life is to skate well on them." The thorniest of social animals, who essentially chased away his own friends with burning brands, now teaches himself to play well with others: "Let us treat men and women well: treat them as if they were real: perhaps they are." It's a good joke, but also a concession. Other people, those assemblages of quivering atoms whom you could never, ever touch, might be more palpable than you thought.

The same thing goes for daily life, so often denounced for its banality—a way of passing the time between visionary moments. "In the morning I awake," Waldo writes, "and find the old world, wife, babes and mother, Concord and Boston, the dear old spiritual world, and even the dear old devil not far off. If we will take the good we find, asking no questions, we shall have heaping measures." There is a contentment here, an acceptance of the world as it is, that we seldom hear from Waldo in his earlier essays.

I don't simply mean that he's playing the contrarian card. He's always done that. He's always been intoxicated by flipping every proposition on its head, just as he advised us to invert the visible world by peering backward through our legs. What he's doing here, though, is urging his readers to dial it down, to stop forcing every moment through a meditative mesh. "The great gifts are not got by analysis," he declares. Then comes an amazing passage, in which Waldo speaks up for the quotidian, for the natural habitat of the normal person:

> The middle region of our being is the temperate zone. We may climb into the thin and cold realm of pure geometry and lifeless science, or sink into that of sensation. Between these extremes is the equator of life, of thought, of spirit, of poetry,—a narrow belt.

He couldn't exactly call himself normal. He could, however, declare himself a citizen of the "mid-world," where none of the great questions have been settled and we all go about our business nonetheless. Nature, previously a window into the sublime, now enters the scene "eating and drinking and sinning." We live in the moment, oppressed by neither future nor past.

Needless to say, there is a price to pay for the loss of eternity. We are, it seems, creatures of limits. Life itself is a "flitting state, a tent for a night." Within its brief span, we are confined to a narrow path, which may be more than enough. The main thing is to go straight down the middle and not worry about the incompatibility between our daily lives and our visionary impulses. The two things cannot be reconciled. Waldo admits as much in a series of short, punchy sentences, like Biblical (or Blakean) proverbs with explosive nose cones. "A man is a golden impossibility," he writes. "The line he must walk is a hair's breadth. The wise through excess of wisdom is made a fool."

. . .

Of course there's more! And of course Waldo tunnels under the mid-world and blows it to pieces—a reliable sapper of his most marvelous conceptions. How reassuring it would be, he muses, if we could "keep forever these beautiful limits, and adjust ourselves, once and for all, to the perfect calculation of the kingdom of known cause and effect." But we cannot. In the midst of our humdrum existence, we are still the recipients, from time to time, of those divine communiques—Waldo calls them "angel whispering." They arrive like transmissions of chaos, whimsy, free will (which, you may recall, we are not supposed to possess). They make us the makers of our own fate, or at least the silent partners in whatever happens.

There is more beyond that. I won't spell it all out. This is more like a surveillance flight over some very extensive terrain, indicating the landmarks and empty spaces. But one thing that must be stressed again is that Waldo's anatomy of grief is also a philosophical investigation. "Grief too will make us idealists," he writes in the opening pages of his essay.

This is not a casual comment. It's an admission that the loss of his son has steered him once again into the whirlpool of skepticism that had intrigued him for decades: into the reality-defiant thought of John Locke and George Berkeley and especially David Hume.

Locke, as I have already noted, was the house philosopher of the Unitarians. He insisted that all human knowledge was data-driven and derived from the senses—or, as he put it, from experience. (There is no way Waldo could have chosen that title for his essay without stirring the Lockean wind chimes in his brain.)

But Hume was more rigorous in paring away the knowable. He threw overboard the same Biblical miracles that Locke had certified as authentic. He also pushed his predecessor's skepticism to new heights, arguing that cause and effect—the cornerstone, you might remember, of Waldo's middle kingdom—was a matter of probability and could not be *known*. Just because we saw a block of ice eventually melt into a puddle of water did not guarantee it would happen again. It was an assumption, a gamble on the part of the human observer.

This is obviously a disquieting argument. It also had profound theological implications, because the Unitarians were great enthusiasts of the argument from design: the idea that the beauty and intricacy of the universe dictated the existence of a Creator. Without cause and effect, that went straight down the tubes, along with any real evidence of the immortal soul. Last but not at all least, Hume's logic, like Berkeley's, suggested that physical reality might well be a dream, vaporous and unverifiable.

That brings us straight back to "Experience," and to the spectral atmosphere of the opening paragraphs. Waldo had engaged with Idealistic thought many other times. On these occasions, he was careful not to scoff at his materialist peers. Yet he nonetheless made the case for the double vision of the Idealist, who "does not deny the presence of this table, this chair, and the walls of this room, but he looks at these things as the reverse side of the tapestry, as the *other end*, each being a sequel or completion of a spiritual fact which nearly concerns him." The same arguments were at the heart of *Nature*, with its layer cake of matter, spirit, and language.

In "Experience," however, the isolating effects of such Idealism are more tragic than they used to be. The solitude is not exhilarating but bitter. Consciousness, which Waldo would have previously touted as the grand prize, turns out to be something of a curse:

> It is very unhappy, but too late to be helped, the discovery we have made, that we exist. That discovery is called the Fall of Man. Ever afterwards, we suspect our instruments. We have learned that we do not see directly, but mediately, and that we have no means of correcting these colored and distorting lenses which we are, or of computing the amount of their errors. Perhaps these subject-lenses have a creative power; perhaps there are no objects.

We are, then, *devices for seeing*—perception is what we are created for, just as Berkeley suggested. We are also incapable of seeing things accurately, or even knowing if those things exist. The transparent eyeball is a failure, afflicted with myopia or blindness. This is one cheerless cul-de-sac. It is a giant experiment in loneliness. Understandably, it kills off all hope of human connection, since the self "ruins the kingdom of mortal friendship and love. Marriage (in what is called the spiritual world) is impossible, because of the inequality between every subject and every object."

God only knows what Lidian made of that last sentence. But it is, honestly, nothing personal—just Waldo conceding that the soul blots out everything else, including your wife's soul, and maybe your dead son's.

Except that he didn't think the dead were truly dead. "It is the secret of the world that all things subsist, and do not die," he wrote, "but only retire a little from sight, and afterwards return again." This wasn't in "Experience," but in "Nominalist and Realist," the penultimate piece in *Essays: Second Series*. It's comforting to come across such a contrary view in the same book. This time around, the universe is additive rather than subtractive. "All persons, all things which we have known, are here present, and many more than we see; the world is full." *The world is full.* A welcome statement from this apostle of emptiness, who on his very deathbed murmured to nobody in particular, "Oh, that beautiful boy!"

10

THE METAPHYSICIAN ON TOUR

"A man must ride alternately on the horses of his private and his public nature," Waldo once noted, "as the equestrians in the circus throw themselves nimbly from horse to horse, or plant one foot on the back of one, and the other foot on the back of the other." But did he truly consort with the American people, those whiskey-drinking and newspaper-devouring masses who were bound, in his view, to transform the world?

The answer is yes. Much of this public life derived from his role as a lecturer—as a key attraction on a circuit that stretched from coast to coast and sustained him for more than four decades.

This circuit was a relatively recent invention. It was only in 1826 that an itinerant educator named Josiah Holbrook showed up in Millbury, Massachusetts. There he persuaded fifty or so citizens to form a local branch of what was to be called the American Lyceum—the name derived from the temple in Athens where Aristotle lectured his young charges.

Holbrook had already spent several years crisscrossing the region, urging tiny hamlets to fund what were essentially natural-sciences think tanks: each would include a library, taxidermized animals, a cabinet of mineralogical wonders, and so forth. That plan never took off. But the idea of a speaker's circuit was a raging success. Soon a dozen nearby villages followed in Millbury's footsteps, and by 1828, there were nearly one hundred outposts of the American Lyceum. Six years later, there were three thousand throughout the United States. In some parts of the country, as one historian of the movement put it, "everyone who could stoop or talk was picking up stones for the Lyceum cabinet or working up lectures for the benefit of his fellow-members." (The bit about stones suggests that Holbrook's dream of geological literacy never quite died.)

Each branch was funded by the locals. In New Bedford, Massachusetts, for example, the Lyceum's charter stated that "one annual fee shall be two dollars, but the sum of thirty dollars paid at any time will entitle a person, his heirs and assigns, to one membership forever." Although the branches were seldom swimming in cash, they mounted ambitious programs from the start—mostly by employing *other* locals as gratis speakers. Not until the mid-1830s did out-of-towners begin traipsing into lecture halls and collecting fees. In this regard, Salem was way ahead of the curve: early on, the organizers doled out a hundred dollars to Daniel Webster, a mind-blowing sum apparently engineered by local son Nathaniel Hawthorne.

Holbrook himself helped to found the Concord Lyceum in January 1829. There were fifty-seven charter members, the eldest being Ezra Ripley and the youngest the twelve-year-old Rockwood Hoar (who would later stare at little Waldo's corpse in such speechless horror). Over the succeeding decades, Waldo delivered no less than ninety-eight lectures at the Concord Lyceum. Sometimes he limited himself to one per annum. On other occasions, he administered them in bunches, covering a farcically wide range of topics: in 1839, for example, he shared his thoughts on protest, love, tragedy, comedy, and demonology.

His appearances in Concord were a public service. He didn't collect a dime for them. But Waldo quickly made a name for himself as a speaker-for-hire throughout New England, whose performances were well worth whatever he was paid.

At first, the fees were fairly modest. When he was invited to lecture in Waltham in the early 1840s, he replied that he would "come for the five dollars offered, but must have in addition four quarts of oats for his horse." (After much discussion, his request was granted.) Soon enough, he became a hotter commodity. In 1847, Thomas Wentworth Higginson, a former minister and Emersonian acolyte who would be best known for his (editorial) relationship with Emily Dickinson, was selecting speakers for the Newburyport Lyceum. He was told to book Waldo no matter who else was on the program, and to pay him twenty dollars rather than the standard fifteen.

"My pulpit is the Lyceum platform," Waldo once declared. His comment gives a sense of how central these engagements became to his imaginative life. All the intensity he had once devoted to his labors as a minister—however badly *that* ended—was now aimed at this new, secular audience. In fact, his appetite for lecturing eventually expanded beyond the Lyceum circuit itself. Instead of waiting for a summons from the good people of Chicopee Falls (where he lectured in 1858) or Kalamazoo (ditto, in 1860), he sometimes set up a series himself, which meant hiring the hall, printing tickets, and reaping the more substantial profits if all went well.

He began this routine in the fall of 1836 when he announced a twelve-lecture series at Boston's Masonic Temple called "The Philosophy of History." He had already scoped out the venue a year earlier, in the hope that Thomas Carlyle might come to America for a series of speaking engagements. In a letter, he told Carlyle that the "expenses of rent, lights, doorkeeper, &c" would amount to twelve dollars per night. Now he went the entrepreneurial route himself, even as he struggled to cobble together the actual material. Writing to his brother William on October 23, Waldo said he was "still scheming my lectures." He added: "How little masters we are of our own wits! Mine run away with me; I don't know how to drive."

The image of Waldo as a frantic teamster of his runaway thoughts has lost little of its freshness. He seemed concerned, too, that the market was saturated. It was true that the vogue for entrepreneurial lecturing had taken off in tandem with the Lyceum mania, so that, in the words of the social historian Carl Bode, "everyone from Harvard professors to phrenologists or outright quacks" was hiring a hall. Waldo hoped to recover his expenses, at the very least. He did considerably better than that. On average, each of his lectures was attended by about 350 people, who had paid two dollars for the entire series.

In a letter to William on March 20, 1837, he wrote: "I found so much audience for my opinions & speculations this winter as to feel much courage to vent all that I find in my manuscripts." He also noted his profits after expenses: $380.

This was a handsome sum indeed for a man whose annual income from his first wife's estate came to about $1,200, which had also been his initial salary at the Second Church. It was a game-changer, in fact, given that Waldo's books hardly turned a profit until much later in his career. He would have described his own vocation as thinker, or poet, or even transparent eyeball. But what he did for a living, in a very real sense, was talk.

. . .

Am I suggesting that he delivered a total of 1,469 lectures over nearly fifty years just for the money? Yes and no. Clearly financial pressure was a big part of it. Waldo acknowledged as much in a January 1843 letter to his young friend Sam Ward, which supports this thesis and undermines it at the same time:

> It is because I am so ill a member of society; because men turn me by their mere presence to wood & to stone; because I do not get the lesson of the world where it is set before me, that I need more than others to run out into new places & multiply my chances for observation & communion. Therefore whenever I get into debt, which usually happens once a year, I must make the plunge into this great odious river of travelers, into these cold eddies of hotels & boarding houses,—farther, into these dangerous precincts of charlatanism, namely, Lectures, that out of all the evil I may draw a little good in the correction which every journey makes to my exaggerations.

There you have it. He needed the cash, especially after the Panic of 1837, which shuttered nine out of ten Eastern factories and cratered the nascent American stock market. Waldo was particularly exposed here because much of his inheritance from Ellen consisted of stocks and bonds. His letters of the period are full of flustered calculations, and as he readily confessed, "I am no very good economist." So his income from lecturing played a bigger and bigger role in keeping the household, and the extended family, afloat.

But, as his letter to Ward suggests, there were other benefits. The Lyceum circuit forced him to leave his hermitage in Concord. It drove him out into the great world, and more specifically, into the American reality he spent so many years exalting in his prose. It was, in a sense, an opportunity to test theory against practice—to see how an entire nation of supposed individuals hung together, particularly in the raw interior of the country, where a rough-and-ready civilization was being made up on the fly.

Waldo also came to view the lecture itself as a new and challenging form. Why should writers continue to churn out poems, plays, epigrams, novels? "A lecture is a new literature," he declared, "which leaves aside all tradition, time, place, circumstance, and addresses an assembly as mere human beings no more. It has never yet been done well. It is an organ of sublime power, a panharmonicon for variety of note."

It was also, crucially, an instrument for *connecting with other people* in real time. For a rocking-chair-bound essayist, this was a necessity. The airless isolation of pure Transcendentalism could turn the audience into an afterthought. But as a man preaching the gospel of the Over-Soul, Waldo was also stumping for communion, and lecturing let him put that idea into action.

He argued that the current must flow in both directions, that speaker and audience alike were to be transformed. The lecturer could consider his talk a success only when he himself was "agitated, and is as much a hearer as any of the assembly. In that office you may and shall (please God!) yet see the electricity part from the cloud and shine from one part of heaven to the other." A tall order, yes. Yet Waldo apparently managed a good many of these galvanic performances, at least to judge from contemporary reports.

Which is not to say that he was a wild-and-crazy presence on the Lyceum stage. Initially, of course, the bar was set low: the early Lyceum was built around sober declamation, more or less a secular version of church on Sunday. But as the years went by, it morphed into entertainment, too. It was a TED talk and standup routine and encyclopedia entry rolled into one. In the middle of the country, it was often the only form of amusement for miles—a frontier multiplex. And some of its stars were

FIGURE 9. RWE in his typical lecture stance. Courtesy of the Concord Free Public Library.

real comedians, like Artemus Ward, whose goofy dialect stories convulsed his listeners for decades. (Abraham Lincoln, who probably heard him perform in person, was such a devotee that he read several of Ward's routines to his stone-faced Cabinet before presenting them with the Emancipation Proclamation.)

Waldo was not a comedian. Indeed, his onstage demeanor was so contained that none other than Artemus Ward once referred to him as a "perpendicular coffin." He stood very still before his audience, his hands folded before him. He wore plain, black, sometimes ill-fitting suits. He didn't gesticulate much. At climactic moments, he might clench his right fist, or make a hammering movement with his left hand, which one onlooker compared to "driving imaginary stakes." Every now and then he shifted his weight, and the audience might be treated to the sound of his creaking boots. Looking back on one such occasion, Julian Hawthorne said, "I do not recall the subject of that lecture, but I can never forget the boots."

Yet his voice, a rich and entrancing baritone, kept his listeners riveted. This was so even when they understood little of what he was saying. James Russell Lowell, who worshipped Waldo while having doubts about his wispier ideas, probably put it best: "We do not go to hear what Emerson says so much as to hear Emerson." He was an oracle, a dispenser of wisdom. It was perfectly fine to sit in the audience while your foot fell asleep and let his words wash over you—to be a passive receptacle, an inlet of the oceanic consciousness he was always talking about.

His habit of shuffling through his manuscript, jumping from one portion to another, probably added some extra suspense. Little did his audience suspect that he was recapitulating his literary methods before their eyes, shaving away transitional passages, juggling epigrams, and following the compositional whim of the moment. He was not merely reading, he was *writing*.

Perhaps that fact, even if dimly intuited, made his lectures a kind of spectacle, a head-scratching thrill ride. An anonymous reviewer in the *Boston Post* described one of Waldo's 1849 appearances in precisely these terms. The star of the show, he wrote, "lets off mental skyrockets and fireworks—he spouts fire, and conjurer-like, draws ribbons out of his mouth. He smokes, he sparkles, he improvises, he shouts, he sings, he explodes like a bundle of crackers, he goes off in fiery eruptions like a volcano." Take *that*, Artemus Ward!

That same review noted that Waldo "inverts the rainbow and uses it for a swing." Herman Melville, who heard him lecture shortly afterward and had clearly read the *Post*'s assessment, dug in his heels at such hyperbole. "No, I do not oscillate in Emerson's rainbow," he wrote to a friend, "but prefer rather to hang myself in mine own halter than swing in any other man's swing." Other listeners were considerably more brusque in dismissing what they viewed as the empty calories of Emersonian prose. One critic, writing in the New York *Knickerbocker*, lambasted Waldo's "high-heeled grammar and three-storied Anglo-Saxon" as a literally toxic experience. "Ralph Waldo is death," he declared, "and an entire *stud* of pale horses on flowery expressions and japonica-domish flubdubs."

Melville's spitballs are offset by the admiring things he said in that very same letter. I would argue that he recognized a kindred, world-devouring spirit with a vocabulary to match—that he felt competitive rather than snidely superior. "Let us call him a fool," he wrote. "Then had I rather be a fool than a wise man." He added: "I love all men who *dive*. Any fish can swim near the surface, but it takes a great whale to go down stairs five miles or more." Melville had not yet begun to write *Moby-Dick*, but his cetacean sketch of Waldo was clearly the highest (or deepest) praise he could offer.

As for that comic riffing in the *Knickerbocker*, it appears to have been a performance piece by a humorist named Jonathan Kelly. *His* readers would have been tipped off by the rhetorical extravagance, which was no less off-the-charts than Waldo's, although its chief ingredients were bombast, blarney, and (as they say in *Blazing Saddles*) authentic frontier gibberish. In fact, Kelly made the connection to Old West braggadocio explicit by calling his subject Roaring Ralph—also the name of a horse-rustling motormouth in Robert Montgomery Bird's popular novel *Nick of the Woods* (1837). Readers would likely have been tickled by the overlap. Hell, maybe some even viewed it as a backhanded compliment.

I linger on these contemporary assessments because it's clear that *something* profound was going on between Waldo and his listeners. The more exalted bits may have eluded some in the room, as did the stubbornly nonlinear flow of his prose. But too many people were too moved on too many occasions for us to pretend that they were simply taking their medicine. Something about Waldo's presence and the things he said penetrated them deeply, and changed them.

I'm going to guess that he, too, was changed. The very fact of an audience put him on alert: he could feel when they were stirred, amused, electrified, indifferent. He was, paradoxically enough, part of the crowd. I also wonder whether his on-the-fly revisions made the lectures slightly more casual and colloquial. He was always a fan of vernacular speech—he loved the conversations he overheard in the street, and found them more vigorous than literary talk. "Cut these words and they would bleed; they are vascular and alive; they walk and run," he wrote. He also compared such language to "a shower of bullets." Who, facing yet another shivering audience in the dead of winter, *wouldn't* want to speak in such a mobile, red-blooded, sharpshooting idiom? We'll never know for sure. There are no recordings of Waldo onstage, and he discouraged reporters from verbatim quotation, since he invariably intended to deliver the same lecture elsewhere and wanted it to stay fresh.

Yet lecturing was communion. Lecturing was Waldo, with his porcupine resistance to his fellow human beings, getting through. If that required some lowering of the rhetorical drawbridge, I'm going to guess that he obliged.

It was Jonathan Kelly, in his Roaring Ralph routine, who insisted that the audience "could no more have deciphered, or translated Mr. Ralph's argumentation, than they could the hieroglyphics on the walls of Thebes." But it was a farmer in Concord who told one observer that he had attended every single lecture that Waldo had ever given at the town's Lyceum—all ninety-eight of them. Hesitating for just a moment, the farmer added: "And I understood 'em, too." How beautiful it must have been for Waldo to be understood at last!

. . .

The sheer quantity of Waldo's onstage appearances—the sheer mileage, not to mention the industrial output of words—would be enough to fill a book. In fact, it has: William Charvat's *Emerson's American Lecture Engagements: A Chronological List*. We won't delve into the entire sequence, of course. Instead we'll take a tiny core sample and let it stand in for the peripatetic whole.

For example: the frigid winter weeks of early 1856. The previous months had already seen Waldo speeding from one engagement to another in New England. In October, Theodore Parker begged Waldo to pinch-hit for him at Boston's Music Hall in mid-November. Waldo was quick to beg off. "I am too closely promised, day by day, now for many weeks or months," he lamented. In December, he added, he would be "forced to go westward once more, sorely against my will." But even before then, he found himself slogging through appearances in Cambridge, Brooklyn, and Salem, where he spoke on two successive nights before decamping to Chicago on December 27.

He traveled there by train. At that point, the trip involved forty-eight continuous hours of transit, and the accommodations were not exactly plush. Charles Dickens, who endured a similar journey little more than a decade before, described it as "a great deal of jolting, a great deal of noise, a great deal of wall, not much window, a locomotive engine, a shriek, and a bell." The cars, Dickens wrote, were like "shabby omnibuses." Each held up to fifty passengers and was heated by a red-hot coal stove in the middle, whose air-rippling effects made everybody look a little ghostly.

Waldo, it should be said, was a professed fan of train travel—at least in theory. "Railroad iron is a magician's rod," he wrote, "in its power to evoke the sleeping energies of land and water." He admired the railroad's acceleration of American reality, and the way it knit together an impossibly diverse and scattered people.

He even *dreamed* about the railroad. Only weeks before his departure for Chicago, on October 4, he recorded in his journal that the previous night, he had imagined himself lost in a cornfield behind his house, then in a small town that somebody identified as Lisbon. "I was got by & by into a railroad car," he recalled, "but was a long way from home." This sounds less magical, more forlorn. Truly, it's hard to picture a man so addicted to solitude having a jolly time amid the sardine-can conditions of the Michigan Southern. For Waldo, it must have felt like Hell on wheels—like perdition with a view. If he encountered a fellow passenger reading a book, he once noted, he felt like hugging him.

A little worse for the wear, Waldo arrived in Chicago on December 29. There he took shelter at the Tremont House for the night. He opened his trunk and was delighted to discover some pears, courtesy of his sixteen-year-old daughter Ellen. He would, he told Lidian in a letter, proceed the next day to Davenport, Iowa, unless snow and ice prevented him from reaching the Mississippi River, which he would cross on foot.

This last mission was less daunting than it sounded. Waldo was an old hand, having crossed the frozen river twice before. Just a few days earlier, one Davenport newspaper described the route as a virtual cakewalk: "The old Father is considered as brought into subjection to the ice king until the warm weather shall set him loose." (The article did acknowledge that earlier in the winter, several travelers had fallen through the ice.)

Waldo lectured at the Congregational Church in Davenport on December 31. A ticket cost fifty cents, and a decent crowd showed up to hear him. We don't know the topic of his lecture—and neither did the audience, to judge from the report in a local newspaper. The reviewer thought the second half of Waldo's lecture better than the first, and all of it fairly amorphous. "He treated laconically upon many subjects," the article recounted, "and all of them he handled skillfully, leaving in his wake a train for thought which will come upon the mind at unexpected moments like a forgotten dream." Waldo, I think, would have regarded that as a roaring success. What better outcome for a lecturer than to warm the brains of your audience with mystical flashes, long after you had departed for your next stop?

His next stop was Rock Island, Illinois. There he spoke on January 1, and although the promotional handbills called him a "celebrated Metaphysician," his topic was more mundane, not to mention identifiable: "England and the English." His fee was forty dollars. Next he moved on to La Salle, and then to Dixon. The rigors of the Midwestern winter were already wearing him down. "A cold raw country this," he wrote to Lidian on January 3, "& plenty of night traveling and arriving at 4 in the morning, to take the last & worst bed in the tavern."

Waldo's visit to Dixon is of particular interest. In our era, the small town along the Rock River has acquired a sepia-tinted mystique as the boyhood home and ideological incubator of Ronald Reagan. The house on South Hennepin Avenue where he grew up is now a patriotic shrine of sorts, the Gipper himself having pocketed a loose tile from the fireplace during a 1984 visit, under which he used to hide stray pennies. Reagan recalled that his childhood in Dixon "was as sweet and idyllic as it could be, as close as I could imagine for a young boy to the world created by Mark Twain in *The Adventures of Tom Sawyer*." If we choose to view Dixon as an epicenter of Americana, then Waldo was more or less present at the creation.

Dixon was so new in 1856 that the town's founder, John Dixon, was still on the scene. Waldo chatted with the "correct quiet man," then eighty years of age, who had worked as a tailor, stagecoach owner, recorder of deeds, and postmaster before running a ferry service on the Rock River. The town was, to an almost comic degree, his creation. He laid out the lots himself. He lobbied to have Dixon declared the county seat—and since this would require a courthouse, he donated the land for Courthouse Square, then sold another eighty acres to pay for the construction of the actual building. With his wife, Rebecca, he helped to found the local Baptist church, and also begged a circuit-riding Episcopal clergyman to stick around. Not surprisingly, the town elected him its first mayor.

The community was, in Waldo's phrase, the lengthened shadow of one man. It seemed to be the work of a self-reliant juggernaut, bending the environment to his own will, making it up as he went along. Surely this was an archetypal American, who had carried out Waldo's recipe for national renewal: "We will walk on our own feet; we will work with our own hands; we will speak our own minds."

Yet Waldo was disturbed to see that the white-maned and venerable Dixon was living in poverty. His situation would have been worse still if Congress had not granted him an additional parcel of land for his service in the Black Hawk War. (Speaking of archetypal Americans: it was during that conflict, in 1832, that Dixon became friendly with both Abraham Lincoln and Jefferson Davis.)

"He who has made so many rich is a poor man," Waldo wrote in his journal, "which, it seems, is a common fortune here." A few pages later, he recorded a conversation on the same theme with a gentleman from Freeport, who insisted that "it is not usually the first settlers who become rich, but the second comers: the first, he said, are often visionary men, the second are practical." Perhaps Waldo, who usually put his chips on the visionary man, was taken aback. But at fifty-three, peddling his wares from town to town like a traveling salesman, he was more practical than he used to be.

. . .

What was Waldo's topic that night in Dixon? He delivered a lecture called "Beauty"—clearly one of his favorites, which he subsequently reprinted in *The Conduct of Life* (1860).

The topic sounds harmless enough. Surely the speaker would touch on sunsets, sacred art, Helen of Troy. All of which means that Waldo's listeners may have been thrown by the first sentence: "The spiral tendency of vegetation infects education also." It's not quite as irrelevant or nutty as it sounds. But it is Waldo who spirals from the outset, Waldo who veers directly into an attack on science as the great slayer and taxidermist of beauty.

First the humble ornithologist gets it in the neck. He fails to divine "what the social birds say, when they sit in autumn council, talking together in the trees. The want of sympathy makes his record a dull dictionary. The result is a dead bird." Then Waldo roughs up the naturalist, the astronomer, and the chemist. In all cases, their great sin is sterility—mistaking the data for the truth. Doctors make the same mistake, as do we for trusting them: "Our reliance on the physician is a kind of despair of ourselves." No, we must look beyond mere surfaces and symptoms if we are to understand beauty.

Waldo punts on defining it, but he is willing to explore some of its earmarks. There is simplicity, there is organic form, and there is flux. Regarding the latter, Waldo asserts: "Beauty is the moment of transition, as if the form were just ready to flow into other forms."

This recalls his earlier definition of power as a bird-like phenomenon hopping from bough to bough, fully itself only in flight. It also suggests Waldo's own resistance to any fixity of form in his prose—thought is always melting into thought, with no concern for orderly transition. He even applies the idea to politics, preferring the fluid motion of incrementalism to the violent bumps and bangs of revolutionary change. Indeed, he suggests that this patient morphing of political progress might eventually lead to women voting, legislating, and driving coaches!

What of personal beauty? It is, Waldo suggests, our natural state—yet sadly watered down by temperamental ugliness and bad genes. Our very faces "are a record in sculpture of a thousand anecdotes of whim and folly." Even the most saintly among us, who should theoretically resemble something from the workshop of Praxiteles, have to reckon with their mixed parentage. "The man is physically as well as metaphysically a thing of shreds and patches," he writes, "borrowed unequally from good and bad ancestors, and a misfit from the start."

For that matter, a pretty face will get you only so far. "Beauty without grace is the hook without the bait," Waldo argues. "Beauty, without expression, tires." Instead, he suggests, beauty is something internal, an aspect of the soul, the opposite of dullness and complacency, which leads Waldo to a line straight out of Oscar Wilde: "The secret of ugliness consists not in irregularity, but in being uninteresting." Indeed, a truly interesting person makes us forget about the question of physical attractiveness. Thinking, perhaps, of Margaret Fuller, whose intellectual vividness promptly burned away Waldo's qualms about her appearance, he writes: "There are faces so fluid with expression, so flushed and rippled by the play of thought, that we can hardly find what the mere features are." To put it another way: the imagination trumps the plodding world of sensory data, and we create beauty where we wish to find it.

This sounds like another reiteration of the feedback loop from *Nature*—the sense that we shape reality even as we perceive it. There, too, he had argued that the humblest physical objects were placeholders for their spiritual counterparts: visible things standing in for invisible ones. Now he takes that argument a step further. All things are essentially *interchangeable* once the white heat of human consciousness is applied to them:

> The feat of the imagination is in showing the convertibility of every thing into every other thing. Facts which had never before left their stark common sense, suddenly figure as Eleusinian mysteries. My

boots and chair and candlestick are fairies in disguise, meteors and constellations. All the facts in Nature are nouns of the intellect, and make the grammar of the eternal language.

Heady stuff for a subzero January night. Again, we don't know what the average citizen of Dixon thought of Waldo's frolics, for which he collected another forty dollars. In a letter to Lidian, he expressed some real affection for "these sinewy farmers of the north," but wondered whether he was connecting with them. "In all that is called cultivation," he wrote, "they are only ten years old, so that there is plenty of non-adaptation & yawning gulfs never bridged in this ambitious lyceum system they are trying to import." We do know that at least one customer had mixed feelings about what Waldo was selling. This was B. F. Shaw, editor of the *Dixon Evening Telegraph*, who liked neither Waldo's high-cholesterol prose nor his bare-bones delivery. "The lecture bore evidence of ripe scholarship," he admitted, "and contained many instances of history, but it had little that was original. It was delivered in a most miserable style."

Shaw's pan appeared in the paper on January 5. No doubt it was passed along to Waldo, but by then he had already read "Beauty" in Freeport, where it was described by the *Freeport Weekly Journal* as "vastly superior to any lecture we have yet had." Win some, lose some.

. . .

His Midwestern tour was not yet over. He traveled from Freeport to Galena, coping not only with the extreme weather and the discovery that all his shirt collars were too small, but with a growing awareness that he had messed up his lecture schedule for later in the month. He begged Lidian to dig out the relevant correspondence from the bureau in the Red Room and send it to Chicago.

Galena, like Dixon, seemed to capture certain American realities in miniature. In this case, it was the classic trajectory of the boom town. The French and the Fox Indians were the first to extract small amounts of galena—i.e., lead oxide—from the soil. By the late 1820s, however, the territory had passed into American hands, and thousands of prospective miners descended upon the area, naming the town after its prize commodity. In the banner year of 1845, nearly fifty-five million pounds of lead were shipped from the mines. Galena had been transformed into a bustling industrial hub overnight. It was, briefly, bigger than Chicago. Then the worm turned: a dwindling demand for lead and the discovery of gold in California in 1849 marked the beginning of a steep decline.

Yet dreams, like local economies, seldom die overnight. Anticipating decades of further prosperity, the town erected the grandiose DeSoto House hotel, whose dining room could seat three hundred guests and whose parlors, according to the *Galena Daily Advertiser*, were furnished with "velvet carpets, rosewood furniture, four large gilt mirrors, sofas, divans, marble-top tables, satin damask curtains, and one of Munn & Clark's best double-round, seven-octave, carved rosewood Piano Fortes." This monument to civic optimism had opened for business the year before Waldo showed up. That was where he stayed, assuring Lidian that he was "comfortably housed" but saying no more about his posh surroundings. Perhaps his silence can be chalked up to the "cruel kindness of a gentleman at Galena," who had invited Waldo to see the celebrated lead mines. The expedition turned out to involve an endless sleigh ride on the frozen Mississippi, after which the traumatized Waldo could, in his own words, "hardly speak."

By January 7 he was in Belvidere, where he read "Beauty" once again. But as he informed Lidian the next day, his tour of the lead mines had laid him low. "Mercury below zero 22° and this the twelfth day of the cold snap," he wrote. "Winter in Illinois has a long whip. To cuddle into bed is the only refuge in these towns." He canceled that night's lecture in Elgin, but pulled himself together sufficiently to speak in Beloit the following night.

There the punishing weather continued. His host made light of it, insisting to Waldo that "we had no cold weather in Illinois, only now & then Indian Summers & cool nights." Waldo, who had endured many a New England winter, thought otherwise. Temperatures this extreme were not merely an inconvenience—they were a metaphysical challenge. So, for that matter, were his listeners, who felt they were owed fifty cents worth of amusement and sometimes voted with their feet when Waldo failed to deliver. These difficulties, he decided, were *good* for him. As he wrote in his journal:

> This climate & people are a new test for the wares of a man of letters. All his thin watery matter freezes; 'tis only the smallest portion of alcohol that remains good. At the lyceum, the stout Illinoian, after a short trial, walks out of the hall. The Committee tell you that the people want a hearty laugh. . . . I must give my wisdom a comic form.

He paused for just a short stay in Chicago on January 12, happy to thaw out after what he described to Lidian as his "cold fortnight's adventures on the prairie." The worst effect of the arctic frigidity, he lamented, was not his sniffles but his inability to work on his latest book. In any case, he was soon off again. On January 16, he spoke in Galesburg, followed by engagements in Peoria, Ann Arbor, Adrian, Sandusky, Cleveland, Columbus, Akron, Hudson, and Ravenna.

Apparently he kept pulling out "Beauty," to erratic effect. He read it in Cleveland on January 23 and in Columbus on January 24, where the *Daily Ohio State Journal* declared that it would "long be remembered as the finest lecture ever delivered at the Atheneum." In Akron, though, the same material got a cooler response. "A large proportion of those who were present," declared a stern notice in the *Summit County Beacon*, "left with a feeling of disappointment." Waldo's wandering muse—even after he had vowed to amp up the comedy!—failed to move the audience. The reviewer lamented his reluctance to brandish "the torch of truth, to guide his hearers to a correct appreciation of the beautiful."

Did Waldo feel hurt by yet another tepid review? It must have disappointed him, aiming as he always did for an electrical exchange between speaker and audience. In his journal, however, he often sounds fired up by his travels. As the brutal cold snap continued, he described his mental state in terms more suggestive of a spring thaw.

"There are times when the intellect is so active," he wrote, "that every thing seems to run to meet it." He compared this abundance to the harvesting of maple syrup, itself the result of a very specific freeze-and-thaw cycle in early spring, when "the maple trees run with sugar, & you cannot get tubs fast enough." The image, with its quasi-sexual invocation of rising sap and woodsy ejaculation, is drawn from Waldo's own experience. The sap is an emblem of New England—and, in his opinion, an abolitionist condiment, since using maple syrup instead of cane sugar was a rebuff to the triangular trade.

How striking, then, to see him immediately link this Yankee plenitude to the Midwestern terrain outside his window. "The hunter on the prairie at the right season," he declares, "has no need of choosing his ground. East, west, by the river, by the timber, near the farm, from the farm, he is everywhere by his game."

Thus did Waldo unite the two regions in his imagination, a no less supple instrument than the telegraph, which he regarded as merely another form of speech. ("Every operator has his own manner or accent," he noted in his journal.) East, west, winter, spring, Waldo transmitted his message—and spent the rest of his life stumbling across the recipients. When he was introduced to Abraham Lincoln in 1862, the embattled president's first remark was, "Mister Emerson, I once heard you say in a lecture, that a Kentuckian seems to say by his air and manners, *Here I am; if you don't like me, the worse for you.*" We don't know exactly when Lincoln, who had his own moment as a Lyceum lecturer in the 1830s, heard Waldo speak. Yet here he was repeating the words back to him, closing the circle that opened each time Waldo stepped onstage in his creaking boots and began to talk.

11

VISIT TO A COLD ISLAND

To thumb through Waldo's account of his Midwestern tour in the winter of 1856 is to be plunged into another age—call it America in the raw. He recorded his other travels in similarly three-dimensional detail. He had a great appetite for facts and an unbeatable ear for colloquial speech, specimens of which he was constantly preserving like botanical wonders. ("Hoosiers are good to begin, but they *cave*," he wrote in 1856—an assessment of the Hoosier-as-warrior that *had* to have been uttered in some rustic tavern, presumably by a non-Hoosier.)

All of this is to say that Waldo could have written an amazing travel narrative about his native land. At one point he did ponder such a project. Some of his peers, such as Bronson Alcott, regretted that he never did "justice to New England" at book length. The closest Waldo came, in the end, was *English Traits*, the very manuscript he was struggling to finish in the early days of 1856. That book was primarily a passive-aggressive valentine to the British Isles. Yet Waldo, who was composing bits of it as he trundled around the frozen interior of his own country, managed to smuggle in an oblique portrait of America around the edges.

No doubt the rough conditions he encountered during his lecture tour made for a heightened sense of contrast between the two nations. American hospitality, Waldo jotted in his journal, "consists in a little fire, a little food, but enough, & and immense quiet. In England, it is a great deal of fine food, & of fire & immense decorum."

England's material abundance, and its much lengthier history, made for an abyss between the great power and its former colony. In comparison, America seemed sprawling, empty, uncouth. Yet the longer Waldo slipped the mother country under his magnifying glass, the more he wondered whether it might be approaching an imperial senescence—a final flowering before it lapsed into a coal-powered, fog-anointed, scone-glutted decline.

Waldo gathered his material on two separate trips. The first followed his exit from the pulpit and nervous collapse in 1833. At that point, he writes in *English Traits*, he was most interested in visiting the human monuments: Coleridge, Wordsworth, Carlyle.

With the latter he would form a lifelong friendship. But in general, such encounters seldom panned out. They were a kind of cultural tourism, Waldo insisted, which encouraged you to overlook the treasures on your own doorstep. "It is probable you left some obscure comrade," he wrote, "at a tavern, or in the farms, with right mother-wit, and equality to life, when you crossed sea and land to play bo-peep with celebrated scribes."

True to form, the two Romantic giants let him down. Coleridge, a stubby chatterbox in a snuff-spotted black suit, spent much of the time denouncing Unitarianism and recycling entire paragraphs from his oeuvre. "The visit was rather a spectacle than a conversation," Waldo ruefully noted.

As for Wordsworth, he greeted his visitor in green goggles, which he wore to alleviate the pain from a recurrent inflammation of the eyes called trachoma. He left Unitarianism alone. Instead he inveighed against the United States, with its excess of sin and scribbling journalists. A friend with some experience of the country, he told Waldo, had assured him that the American "newspapers are atrocious, and accuse members of Congress of stealing spoons!" Wordsworth also condemned Carlyle ("insane") and Goethe's *Wilhelm Meister* ("full of all manner of fornication") before reciting some new poems for Waldo out in the garden. It was, perhaps, more of a genuine exchange than Waldo had enjoyed with Coleridge. Yet Wordsworth, for all his visionary gifts, struck Waldo as "a narrow and very English mind"—a form of consciousness that he would spend much of the book exploring.

This applied in particular to the materials gleaned from his second trip, in 1847. He had been invited to give a series of lectures in Lancashire

FIGURE 10. RWE in 1846, not long before his trip to
Britain and France. Courtesy of the Concord Free
Public Library.

and Yorkshire—in short, to extend his conquest of the Lyceum circuit
to the United Kingdom. In the end, he spoke all over the country, and
in Scotland as well. Now a celebrated writer, he was less interested in
meeting his heroes than in taking the measure of England itself, in all its
power, glory, and artificiality. Its terrain, for example, seemed cultivated
to a fault, with not a hair out of place.

"England is a garden," he wrote. "Under an ash-colored sky, the fields
have been combed and rolled till they appear to have been finished with

a pencil instead of a plough." For an American, this utter triumph over nature was slightly disquieting. Yet Waldo was forced to admit that England was at its zenith, endlessly imitated even by its detractors.

What intrigued him even more than the landscape was the character of its inhabitants. Waldo's title was no accident. He wanted to create an anatomy of Englishness, to establish a genotype for John Bull.

This nudged him into a discussion of race, buttressed by the scientific literature of the era. Waldo, of course, had been an avid consumer of that very literature for decades. I mentioned earlier his 1832 sermon on astronomy, during which he assured his congregation that science would strengthen Christian belief. (Around the same time, he noted that city life would be improved by the installation of a telescope on every street.) He also immersed himself in the latest works on chemistry, botany, geology, and zoology, confident that their discoveries would mirror his own. The aim of science, after all, was "to find a theory of nature." Surely his poetic mode of investigation was pointing him in exactly the same direction.

Needless to say, antebellum science did not exist in a vacuum. Scientific debates rippled out into theology, morals, and philosophy, as they do today. This was no problem for Waldo, who had found these disciplines inseparable to begin with. "The axioms of physics translate the laws of ethics," he wrote. But nowhere was the collision of physics and ethics more combustible than in the scientific debate around race.

At the time, most theorists of race were split into two camps. Monogenists believed that all humans descended from a single origin—from a single pair of beings, who might just correspond to Adam and Eve. In the other camp were polygenists, who argued that God had created the races separately, setting them down on earth in regions best suited to their metabolism and temperament. While each camp was quick to denounce the other, they agreed on one thing: racial hierarchy, arrived at by two different paths. The monogenists assumed that certain racial groups had degenerated over time, leaving the white people at the pinnacle. The polygenists assumed that the races had been unequal from the start, and that their inequality was set in stone. Not surprisingly, this also left white people at the top, in what was presumed to be an eternal arrangement.

Waldo did not fit neatly into either box. Since he viewed human existence as a perpetual flux, he couldn't very well throw in his lot with the polygenists—their notion of history was way too static. The fixed role of races, he wrote, was a "feeble argument." Yet he had some problems with monogeny as well. He certainly agreed with their idea that racial groups might change over time. In this sense he was a transmutationist—a pre-Darwinian believer in evolution. But he did not believe that degeneration was the primary mechanism for such change. Rather, he thought that these transformations unfolded according to divine law, and that they more often involved a kind of ascent: a *progress*. This had been his view since the 1830s, when the poem he affixed to the beginning of *Nature* sketched out a cosmic lesson in upward mobility: "Striving to be a man, the worm / Mounts through all the spires of form." If the humblest creature could climb the evolutionary ladder, why couldn't men themselves?

All of these arguments floated in the background of *English Traits*. In the foreground, Waldo engaged with specific race theorists. There was, for example, the polygenist Robert Knox. In *The Races of Men: A Fragment* (1850), Knox divided humanity into separate species and declared that every aspect of culture flowed from this arrangement. "Race is everything: literature, science, art—in a word, civilization, depends on it," he wrote. An avowed abolitionist, Knox was annoyed to see his work praised by proponents of slavery, and happily anticipated an uprising in America. "A million of slave-holders cut off in cold blood tomorrow," he insisted, "would call forth no tear of sympathy in Europe." Yet his belief in racial difference was absolute. A Black man might well deserve to be free, but he was "no more a white man than an ass is a horse or a zebra."

There was also the monogenist Johann Friedrich Blumenbach, whose division of humankind into five races Waldo must have encountered in the third edition of *On the Natural Variety of Mankind* (1795). Blumenbach was a quintessential Enlightenment polymath, who wrote about everything from tapeworms to melancholy to Alpine crevasses to kangaroos (one of which he kept as a pet). Yet he was best known for establishing a racial hierarchy, with Caucasians, as he called the most purebred white people, at the top and the darker people at the bottom.

To delve into the thoughts of these two gentlemen is to fall into a sinkhole of flickering brilliance and glaring, Klieg-lit stupidity. They were both celebrated as scientific pioneers: Knox in particular was regarded as the most gifted anatomist of the era. Both delivered what seemed to be data-driven insight rather than anecdotal dross. Blumenbach even pushed back, at least from time to time, against the notion that Black people were invariably inferior to their white counterparts—according to one of his biographers, he owned "a library entirely composed of books written by negroes." Yet the thrust of their work, at least as it was absorbed by science-hungry readers like Waldo, was racial typology: race as fate.

Waldo echoed these concepts in *English Traits*. Like Knox and Blumenbach, he tried to heed the anatomical evidence, noting, for example, that the British were physically more robust than other races (very much including Americans). "Other countrymen look slight and under-sized beside them," he wrote, "and invalids." In another wince-making passage, he justified Britain's imperialist plunder of the Indian subcontinent: "It is race, is it not? that puts the hundred millions of India under the dominion of a remote island in the north of Europe." Race made the Celts into Catholics, the Jews into moneylenders—and in the case of Black people, it was "of appalling importance."

I detect a whiff of irony in Waldo's use of "appalling," with its etymological suggestion of paleness. Still, he is preaching the gospel of racial hierarchy here, as he does in other parts of *English Traits*. For this he has been taken to task by such critics as Nell Irvin Painter, in her smart and scathing *The History of White People* (2010). It is a great shame, exactly as Painter says, that Waldo threw his intellectual weight and prestige behind the toxicity of Victorian race theory.

The saving grace, at least for me, is that he couldn't help shooting holes in these ideas even as he was expounding them. They didn't quite feel right to him. So after pleading for the imperishability of race in *English Traits*, he made one of his characteristic hairpin turns.

He decided that the human hierarchies sketched out by Knox or Blumenbach were bogus, or at least blurry. Civilization, custom, the passage of time—they all dull the sharp edges of those racial categories and "eat away the old traits." Waldo also dismissed racial purity as a laughable chimera, turning zoological comparisons like Knox's to very different use:

> Though we flatter the self-love of men and nations by the legend of pure races, all our experience is of the gradation and resolution of races, and strange resemblances meet us every where. It need not puzzle us that Malay and Papuan, Celt and Roman, Saxon and Tartar should mix, when we see the rudiments of tiger and baboon in our human form, and know that the barriers of races are not so firm, but that some spray sprinkles us from the antediluvian seas.

There's a lot going on here, including the sort of proto-Darwinism espoused by the Scottish author and geologist Robert Chambers. The idea that we embodied all previous varieties of life—that we were, in a sense, recovering tigers and reconstructed baboons—certainly rebuffed the ass-versus-zebra scenario sketched out by Knox. If we are composite creatures, isn't race little more than an abstraction?

Waldo doesn't quite go there. He still views the Englishman as a discrete organism, with its own characteristics. Yet that organism is shot through with endless contradiction, so that "nothing can be praised in it without damning exceptions, and nothing denounced without salvos of cordial praise." The Englishman is a mess of impurities, culturally and genetically. Waldo quotes Daniel Defoe's famous line about his countrymen being "the mud of all races," and ridicules any direct line of descent from the Saxons, Jutes, or Frisians.

No, we are talking about an "anthology of temperaments," he insists. This seems like a more generous conception—national character as a kind of porous membrane. Yet in his sketch of *Homo britannicus*, Waldo is careful to exclude the Scots (hobbled by poverty and the "insanity of dialectics") and the Irish (an "inferior or misplaced race"). How the former assessment went down with Carlyle, the choleric Scot who actually makes an appearance later in the book, is not known. He did tell

Waldo that *English Traits* was "full of thoughts like winged arrows," and let the national slander pass without comment.

. . .

Moving beyond the dictates of race, Waldo keeps trying to pin down at least some notion of the English character. They are a logical people, he argues, fixated on cause and effect. For this reason, they "are jealous of minds that have much facility of association"—including, presumably, his own, with its constant lateral leapfrogging from topic to topic. What the English prefer is the comforting hum of machinery. Hence their love of turbines, centrifugal pumps, factories. "Steam is almost an Englishman," Waldo writes. "I do not know but they will send him to Parliament, next, to make laws."

The tone here is lightly satirical, and unquestionably admiring. Yet the British genius for mechanical solutions is also, to Waldo's mind, a defect. Everything on the magical island is somehow *manufactured*. This leads to a pistol-whipping passage in which Waldo seems to retract all the kind things he has said earlier about the so-called beacon of civilization:

> Their system of education is factitious. The Universities galvanize dead languages into a semblance of life. Their church is artificial. The manners and customs of society are artificial—made up men with made up manners—and thus the whole is Birminghamized, and we have a nation whose existence is a work of art—a cold, barren, almost arctic isle, being made the most fruitful, luxurious and imperial land in the whole earth.

Normally, this would be the coup de grâce—why waste any more time praising the victim? Yet Waldo simply moves on, chapter after chapter, expressing his sincere wonderment and comic contempt. His doubts about the triumph of industry sometimes take on a Marxist ring: "A terrible machine has possessed itself of the ground, the air, the men and women, and hardly even thought is free." True, the masters of this all-devouring machinery strike him as essentially benign: "Nothing savage, nothing mean resides in the English heart." What's more, their native good will is intermingled with what he calls a "saving stupidity," which preserves their focus even as it conceals their strength.

Empiricists to their fingertips, they cannot be bothered with the soul. Hence: "Their religion is a quotation; their church is a doll; and any examination is interdicted with screams of terror." This leads to something of a wipeout in the realm of letters, too. Waldo worshipped at the altar of English literature—Shakespeare and Milton were his gods. Yet he judged the national character more generally to be an obstruction when it came to creative writing (a term he coined, for better or worse). The Englishman is "materialist, economical, mercantile. He must be treated with sincerity and reality, with muffins, and not the promise of muffins." Even Alexander Pope, presumably one of the more gifted muffin men, is derided for writing poetry "fit to put round frosted cake."

This is not exactly a measured assessment. Indeed, Waldo's assault on the English race brings to mind his lengthy dust-up with Unitarianism. In both cases, he seems desperate to separate himself from something formative: the urge is vaguely patricidal. Waldo, of course, had been wrestling with these feelings for a long time. A decade earlier, writing in his journal, he had warned himself to avoid the contaminating influence of Europe—and "mainly of England." But it was British *greatness* he was so anxious to dodge: "All genius is fatal to genius. Come not too near." Now that he was actually there, the nonstop stream of comic epithets was a defensive maneuver, and also a means of self-definition. Nothing made him more conscious of his Idealism than being surrounded by an entire nation of muffin-loving materialists. (He was more of a pie man himself.)

And still, England's accomplishments could not be denied. Waldo devotes an entire, awestruck chapter to the *Times*, visiting the newsroom but barred, like all outsiders, from the holy shrine of the editor's office. The paper, he writes, is a "living index of the colossal British power"—an ink-and-paper monument to its fact-devouring readership. Elsewhere he swings by another monument, now in the company of Carlyle, who is never named. The two smoke cigars as they stroll around Stonehenge, sheltering from the wind behind one of the ancient megaliths. "The old sphinx put our petty differences of nationality out of sight," Waldo writes. "To these conscious stones we two pilgrims were alike known and near. We could equally well revere their old British meaning." Can the tribal questions so central to the book finally be evaporating in the presence of something so elemental?

Not really. Soon after, while traveling in a coach to Winchester, Waldo was asked by one of his English hosts to describe America. He had entertained similar queries in recent weeks: one fan in Bridlington asked him if "there were *many* rattlesnakes in the city of New York." Now, however, he was being asked for a more panoramic description. It is an amazing conversation to contemplate, and alas, there is no verbatim transcript.

But Waldo does sum up his answer in a lyrical and homesick paragraph. It crystallizes once and for all that to write about England was to write about America—a wild offspring of the mother country, a kind of doppelgänger whose vast terrain and native energies had yet to be tamed, tamped down, domesticated. England, at its height, was almost over. America had scarcely begun. As he often did, Waldo invested the very landscape with a supernatural freight of power, beauty, and melancholy. The sentences must be quoted at length:

> There I thought, in America, lies nature sleeping, over-growing, almost conscious, too much by half for man in the picture, and so giving a certain tristesse, like the rank vegetation of swamps and forests seen at night, steeped in dews and rains, which it loves; and on it man seems not able to make much impression. There, in that great sloven continent, in high Alleghany pastures, in the sea-wide, sky-skirted prairie, still sleeps and murmurs and hides the great mother, long since driven away from the trim hedge-rows and over-cultivated garden of England.

This is, as I have suggested before, a mythological America—raw material for an Edenic future. Again, its poetic, almost narcotic emptiness omits certain realities, including the prior claims to the same real estate by a multitude of Native Americans and even the fact that much of New

England had been denuded of trees by the time Waldo was writing these sentences. Man, that is to say, had already made something of an impression on this timeless landscape. In many cases, the dew-steeped forests were now pasturage or rotting stumps. Yet Waldo was nonetheless intoxicated by the *idea* of America, so beautifully unfinished and malleable, a vast habitation of the spirit with, for the most part, nobody home.

He returned to this theme in the final section of *English Traits*. The text is, in fact, a speech he gave in Manchester, following remarks by the calico king and free-trade crusader Richard Cobden, the illustrator George Cruikshank, and a letter of apology from Charles Dickens, who was busy that night. It was, in other words, a kind of pep rally for the very notion of England, and Waldo mostly rose to the occasion. He praised the "moral peculiarity of the Saxon race" and its "habit of friendship," whose adhesive qualities made the "superficial attachments" of other nations look flimsy, if not downright treacherous.

"All hail!" he exclaimed, "mother of nations, mother of heroes, with strength still equal to the time; still wise to entertain and swift to execute the policy which the mind and heart of mankind requires in the present hour." The rolling periods, the Johnsonian parallelisms, were pure catnip for Waldo's audience. Here was an American, they must have thought, who respected his cultural elders.

Yet at the very end, before plopping back into his seat, he delivered the shiv. What if, hypothetically speaking, England should fail in its highest aspirations? What if this mightiest of nations should choke on its own cornucopia of buttons and bolts, stoves and saucepans, tweezers, trinkets, toilets, tea chests, the million-and-one gimcracks known collectively as Birmingham toys?

Waldo didn't say that such a calamity *would* happen. In the lavish setting of the Free Trade Hall—a shrine to British mercantile genius, built on land donated by Cobden himself—his speculation may have sounded like an apocalyptic afterthought. But both his speech and *English Traits* end with what is essentially a dose of Manifest Destiny. If England should falter, Waldo says, "I will go back to the capes of Massachusetts, and my own Indian stream, and say to my countrymen, the old race are all gone, and the elasticity and hope of mankind must henceforth remain on the Alleghany ranges, or nowhere."

It was an ankle-biting farewell to a nation he would visit only once more in his life, in 1873, by which time his prediction had begun to come true. At that very moment, America's economic might was finally catching up with Britain's. Within a couple of decades, the old race, those cordial forebears whom Waldo called "Patagonians of beef and beer," would be left behind.

12

KNOCKING DOWN
THE HYDRA

The upstairs study at the Old Manse, the ancestral redoubt where Waldo wrote *Nature* and spent a good many happy hours, is an inviting room. During the New England winter, a constant blaze in the fireplace once kept the room warm and smudged the walls, now handsomely wallpapered, with smoke. There was a chair with a built-in desk, and a sofa, and a mirror, and a peekaboo view of the Concord River through the trees.

But if you exit the study, and turn left, and climb the stairs, you find yourself in the attic. Much of this space is raw and unfinished, as it was in Waldo's day. There is a small office-plus-alcove toward the rear, called the Prophet's Chamber, where not only Waldo but visiting preachers would take their sermons-in-progress for a test drive, declaiming to the rough planking and whitewashed walls. These visitors to the chilly attic treated the space as a rhetorical laboratory. But the regular residents, for a decade or more, were slaves.

This was not during Waldo's time. Slavery was outlawed in the state of Massachusetts in 1783. But his grandfather, the Reverend William Emerson, who built the Old Manse in 1770, counted several human beings as his property, including a trusted and longtime retainer named Frank.

The fact that William Emerson was a fierce proponent of American independence, who compared the heavy hand of British rule to "the shackles of slavery," produced not a jot of cognitive dissonance. Indeed, this gift for compartmentalization (a national pastime to this very day) led to constant paradox, mostly grim, often surreal. When, for example, the British regulars marched on Concord on April 19, 1775, William Emerson hustled out to join the insurgent Minutemen. As the British approached the Old Manse, Frank grabbed an axe to defend the household and burst into his mistress's bedroom, crying out, "The Red Coats have come!" Phebe Emerson fainted dead away—not at the prospect of British interlopers, but at the sight of a Black man holding a weapon in her bedroom.

Despite this incident, Frank was left to protect the family in 1776 when William Emerson decamped to Fort Ticonderoga, where he served as chaplain to the Continental Army. What happened to this faithful retainer *after* the war is unknown. Family lore suggests that he was manumitted—but like so many of his peers he vanished from the historical record, very much including the Emerson household inventory, where he customarily would have been listed among the curtains, wigs, and tea set.

On the other hand, a small population of free Black people did settle in Concord during the postwar years. In several cases, they were former slaves who had fought for the Continental Army and won a sort of de facto emancipation for their efforts. Some settled on a fringe of undesirable land adjacent to what the townspeople called the Great Field. Others built a community in the equally undesirable woods around Walden Pond. Unlike Thoreau, who would eventually take up residence in the same spot and erect his modest shrine to self-sufficiency, they weren't seeking shelter from the straitjacket of civilization. They had simply been driven to the outskirts of town by white hostility, the locals having little sympathy for Black freedom, especially when it involved human beings who had once been their property.

The population of this embattled community had never been large— two or three dozen at the most. Their numbers soon dwindled. By the time Thoreau arrived on the scene, these people of color were mostly gone—although recently enough that he could take the reader on a spectral tour of the neighborhood in *Walden*, noting the "half-obliterated cellar hole" where Cato Ingraham had dwelled, or the wild remnants of

Brister Freeman's old apple orchard. They were, in a sense, already phantoms. Indeed, one of the only documented artifacts of this vanished community, now in the Concord Museum, is a mirror, whose silver foil has long since flaked away. What better emblem of invisibility?

I am not scolding Thoreau for his elegiac paragraphs. Nor am I taking Waldo to task for the sins of his grandfather—the slaveowner who died a patriot's death in 1776, of typhus. Yet these things, too, seem emblematic. In the study at the Old Manse, three generations of Emersons worked at their emancipatory tasks, while, at least for a time, the human chattel slept upstairs. Black people, free or enslaved, were the ghosts in the attic. They haunted the collective conscience of the age, which responded with apathy or outrage or self-inflicted amnesia.

. . .

There were few if any opponents of slavery in Concord prior to the 1830s. After that, the movement began to gain some traction there and throughout Massachusetts, partly fueled by the success of William Lloyd Garrison's fiery newspaper, *The Liberator*. The New England Anti-Slavery Society got underway in Boston in 1832, and local branches popped up in communities throughout the region. Five years later, readers will recall, Lidian Emerson was among the sixty-one women who founded the Concord Female Anti-Slavery Society. Yet even these vanguard abolitionists were likely to embody the sort of paradox that I mentioned in connection with the Reverend William Emerson. That is, many of them found slavery abhorrent as an institution while assuming that Black people were nonetheless inferior to their white counterparts. This was conventional wisdom in Waldo's era. It was buttressed by the kind of bogus science that he would come to expound in *English Traits*—the skull measurements, the fanciful hierarchies, the politics of pigmentation—but plenty of people believed it without ever reading a page of Johann Friedrich Blumenbach.

I'm not talking about whip-wielding sociopaths here. I'm talking about the heroic figures of nineteenth-century America, the people who were supposed to levitate above the follies of the age by their intellectual bootstraps. So we have Abraham Lincoln declaring that he would never "introduce political and social equality between the white and black races," and Theodore Parker insisting that "an Anglo-Saxon with common sense does not like the Africanization of America." Walt Whitman, too, was dead set against the amalgamation of the races, posing the perennial question: "Is not America for the Whites?" Elizabeth Cady Stanton bitterly resented the passage of the Fifteenth Amendment in 1870, fuming that "Sambo" had beaten white women to the ballot box. Even William Lloyd Garrison, who devoted just about every waking moment of his life to the annihilation of slavery, ascribed the oratorical magic of his greatest protégé, Frederick Douglass, to the "power of an unsophisticated mind."

We could go on in a similar vein for hours. Searching for the ruinous flaw or self-immolating utterance has become a reflex—a way to bring the so-called giants down to our own level, or maybe something lower. In lots of cases, this seems warranted. So many reputations depend on the avoidance of just a few key facts; so much of what we learned in history class is little better than mythologizing dross. More truth is always better. Yet the flip side of this compulsive candor is a hectoring perfectionism—a desire to prove that Achilles was, in the end, all heels and nothing else.

If Lincoln and Parker, Whitman and Stanton and Garrison, had done nothing but exemplify the most destructive notions of the day, we would be quite justified in kicking them out of the pantheon. We could write them off as standard-issue bigots and be done with it. Frustratingly, however, they were composite creatures, visionaries with blind spots. They were also self-correcting, to an extent that should impress us nearly two centuries later, since we happen to be wrestling with some of those very same notions, preserved in an amber of shame and denial. Lincoln, for example, moved far beyond his early, ugly, and (most likely) politically calculating statements about racial equality. Garrison surely countermanded his crack about Douglass's unsophisticated mind by praising the former slave's abolitionist newspaper, *The North Star*, as "another proof of his genius."

And what of Waldo? He, too, began with some of the right ideas and some of the wrong ones. What matters most is his trajectory, and where he ended up. But at a very young age, he asserted both his fealty to an absolutist version of abolitionism and his foolish ideas about Black inferiority.

He went on the record early. Waldo was only nineteen when he wrote in his journal: "No ingenious sophistry can ever reconcile the unperverted mind to the pardon of *Slavery*; nothing but tremendous familiarity, or the bias of private *interest*." That would seem to be it in a nutshell, right? The blanket condemnation, and the understanding that the most vigorous defenders of human chattel would be those tainted by habit and economic gain, makes me want to cheer. The problem is that Waldo filled some of the adjacent pages in that same journal with schoolboy speculations about racial hierarchy. Some of this material is hard to read: "I saw ten, twenty, a hundred large lipped, lowbrowed black men in the streets who, except in the mere matter of language, did not exceed the sagacity of the elephant."

To be fair, Waldo is playing devil's advocate here. He's consciously marshalling the proslavery arguments so that he can, as he puts it, "attempt to knock down the hydra." Yet he is channeling the monster a little too effectively—he's halfway to convincing himself, and it shows. Sure, he seems to be saying, slavery is immoral on the face of it, but isn't the question of Black inferiority still worthy of a thought experiment?

If so, it was an experiment involving no actual data. After all, Waldo knew as much about Black people as he did about elephants: almost nothing. He was unlikely to have conversed at length with any person of color, or even encountered any on a regular basis. In 1820, right before Waldo confided those thoughts to his journal, there were only 1,726 Black Bostonians out of a total population of 254,674. Concord, as I have noted, had already squeezed out most of its people of color from Walden woods, although a couple dozen remained in the area.

As a budding race theorist, then, Waldo was operating in a vacuum. His thoughts on the topic were notable not for their ugliness, not for their callowness, but for their utter conventionality. Most white Americans thought exactly as he did about Black Americans. In that sense, he was simply reading his lines from a cultural script. In due time, he would be horrified by that sort of vacant assent to the hive mind—but not quite yet.

. . .

It would be fair to say that I'm squirming here. In a sense, I have been squirming through the past three decades of Waldo's life, waiting for him to rectify his early indifference to racial justice. To write about the Transcendentalist prophet and champion sentence-wrangler was pure pleasure. To absorb his panoply of losses was painful, yet also a lesson in empathy and immediacy—grief is like one of those rare isotopes, with a half-life beyond our reckoning. But when it came to the biggest ethical challenge of his day, Waldo was, let's say, a slow learner. I knew how the story ended, knew that he ultimately responded to the better angels of his nature. Still, I wanted him to hurry up. The sooner he moved upstream, out of the warm pool of moral laxity in which most of his contemporaries were happy to paddle, the better. I wanted my hero to behave like one.

Waldo himself was big on heroes. In 1850, he published an entire book about them, called *Representative Men*, which was essentially a tour of his personal pantheon. There they were: Plato, Swedenborg, Montaigne, Shakespeare, Napoleon, and Goethe. With at least half of these gentlemen he had serious problems. Swedenborg, his early idol and Virgilian guide to the world of the spirit, now struck Waldo as unreadable, his books notable for having "no melody, no emotion, no humor." Napoleon had the nerve to smash the *ancien régime* to pieces, but was also a monster of egotism who destroyed France and cheated at cards. It's no surprise that Waldo, whose entire philosophical outlook was built on kicking history to the curb, would have mixed feelings about his heroes. They were emissaries from the past, which he both loved and despised, and father figures (ditto, more or less).

Yet he recognized that such figures were not only useful but essential. "It is natural to believe in great men," he wrote. Like it or not, they saturated our existence. "Their names are wrought into the verbs of language," he went on, "their works and effigies are in our houses, and every circumstance of the day recalls an anecdote of them."

In theory, of course, we should be impervious to their good influence. That was Waldo's gospel, which he preached over and over—there was no chink in the armor of individualism large enough to admit a role model. He was perfectly glad to play this card again in *Representative Men*, while also suggesting that such heroic figures make our solitude a little less watertight:

> We swim, day by day, on a river of delusions, and are effectually amused with houses and towns in the air, of which the men about us are dupes. But life is a sincerity. In lucid intervals we say, 'Let there be an entrance opened for me into realities; I have worn the fool's cap too long.'

The gatekeepers to reality, you might say, are heroes. They usher us in, simply by defying the backwash of received opinion. They oxygenate the very atmosphere, which Waldo views as dangerously polluted: "The ideas of the time are in the air, and infect all who breathe it." They shame us, they prod us, they inspire us, and somehow diffuse their greatness into the population at large, perhaps through some mysterious delivery system like the Over-Soul. Remarkably, it takes only a few such figures to uplift an entire society. "What indemnification is one great man for populations of pigmies!" Waldo exclaims, sounding a bit like the churlish Carlyle but with less emphasis on the sheer puniness of the regular folks.

In any case, it's Waldo's own progress from pygmy to giant that concerns me here. After the youthful jottings I mentioned above, he never completely stopped mulling over the issue in his journals. Still, for a long time, his public utterances were few and far between. In his very first sermon—the one that precipitated his physical collapse, in 1826— he urged his listeners to take heed of "the slave's misery as they cross his path in life." He also invited such abolitionists as Samuel May and Arnold Buffum to preach from his pulpit at the Second Church during the early 1830s, which must have offended a fair number of his parishioners. (May had a particular gift for riling up the audience, and was later burned in effigy by his fellow citizens in Syracuse, New York.)

The political turbulence of the decade, however, made it harder and harder to stay mum. By the mid-1830s, the topic of abolition was so incendiary that it was banned from the (literal) corridors of power: the "gag rule" of 1836 decreed that any antislavery petition brought before the House of Representatives would be immediately and permanently tabled. At the same time, the public debate grew ever more fiery, a war of words that increasingly erupted into actual violence.

Waldo was under pressure, both internal and external, to speak up. Yet he resisted. As a Transcendentalist, he still hoped for a revolution in consciousness, which meant that all of the world's evils would be essentially self-erasing. Slavery, in this view of things, would simply collapse under the weight of its own wickedness. For that matter, the Unitarians, who had left a deep mark on Waldo despite his frequent complaints about them, argued that the human soul had to be perfected as a whole, not repaired on a piecemeal, issue-by-issue basis.

Still, his silence made him uneasy. In an 1837 journal entry, he excoriated himself for his own inaction: "A friend of the slave shows me the horrors of Southern slavery—I cry guilty guilty guilty!"

It was an incident of violence that first pushed Waldo into the public fray. On November 7, 1837, a mob in Alton, Illinois, attacked a warehouse where Elijah Lovejoy, a minister and abolitionist newspaper editor, had hidden his printing press. There was an attempt to burn down the building, and when Lovejoy emerged to stop it, he was shot five times in the chest. His corpse lay out in the street until the next morning. As for his press, it was broken into pieces and hurled into the Mississippi River.

Waldo viewed Lovejoy as a double martyr. He had died for the antislavery cause, of course, but also for free speech, which was the only real conduit for Unitarian-style moral suasion. "The brave Lovejoy has given his breast to the bullet," Waldo wrote in his journal, arguing that the victim had perished "for humanity & the rights of free speech & opinion."

Straddling these two issues, Waldo decided to mount the podium that same month. He declared his readiness to speak out—and was momentarily rebuffed when most of the venues in supposedly freedom-loving

Concord declined to host the event. Where he spoke is still unclear, but in the end he delivered what was by all accounts a watery and unsatisfying address.

The speech itself is lost. But some small, fossilized bits appear in James Elliot Cabot's authorized biography, and they show Waldo leaning heavily on the free-speech angle, as if the biggest civic challenge of the moment were to find a decent auditorium. "Even the platform of the lyceum," he laments, "hitherto the freest of all organs, is so bandaged and muffled that it threatens to be silent." He then bends over backward to acquit the slaveowner of any substantial sin—*not* because slavery is anything less than monstrous, but because the average citizen of the North is little better as a moral animal. "Let him not exaggerate by his pity and his blame the outrage of the Georgian or Virginian," Waldo insists, "forgetful of the vices of his own town and neighborhood, of himself."

The myopia is maddening. Of course it took a certain courage to recognize your own likeness to the slaveowner. It would have been more courageous still to acknowledge the complicity of the North and South. Waldo was certainly aware of the economic embrace that united the two regions, which had caused Charles Sumner to excoriate "the lords of the lash and the lords of the loom," explicitly roping in the owners of the New England mills who depended on Southern cotton for their prosperity.

But Waldo simply could not shake off his idea that freedom was an individual matter, eked out by the individual soul—that metaphysical manacles were roughly on par with physical ones. He also had scant patience for what he saw as the monomania of the great reformers. These fiery figures, he wrote in "Lecture on the Times," were "narrow, self-pleasing, conceited men, and affect us as the insane do. They bite us, and we run mad also."

Abolitionism, in other words, was a form of rabies. Waldo would spend the next few years avoiding it, digging himself deeper into his bunker of spiritual self-care. Yes, he did break his vow against political action just a year later, when he sent a furious open letter to President Martin Van Buren protesting the expulsion of the Cherokee from their ancestral homelands. On that occasion, he did not mince words. He tipped his hat to the giant task facing the tribe—to "redeem their own race from the doom of eternal inferiority," mainly by behaving like white people. But most importantly, he insisted that the Cherokee must be treated like human beings, and that the failure do so would bring shame upon the entire nation.

"We only state the fact," he wrote, "that a crime is projected that confounds our understandings by its magnitude—a crime that really deprives us as well as the Cherokees of a country; for how could we call the conspiracy that should crush these poor Indians our Government, or the land that was cursed by their parting and dying imprecations our country, any more?"

This sizzling protest was published in several newspapers. Whether Van Buren ever read it is an open question. He evicted the Cherokee right on schedule, whatever Waldo (or the U.S. Supreme Court, in *Worcester v. Georgia*) said to the contrary. But even before this catastrophic outcome, Waldo felt discouraged by his foray into public debate. "This stirring in the philanthropic mud, gives me no peace," he lamented in his journal. "I will let the republic alone until the republic comes to me." Could there be a less promising recipe for political activism? Yet the republic—or at least its ideological agonies—would eventually claim his attention.

. . .

What changed? Partly it was a growing sense that his temperamental aversion to the abolitionists was trivial and wrong. There was much to overcome here. In his journal, right after complaining about the philanthropic mud, he denounced antislavery rallies in weirdly pornographic terms: "The speakers warm each other's skin & lubricate each other's tongues & the words flow, & the superlatives thicken, & the lips quiver." It's as if the communion of public speaking, so bracing to Waldo on the Lyceum circuit, took on an erotic ickiness when the topic was politics.

Yet his exposure to the great figures of the movement, either at meetings or in private, gradually won him over. He came to praise William Lloyd Garrison's tenacity and eloquence, declaring him "armed with all the weapons of a great Apostle." Lucretia Mott, he decided, was a "noble woman." When Wendell Phillips's antislavery address struck one audience member at the Concord Lyceum as "vile, pernicious, and abominable," Waldo insisted that he be invited back for the next season. Their heated rhetoric and monomania aside, these people compelled Waldo's respect and, eventually, his deep admiration.

Also, Waldo had experienced his own share of brickbats as a result of the Divinity School Address. This was in 1838—which is to say, just months after his tepid debut as an abolitionist speaker and his missive to Van Buren. He had suffered a mild dose of public opprobrium, in the form of Andrews Norton's attacks. He had been called an infidel and a mad dog (more or less what he later called the abolitionists). But Garrison, for example, had dealt with far worse. Mobs jeered at him and pelted him with rocks, a gallows had been erected in front of his Boston office, and the Georgia legislature offered $5,000 to anybody who would drag the bald and bespectacled agitator down South for punishment. Here was one of those moral exemplars, those representative beings whose greatness spreads like a contagion. Surely this "agent of good," as Waldo would later describe him, deserved his wholehearted support.

The other factor, crucially, was an influx of knowledge. I have already noted Waldo's paucity of direct experience, or even dutiful fact-finding, when it came to the evils of human chattel. His antislavery barbs, on the rare occasions that he issued them, were aimed at an abstraction—a despicable blank. His schooling took a great leap forward, however, in 1844, when the Women's Anti-Slavery Association of Concord asked him to speak at their annual celebration of emancipation in the British West Indies.

This time, he embarked on a full-body immersion in the literature. He pored over Thomas Clarkson's *The History of the Rise, Progress, and Accomplishment of the Abolition of the African Slave Trade by the British Parliament*, a massive synthesis of evidence and argument that had actually played a big role in ending slavery on British soil. It was, in that sense, an activist document—just what Waldo needed to read at that very moment. The author had interviewed a multitude of sailors, overseers, surgeons, merchants, and other participants in the trade, and the accretion of detail was overwhelming. On a typical page, Clarkson recounted how one slave had been shoved into a cauldron of boiling cane juice, while another was whipped until unconscious, then dragged by her legs to the hospital, where she died. No system of moral equivalence could make these things acceptable. Nor was there any way to soften the shock of the book's infamous visual exhibit: a fold-out illustration showing how 454 shackled Africans were crammed belowdecks on a Liverpool-based slave ship.

Waldo also read *Emancipation in the West Indies: A Six Month's Tour in Antigua, Barbadoes, and Jamaica, in the Year 1837*. The authors, James Thome and Joseph Kimball, had traveled to the islands to chronicle the aftermath of abolition. Proslavery advocates had predicted a race war, followed by economic collapse—and probably even Waldo had been nervous about the outcome of this societal experiment. But three years after 750,000 enslaved people had been granted their freedom, there was no bloodbath, no reversion to the Stone Age. Instead, the authors found much calm, diligence, prosperity, and the delightful surprise of a multiracial crowd at a Wesleyan chapel in Antigua. There one could see, in adjacent pews, "the ebon hue of the negro, the mixed tint of the mulatto, and the unblended whiteness of the European. Thus they sat in crowded contact, seemingly unconscious that they were outraging good taste [and] violating natural laws."

Buttressed by this mass of data—by a thousand specimens of the actual—Waldo took to the podium on August 1, 1844. Since all the churches in Concord had declined to host his lecture, he agreed to speak at the courthouse instead. But the ecclesiastical sabotage continued when the sexton of the First Parish Church scorned any suggestion that he ring the town bell to summon the audience. It was left to Thoreau to ring the bell, after which the church was locked to prevent any further abolitionist mischief.

The lecture itself was a revelation. Gone was the mushy equivocator of his 1837 address, with its bait-and-switch focus on free speech and odd empathy for the slaveholder. Waldo, so skittish about the fire-breathing rhetoric of the great reformers, was now emitting some flames of his own.

In his very first sentence, he seems to make amends for his earlier airiness on the topic. They are meeting, he tells his audience, on the anniversary of a day that "gave the immense fortification of a fact—of gross history—to ethical abstractions." No more theory, he proclaims. The crisis of slavery calls for practice, which in the case of a writer means words as sharp and obdurate as stones, and no looking away, no matter how ugly the reality. Hence his plunge into the scarifying details. Most of these Waldo gleaned from the two books mentioned above, and he insists that his audience treat them as *real*, not secondhand goods. They will recoil, he says, with the very core of their being. "The blood is moral," he writes. "The blood is anti-slavery; it runs cold in the veins: the stomach rises with disgust, and curses slavery."

Waldo narrates the history of British emancipation, dwelling on its happy ending. Yet he is realistic about the entrenched evil of slavery. "The habit of oppression," he concedes, "was not destroyed by a law and a day of jubilee." Nor do improved economic arrangements instantly erase the damage of the preceding ones—especially, Waldo notes, when they were not strictly economic in the first place. Slavery, he argues, flows not only from greed but from an even darker instinct in the plantation owner: "the love of power, the voluptuousness of holding a human being in his absolute control." It must not be smuggled into the conversation as merely one more or less palatable form of labor. It is a deformation of the spirit, for both parties.

He is scathing, too, on the complicity of the American consumer— even those dwelling in the morally hygienic North. They delight in the products of slavery while strategically avoiding the question of who produced them, and at what cost:

> If any mention was made of homicide, madness, adultery, and intolerable tortures, we would let the church-bells ring louder, the church organ swell its peal, and drown the hideous sound. The sugar they raised was excellent: nobody tasted blood in it. The coffee was fragrant; the tobacco was incense; the brandy made nations happy; the cotton clothed the world. What! all raised by these men, and no wages? Excellent! What a convenience! They seemed created by providence to bear the heat and the whipping, and make these fine articles.

The irony here is expert and, one would think, impossible to overlook. But just in case, Waldo is careful to refute that final sentence.

Emancipation in the West Indies is a cause for celebration precisely because it exploded the myth of Black inferiority. "A man is added to the human family," he declares. "Not the least affecting part of this history of abolition, is, the annihilation of the old indecent nonsense about the nature of the negro."

For just a moment Waldo seems to dip his toe into Darwinian waters: only the strong, he suggests, will survive the culling. But he means strength of *mind*. "Ideas only save races," we read. And then, instead of evoking the racial hierarchies he would later preach in *English Traits*, he declares them irrelevant. "The might and right are here: here is the anti-slave: here is man: and if you have man, black or white is an insignificance."

It's an amazing sentence, with its equalizing string of colons and insistence that the pith of a human being is the free play of intellect, that skin color means nothing at all. Waldo takes it a step further. To the Black man in full possession of his mental freedom, he grants a kind of superhero status. "His skin and bones," he writes, "though they were the color of night, are transparent, and the everlasting stars shine through, with attractive beams." The transparency recalls Waldo's ecstatic moment as an all-seeing eyeball on the village common. It suggests, too, that his version of Transcendentalism, so often lampooned for endlessly huffing its own vapors, has made landfall at last in the world of politics, struggle, suffering.

That's certainly how the speech was greeted by his peers. Garrison celebrated it in the *Liberator*, and the author and abolitionist George William Curtis, who was on hand for the event, noted the change in tone: "It was not of that cold, clear, intellectual character that chills so many people, but full of ardent Life." Once the speech was available in pamphlet form (largely Thoreau's doing), Wendell Phillips handed out copies for years afterward. Like it or not, Waldo was now admitted to the abolitionist fold. But could a man so thoroughly opposed to crusades become a reluctant crusader?

13

HIGHER LAWS

Waldo's reservations about political activism never vanished entirely. He always wondered whether he could accomplish more for the world by continuing his existential explorations in his rocking chair. As he noted in his journal during this period: "I do not and can not forsake my vocation for abolitionism."

What changed, perhaps, was the very idea of his vocation—his calling. The crimes of the era, the follies of the tribe, were no longer distractions to be drowned out by Transcendentalism, with its narcotic and noise-canceling properties. They were, instead, spiritual battles fought in the material world, by human beings as fallible and furious as he was. He had no choice but to join them.

Hence his slowly accelerating commitment to the antislavery cause. Waldo spoke out again a year later, at a sizable abolitionist rally in Waltham. In this case, too, the manuscript of his speech has been lost, but bits and bobs can be reconstructed from newspaper reports and journal fragments. In what feels like a very contemporary note, he dwelled on what we would now call the n-word. These two syllables, he argued, embodied all the fraudulent arguments about Black inferiority. He ridiculed the notion that "the Creator of the Negro has given him up to stand as a victim of a caricature of the white man beside him; to stoop under his pack, and to bleed under his whip."

Waldo attended meetings, sent letters of support, spearheaded petitions. He refused to appear at the New Bedford Lyceum as long as the organizers maintained their policy of segregated seating for Black audience members. He gave another speech in Dedham in July 1846, lavishing praise on the abolitionists he had once mocked, calling them "the true successors of that austere Church, which made nature and history sacred to us all in our youth." He also saluted their refusal to "defer to the solemn nonsense of existing things," which sounds less like a Puritan and more like himself.

. . .

There was a brief intermission in these activities, since Waldo spent nearly nine months in England and France during 1847 and 1848. Perhaps the distance from his homeland allowed his abolitionist ardor to cool. But there was continuity, too, since he was soon faced with another ferment of political struggle, this one focused on class rather than race. In February of 1848, while he was in Glasgow, revolution broke out in France: within a few days, mobs clashed with the military in Paris and drove King Louis-Phillipe from the throne. This was epochal enough. What followed, though, was a chain reaction of insurgencies throughout the continent. There were uprisings in Italy, Hungary, Prussia, Poland, and Romania, and the Austrian chancellor Klemens von Metternich, long regarded as the supreme puppeteer of European stability, fled Vienna in a panic.

Meanwhile, England had its own class war to deal with. For the past decade, the British establishment felt itself increasingly menaced by the Chartists. This quasi-socialistic movement took its name from the so-called People's Charter, a list of elementary rights including universal suffrage, annual elections, and the secret ballot. Chartism's initial focus, in other words, was electoral reform. But the movement soon became the voice of Britain's working people, whose sheer numbers sent a collective chill through the political class. In 1842, for example, the Chartists had submitted a petition to Parliament signed by *three million* Britons. Six years later, just as Waldo returned to London from Glasgow, the Chartists staged a demonstration in Trafalgar Square, followed by three days of looting and rioting.

Waldo, then, was able to observe this tumult at close quarters. On March 8 he attended a Chartist meeting in Holborn, admiring the leadership but distinctly nervous about the rank-and-file, whose motto he noted in his journal: "Every man a ballot & every man a musket." He approved of their aims while recoiling from the prospect of violence, just as he recoiled from the redistributionist schemes being touted by the French. Wouldn't the confiscation of private property "remove the motive to industry"?

Yet he also considered the moment a trial by fire for any respectable thinker, who must not shrink from it. "I fancied, when I heard that the times were anxious & political, that there is to be a Chartist revolution on Monday next, and an Irish revolution in the following week, that the right scholar would feel—now was the hour to test his genius." It was in this spirit, perhaps, that Waldo decided to visit Paris and observe the people's republic firsthand. He arrived there on May 6. Over the next three weeks he sampled a smorgasbord of socialist oratory, visited with Alexis de Tocqueville, and saw exactly how the revolution eats its own. That is, he watched the unfolding of a counter-coup, as the radicals tried to unseat the moderates in the National Assembly—at gunpoint.

The attempt failed, to Waldo's relief. So did the Chartist rebellion, which fell apart right before his departure for Paris. Still, he found himself powerfully drawn to the idealism that had underpinned the pan-European uprisings in the first place. Those impulses, as he wrote to Lidian, struck him as fundamentally human and beyond politics. "The deep sincerity of the speakers who are agitating social not political questions," he declared, "and who are studying how to secure a fair share of bread to every man, and to get God's justice done throughout the land, is very good to hear."

The fact is that Waldo thrilled to the revolution and feared the revolution. Its bold rhetoric, with the promise of a brave new world, sometimes resembled his own. Yet the idea of transforming societies now left him skeptical, and he wondered in his journal whether any such utopia could be created from the bottom up: "When I see changed men, I shall look for a changed world." On the other hand, who was more convinced of the capacity of human beings to *change themselves* than Waldo? His ability to hold such contradictory positions in his head was an old habit,

also a standard operating procedure. Whether it was conducive to getting God's justice done is a different question altogether.

. . .

Sometimes the contradictions took their toll. After his return home to
Concord, he recorded a disturbing dream in his journal, essentially a
screaming match between himself and some nameless wraith. Toothless
and feeble, Waldo reports, he "could not articulate, & the edge of all my
taunts & sarcasms, it is to be feared, was quite lost." This nightmare of
speechlessness was interrupted only when Lidian, hearing the rattle in
his throat, shook him. "One day we shall wake up from this longer confusion," Waldo speculated, without wondering why the two halves of
his psyche were in such violent contention.

But in 1848 it wasn't only Waldo who was being torn in two. The country was coming apart at the seams. The contradictions enshrined in the
constitution—its espousal of human freedom *and* its tactical embrace of
a slaveholding culture—were becoming impossible to sustain, especially
as the nation expanded. The Mexican-American War, a two-year-long
land grab predicated on shaky claims of Mexican aggression, upped the
ante still further. When the Treaty of Guadalupe Hidalgo was signed in
February 1848, the United States prepared to absorb another 525,000
square miles of territory. From this windfall would be carved, in part or
whole, Arizona, California, Colorado, Nevada, New Mexico, Utah, and
Wyoming—igniting another firestorm about the balance of free states
and slave states.

Waldo had predicted a disaster early on. "The United States will conquer Mexico," he wrote in his journal, "but it will be as the man who
swallows the arsenic which brings him down in turn. Mexico will poison
us." It wasn't that Waldo, with his mythological conception of his own
country, was completely opposed to Manifest Destiny. But he anticipated
and dreaded the effort to expand slavery into this vast new terrain.

The election of Zachary Taylor as president, in November 1848, was
touted as a potential panacea. To a startling degree, he seemed to per-
sonify the deep fissures of the country. Born in Virginia to an old New

England family, Taylor was both a fan of the abolitionist firebrand William H. Seward and an enslaver himself. ("We prefer Old Zack with his sugar and cotton plantations and four hundred negroes," declared one Virginia newspaper.) Might not he bridge the yawning gaps in the body politic? Shortly after his election, Taylor tried to calm the waters with a propitiatory speech. He urged his fellow Americans to avoid "those exciting topics of a sectional character which have hitherto produced painful apprehensions in the public mind." *Don't worry, be happy*, was the basic message.

It didn't work. Southerners threatened to secede, Northerners fulminated against the wickedness of slavery, and legislators got into frequent brawls on the floor of the U.S. Congress. Taylor, meanwhile, infuriated slaveholders by urging that California be admitted as a free state. When they accused him of Yankee-style treachery, he promised to personally lead an army south of the Mason-Dixon line—no meager threat from a military icon who was said to dodge enemy fire by standing on his saddle and allowing the cannonballs to pass between his legs.

Perhaps Taylor's strong-arm tactics might have kept the South in check, at least for a while longer. But at an Independence Day celebration in 1850, the president attempted to cool down by stuffing himself with cherries and iced milk—and died five days later, mostly likely of salmonella. His successor, Millard Fillmore, shared most of Taylor's Free Soil beliefs, but was a machine politician rather than a mobster in epaulettes. *His* solution to preserve the imploding Union was to back the Compromise of 1850, a package of eight resolutions hammered out by Henry Clay and Daniel Webster, with South Carolina's John C. Calhoun acting as a slavery-loving, nullification-preaching wingman.

This last-ditch effort threw multiple bones to both sides. It ultimately admitted California as a free state, settled a Texan boundary dispute, and abolished the slave trade in Washington, D.C. (without, however, freeing any currently enslaved people in the nation's capital). In a self-defanging move, it denied Congress's power to regulate the interstate slave trade. It also fortified those laws already on the books that demanded the return of fugitive slaves to their owners. This was a provision dearly desired by Southern planters, who had seen a slow seepage of their property to the North and wanted the mushy language of the constitution firmed up in their favor.

There were months of fiery, leather-lunged debate. Clay spoke while brandishing a sliver of wood from George Washington's coffin (or so he claimed). Webster, in his famous speech on March 7, compared the prospect of disunion to "the wreck of the universe." The cadaverous Calhoun, dying of tuberculosis and too weak to deliver his own speech, predicted that the admission of California as a free state would "destroy irretrievably the equilibrium between the two sections."

In the end, after further finessing, the package was broken down into separate resolutions. These passed in September along strictly sectional lines, with no real middle ground. President Fillmore called this jerry-rigged arrangement a "final settlement." As it happens, its fate was rather less Ozymandian. It fell apart just four years later, when the urgent necessity of stealing more land from the Indians led to the admission of two more potential slave states, Kansas and Nebraska, and upset what had been a very precarious applecart to begin with.

. . .

Readers will have noticed a great deal of politics in the preceding pages. I have seldom gotten down in the weeds like this in earlier chapters—but that is precisely the point. Politics had bored its way into Waldo's life, and his entire household followed the events above with edge-of-the-seat attentiveness. Lidian read Daniel Webster's March 7 speech with what her daughter later described as "grief and indignation"—in fact, the date was marked as an antiholiday at Bush for years afterward.

When nearly a thousand worthies in Boston published an open letter in support of that very same speech, Waldo despaired. "This was a day of petticoats, a day of imbecilities," he wrote in his journal. The signatories struck him as the clapped-out dregs of Massachusetts society. "They are the names of aged & infirm people," he fumed, "who have outlived everything but their night cap & their tea & toast." But his irritation over the letter was only the beginning. Webster's speech had wounded him deeply: one of his heroes had abandoned his principles to shake hands with the slave power. Venting his anger a few months later, Waldo wrote: "The word *liberty* in the mouth of Mr. Webster sounds like the word *love* in the mouth of a courtezan."

Yet his shock at Webster's treachery paled beside his reaction to the Fugitive Slave Act, a key provision of the Compromise of 1850. Americans in free states were already obliged by law to return runaway slaves to their owners. This squalid obligation had been forced into the constitution, a logrolling sop to the South that carefully avoided the word *slave*. The mealymouthed clause merely noted that any "person held to service or labour" with the gall to flee to another state must be promptly restored to "the party to whom such service or labour may be due."

Still, this provision had been slackly enforced. Many free states approached it with foot-dragging indifference. Many, too, passed what came to be known as personal liberty laws, which granted runaways the right to a trial by jury, habeas corpus, and other judicial protections. The time and money involved in such trials enraged slaveowners. Meanwhile, fugitives frequently took the opportunity to slip over the state line while the legal gears were grinding away.

The new statute was an attempt to close all such loopholes. Now U.S. marshals and their deputies were obliged to assist in the return of runaways. Any officer who declined to carry out this task would be fined a thousand dollars—a high price for a fit of conscience. There would be no more trials, no more running out the clock. Also, the costs of rounding up fugitives would be paid by the national government, essentially federalizing the whole operation: the United States had transformed state-sponsored kidnappings into official policy. Last but not least—especially in the eyes of an agonized Waldo—the law made all Americans into its accomplices. It was now a serious crime to harbor runaways or obstruct their capture. In fact, a federal marshal could literally deputize any person on the spot: a kind of magic trick, turning ordinary citizens into snitches, quislings, enforcers.

This was the last straw for Waldo. It drove him into a fury, which spilled out over more than eighty pages of his journal and several impassioned speeches. You might say (and some skeptics *have* said) that it was primarily a personal affront: that his right to keep his hands clean while simultaneously decrying the evil of slavery had been snatched away. I don't agree. Waldo had more than once acknowledged the complicity of North and South when it came to human chattel. This was the final, logical outcome of that cozy relationship. Every American was now as guilty as the next, a point Waldo had made, somewhat airily, in his very first address on the subject.

It is true that in his journal, he drew a distinction between his long-distance abolitionism and the arrival of the issue on his very doorstep. "This is not meddling with other people's affairs," he wrote. "This is other people meddling with us." Yet his hatred of the law was not simply an expression of moral fastidiousness or sectional pride. He was repelled by the thought of assisting in the capture of "a human being who has taken the most frightful risks of being shot or burned alive, or cast into the sea, or starved to death or suffocated in a wooden box." A runaway was a hero. The law that opposed him was, in Waldo's view, pure barbarism. It compelled the citizenry of Massachusetts to kidnap the runaway and "send [him] back again a thousand miles across the sea to the dog-hutch he fled from. And this filthy enactment was made in the 19th Century, by people who could read & write. I will not obey it, by God."

At first, Waldo pinned his hopes on passive resistance. Despite the law's many toxic provisions, he assumed that his fellow citizens would refuse to enforce them. For a very brief period, this appeared to be true: several attempts to abduct fugitives from the streets of Boston were foiled.

But on April 3, 1851, a seventeen-year-old runaway named Thomas Sims was snatched up by authorities and imprisoned in the courthouse, which was itself sealed with heavy (and symbolic) chains. He was marched to a waiting ship nine days later, with 250 U.S. troops on hand to prevent any last-minute rescue, and returned to Savannah. There he was flogged in public on April 19. This was, not coincidentally, the anniversary of the Battle of Concord and Lexington, and a stinging reminder to people like Waldo that the moral high ground claimed by the North meant nothing to the South.

A week after Sims was whipped, Waldo accepted an invitation from the town of Concord to speak out on the Fugitive Slave Law. His address, delivered on May 3, was a scorcher: the angriest, darkest, and most ferocious of his career. "The last year has forced us all into politics," he began. But instead of issuing the usual disclaimer about his failings as a political animal, he plunged straight into what he viewed as the moral catastrophe of the new statute. It was, he thought, a kind of plague:

> We do not breathe well. There is infamy in the air. I have a new experi-
> ence. I wake in the morning with a painful sensation, which I carry
> about all day, and which, traced home, is the odious remembrance of
> that ignominy which has fallen on Massachusetts, which robs the
> landscape of beauty, and takes the sunshine out of every hour.

In Waldo's view, the passage of the law (and the shuffling acquies-cence of his neighbors) shredded every piety about the United States. "The popular assumption that all men loved freedom, and believed in the Christian religion, was found hollow American brag," he laments. He acknowledges that other nations, too, have their structural defects or original sins, but nothing can compare to the "greatest calamity in the universe, negro slavery."

Invoking the principle of higher law, he ties slavery to mercantile greed—both trample underfoot the very notion of morality. "I thought it was this fair mystery," he declares, "whose foundations are hidden in eternity, which made the basis of human society, and of law; and that to pretend anything else, as, that the acquisition of property was the end of living, was to confound all distinctions, to make the world a greasy hotel, and, instead of noble motives and inspirations, and a heaven of companions and angels around and before us, to leave us in a grimacing menagerie of monkeys and idiots." This was not garden-variety platform rhetoric. It transformed politics into bleak poetry—who else would have set Hell in a greasy hotel (and Waldo had stayed in plenty of those)? It also attempted, as per Waldo's old preference, to diagnose the nation's ills as broadly as possible, rather than inveighing against slavery in isolation.

If all the evils were daisy-chained together, so were all the culprits. "Great is the mischief of a legal crime," Waldo insists. "Every person who touches this business is contaminated." But some were more contami-nated than others—and predictably, Waldo now wheeled around to pour his scorn on Daniel Webster, the god who had failed. All New Englanders, he insisted, were now united in this disdain.

"They have torn down his picture from the wall," Waldo reported, "they have thrust his speeches into the chimney." The "one eminent American of our time" has shamed himself beyond redemption. Waldo's final verdict on him slips into surrealism, followed by low comedy. "All the drops of his blood have eyes that look downward," he writes. "It is neither praise nor blame to say that he has no moral perception, no moral sentiment, but, in that *region*, to use the phrase of the phrenologists, a hole in the head."

The solution, he thought, was simple. The law must be struck down; slavery must be confined to the slave states, then wiped out entirely. But what was simple in theory was more complicated in practice, and Waldo toyed with various versions of abolition, including one in which American enslavers, like their West Indian counterparts, were compensated for their lost property. The cost would be great, he allowed—but so what? American generosity, and American ingenuity, would take care of it. "Let them confront this mountain of poison—bore, blast, excavate, pulverize, and shovel it once for all, down into the bottomless Pit," he wrote. "A thousand millions were cheap."

His own state, Waldo promised, would lead the way. "Massachusetts is little," he wrote, "but, if true to itself, can be the brain which turns about the behemoth." Perhaps this was a bit of red meat for the citizens of Concord. It also narrowed the issue back down to geographical purity, as if what was most urgently needed was a cordon sanitaire just south of Springfield. Still, I think he meant it. A heroic human being was, as the military say, a force multiplier—a phrase Waldo probably would have enjoyed. Why couldn't a heroic state function the same way?

. . .

There were more speeches. I won't gloss them all. What matters most is the intensity and duration of Waldo's commitment to abolitionism. Throughout the 1850s, as the country moved closer and closer to the precipice—as the feckless Fillmore was followed by Franklin Pierce, then by James Buchanan (whose great claim to fame was cheerleading the disastrous Dred Scott decision)—Waldo kept up his devotion to the cause.

For starters, he took to the campaign trail. In May 1851, Waldo stumped on behalf of John Gorham Palfrey, with whom he had a somewhat spotty relationship. The two had traded barbs in the past, and perhaps Lidian's old attachment to Palfrey—she had adored his preaching when he was a freshly hatched minister at Boston's Brattle Street Church—produced some alpha-male friction as well.

Still, Palfrey was now a Free Soil candidate for a congressional seat. Waldo spoke on his behalf throughout Middlesex County, mostly repeating his Fugitive Slave Act address. For his efforts he was ridiculed by one of the Boston papers, whose correspondent suggested that he was not "a reliable authority on questions of morals, or a safe guide in the affairs of life." He was also booed and hissed when he spoke at Cambridge, the culprits being rowdy Harvard students who repeatedly cheered for Daniel Webster.

Waldo glumly noted the electoral results in his journal: Palfrey lost by a margin of just ninety-five votes. The outcome may have discouraged him. It did not stop him from speaking out, nor from boosting the abolitionist cause in other ways.

A few months after Palfrey's defeat, for example, he donated money to assist a runaway who was passing through Concord en route to Canada. In 1852, he contributed a poem, "Liberty," to a collection called *Autographs for Freedom*, which was a fundraising vehicle for Frederick Douglass's newspaper. In 1854, he gave another major address on the Fugitive Slave Act, timed to coincide with the fourth anniversary of Webster's despicable March 7 speech.

This time he spoke at the Broadway Tabernacle in Lower Manhattan. This spacious church happened to be a magnet for antislavery activists (and the site, according the *New York Herald*, of frequent "spiritual harangues, anniversaries, lectures, [and] laughing gas exhibitions"). In one powerful passage, Waldo again excoriated the ugly essence of slavery, its transformation of human beings into commodities, into *things*:

It was a question, whether man shall be treated as leather? Whether the negroes shall be, as the Indians were in Spanish America, a species of money? Whether this institution, which is a kind of mill or factory for converting men into monkeys, shall be upheld and enlarged?

He also had some choice words for America's lily-livered political class, which had been quailing before the slave power for years. "They had no opinions," he wrote, "they had no memory for what they had been saying like the Lord's prayer, all their lifetime; they were only looking to what their great captain did, and if he jumped, they jumped—if he stood on his head, they did."

Their great captain was, of course, Daniel Webster, who comes in for another drubbing here. But Waldo has other targets in mind: the laws, the courts, the legislature, all the pillars of civic life that have left the edifice of slavery securely in place. There was also the Christian church, that frequent source of proslavery rhetoric. "These things show that no forms, neither Constitutions nor laws nor covenants nor churches nor bibles, are of any use in themselves; the devil nestles comfortably into them all," he insists. "There is no help but in the head and heart and hamstrings of a man." This was what he could offer: a singular conscience, issuing his spiritual harangue.

Waldo had mixed feelings about his appearance. The size of the crowd (the Tabernacle had a capacity of 2,400) spooked him, as he noted in his journal: "I was most thankful to those who stayed home." Still, he soon began work on another address. This was his "Lecture on Slavery," first delivered at the Tremont Temple in Boston in January 1855. Now he placed the issue of slavery in a broader philosophical context, while mostly heeding his own dictum for political speech: "One must write with a red hot iron to make any impression." He also pushed back against his own reputation as an evangelist of individualism by exalting the power of communal action. "It is so delicious to act with great masses to great aims," he declared—an assertion that probably would have made him snort just a decade earlier.

He delivered "Lecture on Slavery" at least seven more times, in Worcester, Philadelphia, New York City, Syracuse, and various other venues. It was followed by more speeches, more fundraising, more philanthropy. Waldo donated money to Free Soil fighters in Kansas. He donated money once again for the defense of John Brown, who had stayed at Waldo's house prior to the ill-fated assault at Harpers Ferry, and whose children would subsequently be educated with his own.

When the Civil War finally erupted in the spring of 1861, he welcomed what he saw as an apocalyptic effort to destroy slavery once and for all. (After a visit to the Charlestown Navy Yard, this peaceable man was heard to declare: "Gunpowder sometimes smells good.") And on January 1, 1863, when the Emancipation Proclamation went into effect, Waldo read a new poem, "Boston Hymn," to a crowd assembled at the city's Music Hall. Much of it was patriotic boilerplate, and perfectly serviceable as such. But in one stanza, he spelled out the old idea of compensating slaveholders for their lost property, then inverted it:

> Pay ransom to the owner,
> And fill the bag to the brim.
> Who is the owner? The slave is owner,
> And ever was. Pay him.

In the blink of an eye, the image of the enslaved human being as a passive participant in an economic arrangement is smashed to pieces. The only person entitled to be paid for his years of backbreaking labor *is the slave himself*. The slaveowner, finally a contradiction in terms, is owed nothing. Waldo, who had once endorsed such compensatory schemes, now dismissed them. The lines are terribly moving, especially when you consider the context of the evening.

They were moving in other contexts, too. In January 1864, Thomas Wentworth Higginson, who was then commanding an all-Black regiment in South Carolina, informed Waldo that the regimental surgeon had read "Boston Hymn" to the troops. "I vividly recall the thrill that went through me," Higginson wrote, "as he read the grand verse beginning, 'Pay ransom to the owner.'" The troops also seem to have been thrilled. As Waldo's correspondent assured him: "They understood every word of it."

. . .

It would be nice to report that Waldo's steady (you might even say heroic) progress from Transcendental bystander to full-tilt abolitionist wiped out his old, bad ideas about race. After all, this was the man who declared that the very emblem of America should be the "negro soldier lying in the trenches by the Potomac with his spelling book in one hand and his musket in the other." Didn't that self-made (and also heroic) figure deserve his complete respect—and the jettisoning of all that racialist baggage?

No such luck. The good and the bad—the exalted and excruciating—coexisted in Waldo's mind until the very end. In many cases, it wasn't the antipodes of Black and white that ran his thinking into the ditch. His ideas about racial caste retained their national or tribal emphasis, as per the Saxon worship in *English Traits*. There was, for example, his memorably weird formulation in "Fate," published in *The Conduct of Life* (1860). Positing a world in which Nature crushes any weakling—or weak race—in her path, he writes:

> The German and Irish millions, like the Negro, have a great deal of guano in their destiny. They are ferried over the Atlantic, and carted over to America, to ditch and to drudge, to make corn cheap, and then to lie down prematurely to make a spot of green grass on the prairie.

As we have seen, Waldo despised the concept of men-as-things. Here he seems to welcome, or at least accede to, men-as-fertilizer—the supposedly lesser races as agricultural fodder, who will themselves nourish the earth after a short period of exploitation. True, his tone is tricky here. I'm not sure his heart is with the exploiters, nor that pegging the value of a human life to the price of corn is in any way attractive to him.

Yet he accepts this ugliness as fated, inevitable. He outsources the cruelty to Nature, you could say, which impersonally culls the "conditional population" of the planet.

Elsewhere, though, his specific prejudices regarding Black people rose to the surface. Higginson suggests in his memoirs that Waldo blackballed Frederick Douglass from membership in the Town and Country Club, a short-lived cigar-smoking aggregation meant to unite urban swells with rural parsons. Recent research indicates that this is nonsense. Waldo actually argued that Black applicants *should* be admitted to the club: "With regard to color, I am of the opinion that there should be no exclusion. Certainly, if any distinction be made, let it be in the colored man's favor." (He did, however, oppose admitting females of any color, out of concern that the club might turn into a "saloon for ladies.")

Higginson, a Waldo-worshipper, seems to have made an honest mistake here. But what truly interests me is another assertion in the same passage. "Emerson," Higginson writes, "as he himself admitted to me, was one of that minority of anti-slavery men who confessed to a mild natural colorphobia, controlled only by moral conviction."

Let's assume it's a verbatim quote. Here was Waldo, then, pleading guilty to the baked-in bigotry of his era—to the instinctive anxiety of white people in the face of their Black counterparts, which can still be observed on the streets of any big American city at any hour of the day or night. His honesty is bracing. Even more bracing is the assumption that such feelings must be overridden, that human consciousness is incessantly self-correcting.

Indeed, self-correction was at the heart of Waldo's personality, and his genius. He recognized that his truth-seeking would lead to a great many contortions, qualifications, paradoxes. No reader can fail to notice these things piling up on the page. When Nell Irvin Painter delivered her stinging verdict on *English Traits*, she conceded that one crucial chapter "contradicts itself in tone and in word." For her, this was a typical habit of race theorists. For me, it's a typical habit of Waldo's—and, again, the book's saving grace. As I suggested earlier, I think he sensed that part of his argument was rotten, perhaps in ways he didn't grasp. It was conscience, then, or moral conviction, that tinkered with the tone and subtly discredited the very sentences he had just written.

Nowadays, we might call this self-correcting imp the unconscious. At times, Waldo talked about it in similar terms, albeit with some confusion about which half of the mind had the upper hand. "A man finds out that there is somewhat in him that knows more than he does," he wrote in his journal. "Then he comes presently to the curious question, who's who? which of these two is really me? the one who knows more, or the one who knows less? the little fellow, or the big fellow?"

It's a trick question. The answer is both. Waldo was the apostle of freedom *and* the race huckster, the ignorant schoolboy *and* the diagnostician of the American dilemma. He knew more than he knew, and less. What he did finally comprehend was that all Americans had drunk from the same poisoned cup—we are drinking from it still—and that the only antidote was a communal one. "We are all boarders at one table," he wrote back in 1840, when he was supposedly worshipping at the atomizing altar of individualism. "White man, black man, ox and eagle, bee, & worm." He said plenty of other things, too, but I prefer to listen to the part of Waldo who knew more, and who understood that we would be redeemed together or not at all.

14

AN INSPECTION
OF THE WRECK

Waldo foresaw his old age and death from the time he was a young man. In one journal entry, he telescoped his entire life into what we would now call a bullet list, starting in the nursery and concluding at the cemetery: "Toys, dancing school, Sets, parties, picture galleries, sleighrides, Nahant, Saratoga Springs, lectures, concerts, sets through them all, solitude & poetry, friendship, ennui, desolation, decline, meanness, plausibility, old age, death." He was, at the time of this gloomy précis, all of thirty-eight years old.

As it happens, his forecast was wrong on quite a few counts. For starters, he beat the actuarial odds. In 1860, as the Civil War broke out, the life expectancy for a typical American was 39.41 years (and the number dipped even lower during the conflict, for obvious reasons). Waldo was just a few weeks shy of sixty-two when the Army of Northern Virginia lay down its arms at Appomattox. The war had also solidified his reputation as America's leading thinker—its stoop-shouldered sage and village elder. It thrust him into public life as never before.

In early 1862, for example, he visited the capital. Over the course of two chilly days, Waldo lectured at the Smithsonian, was squired around the corridors of power by William H. Seward (who told him a "smutty" story that Lincoln himself had urged Seward to sanitize), and twice met with the president, once while Lincoln's two young sons were having their hair cut at the White House. Here was Waldo at the summit of the great world, consorting with the men who moved the levers of life and death. To be treated as their peer was doubtless a strange and marvelous sensation.

All of this meant that he entered the postwar era on a roll. His lecturing career had never dwindled entirely, even in the midst of wartime turbulence. In 1863, for example, he did another Midwest tour, swinging through Cleveland, Detroit, Ann Arbor, Milwaukee, Racine, Beloit, Chicago, and Indianapolis.

But Waldo picked up the pace during the second half of the decade. In 1867, at his peak, he gave eighty lectures. His presence on the podium was still impressive, although his old-fashioned clothing and lofty vibe may have increasingly struck audience members as something out of a tintype. (Attending one of those 1867 lectures, James Russell Lowell noted, "It was as if a creature from some fairer world had lost his way in our fogs.") Yet he remained a popular draw on the circuit. Perhaps he, too, was now viewed as an emissary from the past—from a simpler, preindustrial, more idealistic version of America. He would have hated the idea.

He meanwhile won his share of autumnal honors. Some of these were symbolic: branding exercises, more or less. Hence he was appointed vice president of the New England Woman Suffrage Association (despite his insistence that women be barred from the Town and Country Club) and the Massachusetts Society for the Prevention of Cruelty to Animals (despite his panting eagerness to shoot a deer during a prewar camping trip).

Even Harvard, which had shunned him for decades in the wake of the Divinity School Address, seemed eager to kiss and make up. In 1866, the university granted Waldo an honorary doctorate and elected him to its Board of Overseers. The next year, he lectured once again at the mother ship of Boston Brahminism.

His renewed relationship with his alma mater certainly meant something to Waldo, and he worked hard to make himself useful to the board. Still, his resentments seem to have persisted. In 1868, amid journal jottings about his Harvard duties, he drew up a list of the school's defects. One was: "Instead of an avenue, it is a barrier." Another, perhaps more personal item: "It gives foolish diplomas of honor to every old clergyman, or successful gentleman who lives within ten miles."

. . .

His writing, however, had slowed down. This wasn't immediately apparent, since Waldo's prose showed up in book form long after it had been composed, in that classic light-from-a-distant-star fashion. He would rough out the sentences in his journal, road test them repeatedly in the American heartland, then finally allow them to be typeset. So it was that *The Conduct of Life* (1860), which continued to sell throughout the decade, contained lectures that he had been delivering since the early 1850s.

The book, among his most popular, is a strange one. Very much a product of the Lyceum circuit, it is more plainspoken and prescriptive than his earlier work. As the title suggests, it is the closest Waldo ever got to a self-help manual. It dispenses advice. It tells you to work hard, brush your teeth, stay focused. It wrestles with what the author, in "Fate," calls "a practical question of the conduct of life. How shall I live?"

In this essay, the first in the collection, Waldo is still working out the great polarity that had fascinated him since his boyhood: fate versus freedom. Were we helpless passengers in our progress through life, or were we steering the vehicle? Waldo's dedication to self-reliance, and his own record of extricating himself from familial and societal straitjackets, would suggest the latter. Yet his weary recognition of his own limitations, and even the trace elements of Calvinism in his intellectual makeup, suggest otherwise. The mightiest of individuals cannot blaze their own trails for long. In fact, most of them, given enough time, revert to the mean—they are swallowed up once again by the tribal, the generic, the sum of their origins.

Waldo articulated this most amusingly in what I like to call the Pumpkin Paradigm. "We fancy men are individuals; so are pumpkins; but every pumpkin in the field, goes through every point of pumpkin history." It's a big step down, you might say, from the raging prophet to the soft-centered squash. But nobody who has survived to the age of fifty truly thinks the universe will do their bidding. Life on earth offers too much evidence to the contrary. Dreams deflate, friendships fade, bones break, as do hearts, in no particular order. We are simply not in control.

Hence the whip hand given to fate in this particular essay. Its sheer cruelty grants it an irresistible edge. "Providence has a wild, rough, incalculable road to its end," Waldo writes, "and it is of no use to try to whitewash its huge, mixed instrumentalities, or to dress up that terrific benefactor in a clean shirt and white neckcloth of a student in divinity." Surely the former student in divinity felt himself implicated in this losing battle! He even hoists a kind of white flag: "Every spirit makes its house; but afterwards the house confines the spirit." This recantation of his own earlier credo, with its suggestion of house arrest, is a sad thing to encounter.

Having started down the path of revisionism, Waldo keeps going. Nature, so eloquently celebrated in his first book, is now another word for fate. Nature is "the tyrannous circumstance," the snapping jaw of the material world, devouring entire races in her maw. From this point of view, the planet boasts nothing but a "conditional population"—temporary residents about to be crushed beneath the Darwinian steamroller.

The individual, too, operates within the narrowest zone of autonomy, "hooped in by a necessity, which, by many experiments, he touches on every side, until he learns its arc." Here, and elsewhere in the essay, Waldo seems to be approaching a Carlyle-style ground zero, where the helpless humans are miserable by design.

Yet freedom is still in the game. "Fate has its lord," Waldo notes, "limitation its limits." He's talking about power (yet another word for freedom, and yes, the terminological fog can be hard to navigate). Each person, we read, is not merely a physical fact but a staging ground for the clash between these forces—a "stupendous antagonism, a dragging together of the poles of the Universe." And how does a person make use of these friction-fed energies? By thinking. "Every jet of chaos which threatens to exterminate us," he writes, "is convertible by intellect into wholesome force." This push-and-pull relationship is what makes us free. Conveniently, perhaps, it also resolves so many other conflicts into a beautiful blur, ensuring that "plaintiff and defendant, friend and enemy, animal and planet, food and eater, are of one kind."

This is not so far from Waldo's old doctrine of compensation. But it now feels less like wishful thinking, more like a bruised acceptance of reality—of its buzzing confusion, its brutality and beauty. He knew so much more about life (and death) than he had as a starry-eyed visionary during the 1830s. There was more pain in his heart, more dirt under his fingernails, more familiarity with the slow-acting drug of disappointment. Yet his weary truce with reality did not prevent him from juggling every master metaphor at his disposal: fate, freedom, power, nature, thought. He now felt that he could treat them as interchangeable currencies.

Which explains why "Power," discussed in the essay right after "Fate," is both the cognitive slayer of iron necessity and whatever else Waldo wants it to be. It is a belief in cause and effect. It is a tapping into the raw energies of nature. It is, weirdly, political populism, about which Waldo was not always so sanguine, although here he writes: "The instinct of the people is right." It is also a font of cheerful maxims that finally land Waldo in the self-help camp: "Practice is nine tenths. A course of mobs is good practice for orators. All the great speakers were bad speakers at first." Power is powerful enough to populate a multitude of coffee mugs and refrigerator magnets more than a century after Waldo's death. It is also interchangeable with another of his master metaphors, perhaps the worldliest of them all: money.

· · ·

Or so Waldo argues in "Wealth." Money, says this avatar of immateriality, springs from "applications of the mind to nature." This formula could have occurred in his earliest work, but the ringing of the cash register in the background gives it a very different flavor. Not only does Waldo prescribe the Calvinist work ethic; he makes affluence into a necessity. "Will a man content himself with a hut and handful of dried peas?" he asks. "He is born to be rich." Such statements must have galled, say, Thoreau, very much a hut-and-peas man himself. They also seem to fly directly in the face of Waldo's earlier distaste for getting and spending as operative principles for living.

Perhaps aware of this contradiction, Waldo falls back on his supply of fungible metaphors. If the mindless accumulation of luxuries "were the main use of surplus capital," he allows, "it would bring us to barricades, burned towns, and tomahawks, presently." But sensible plutocrats have their minds on loftier things. "Power is what they want," Waldo writes, which consists of the ability to "give legs and feet, form and actuality to their thought." We have circled back to the multivalent topic of the previous essay. Wealth is among the raw energies of nature. Merchants are therefore Periclean figures who just happen to have gigantic bank accounts, who wield power in the form of cash.

I suppose there is a certain logic here. Money is a symbolic thing, a system of correspondences worthy of Swedenborg. A slip of paper, essentially worthless, is deemed interchangeable with a hot meal, a pair of shoes, a telescope, a flock of sheep. Its value is pegged to a lump of metal, also essentially worthless. The poetry of these equivalences— and their function as acts of faith between buyer and seller—must have appealed mightily to Waldo.

He could have left it there, in the realm of metaphor. He could have stopped at noting the dollar's "susceptibility to metaphysical changes. It is the finest barometer of social storms, and announces revolutions." But instead he pressed right on into the Great Dismal Swamp of economic theory, aligning himself with the laissez-faire arguments of Adam Smith (whose *Wealth of Nations*, he once told a Boston audience, was a "book of wisdom" on par with *Paradise Lost*). It is dizzying to see how Waldo, having finally accepted the need for a strong government when it came to the destruction of slavery, was eager to bar it from economic life. Instead, we were supposed to rely on the Invisible Hand, that mystical masseuse of human behavior:

> Wealth brings with it its own checks and balances. The basis of political economy is non-interference. The only safe rule is found in the self-adjusting meter of demand and supply. Do not legislate. Meddle, and you snap the sinews with your sumptuary laws.

Here, in a nutshell, is what made Waldo into a patron saint (or at least a mascot) for the industrial buccaneers of the Gilded Age. He gave metaphysical oomph to what was economic orthodoxy—that regulation of trade was not only a drag on prosperity but against nature.

It wasn't only his laissez-faire beliefs, however, that made him such a congenial figure. Self-reliance, and Waldo's hearty enthusiasm for Anglo-Saxons at the helm, shaded directly into the social Darwinism of the day. His influence went to the very top. Herbert Spencer, the uber-Darwinist who coined the phrase "survival of the fittest," met Waldo during his British tour in 1847. He had admired Waldo's work since he was a young man. In his memoirs, he recalled reading one of the essays aloud to a friend, who likened the experience to "distant thunder."

When Spencer hung out with Andrew Carnegie, another admirer of the essays, at London's Grand Hotel, these two worthies talked about— that's right, Waldo. As for Carnegie himself, when he showered four Scottish universities with U.S. Steel bonds in 1901 and was appointed rector by a grateful St. Andrews, his inaugural speech came straight out of the Emersonian playbook. "You are responsible only for action in obedience to the judge within," Carnegie declared. He added, with a bit of Waldo-style asperity toward the past, "All revelations through books written thousands of years ago with their inevitable mistranslations, omissions, admissions, and errors, are useful only as they may lead you to the good and the true."

For Carnegie, of course, self-reliance entailed extraordinary generosity. His was the wallet that launched a thousand libraries. Yet it was accompanied by a paternalistic refusal to pay a decent wage, since his workers were judged too feckless to manage their own money. Visionary and cheapskate did not strike him as contradictory roles.

In this sense, too, his embrace of Waldo has a certain logic. Waldo read the economists (not only Adam Smith but also Thomas Malthus) for, as he liked to say, the lusters. That is, he took from them what interested him and left behind the remainder. He also ran their ideas through the distillation rig of his brain, boiling them down to a kind of metaphorical liquor.

This is why it's so hard to pin down his political or ideological or economic beliefs. He never lingered for long in the weeds of any particular policy debate—the reader always senses an updraft toward general principles. What Waldo saw, early on, was a perpetual battle between the Establishment and the Movement (phraseology that he invented!). What he saw, later on, was that the two parties were constantly changing places, that a conservative was a radical who had put on thirty pounds and taken out a mortgage. Later still, he must have recognized that the banked fires of his own thought had become perfectly palatable to the wealthiest Americans. He was now, in other words, the Establishment.

It's quite likely that Waldo's vogue among the industrialists extended the shelf life of his work for several decades. By 1876, when Octavius Frothingham published his classic *Transcendentalism in New England: A History*, he was already engaging in cultural archaeology. It had long been the fashion, the author wrote, "to laugh at Transcendentalism as an incomprehensible folly." Frothingham's account of the movement, whose caboose he had boarded very late in the game, remains an excellent read. Still, his defensive tone is telling. The prophetic stars of the 1840s were dimming, dying—or, like Bronson Alcott, looking back at their heyday as an era of "cheerless anxiety and hopeless dependence." Their ideas now struck post–Civil War America as so much mystical tinsel. Yet an exception was made for Waldo, smuggled into the Gilded Age as a patriotic action figure and champion of wealth.

This is, at the very least, a distortion. Waldo had been a sharp critic of mercantile society since he was a young man. Looking back on his youth from the vantage point of 1867, he decried the rise of the plutocrat and the consequent cheapening of American culture. "The stockholder has stepped into the place of the warlike baron," he wrote. "The nobles shall not any longer, as feudal lords, have power of life and death over the churls, but now, in another shape, as capitalists, shall in all love and peace eat them up as before." Skeptics will respond that Waldo, too, was a stockholder, courtesy of his wife's inheritance, whose own fortunes rose and fell with the gyrations of the market. There is some truth to this. As the owner of sixty-seven shares in the City Bank, he wished it to prosper—and felt the same way about the Atlantic Bank (nineteen shares) and the Boston and Roxbury Mill Dam (thirty-one shares). The dividends from these assets propped up his life as surely as his income from lecturing.

Yet I don't think they disqualify him from making shrewd judgments about the mixed blessing of capitalism. When he viewed the latter as one more channel for the raw energies of mankind—a form of tilling the soil by remote control—he tended to be more forgiving, even enthusiastic. It was yet another self-correcting system, a great machine that was responsive, like everything else, to the rules of compensation. Why shouldn't it reflect those inner realities that Waldo had cherished throughout his entire life? "The counting-room maxims liberally expounded are laws of the Universe," he insisted. "The merchant's economy is a coarse symbol of the soul's economy." Capitalism was, in this sense, one more spiritual practice, however red it might be in the tooth and claw.

Money, too, was not necessarily bad. Perhaps it was a dirty word for a pure Transcendentalist, but its operations were marvelous—it turned one thing into another, which was the bedrock of Waldo's thinking to begin with. "A dollar is not value," he wrote, "but representative of value, and, at last, of moral values." That last clause is a dubious leap, you might argue. To recognize a wrinkled dollar bill as a metaphor is one thing; to view it as an instrument of virtue is another. Yet Waldo, that hater of stasis, saw almost any process of ongoing transformation as inherently good. He could be quite effusive about it. "Money," he memorably declared, "which represents the prose of life, and which is hardly spoken of in parlours without an apology, is, in its effects and laws, as beautiful as roses."

At other times, though, he was less enchanted by the dance of dollars and cents. He understood that the gap between the rich and poor was deeply divisive, that property itself could be a form of predation. His portrait of Napoleon in *Representative Men* concludes with a socialistic outburst that is almost biblical in its wrath. Here are words to warm the heart of the Occupy Wall Street enthusiast, or indeed anybody else turned off by the acquisitive antics of our current billionaire class:

> As long as our civilization is essentially one of property, of fences, of exclusiveness, it will be mocked by delusions. Our riches will leave us sick; there will be bitterness in our laughter; and our wine will burn our mouth. Only that good profits, which we can taste with all doors open, and which serves all men.

Our principles, of course, do not exist in a vacuum. It seems likely that Waldo's wealth-hating impulses were softened by the fact that his younger daughter had married into it. Edith Emerson became, in October 1865, the wife of William H. Forbes. His father, John Murray Forbes, was a major American tycoon and on-the-fly diplomat, whom Waldo had actually run into during his tour of the dingy State Department in 1862.

Waldo regarded Forbes as a kind of capitalist superman. "I think this is a good country," he wrote, "that can bear such a creature as he is." It was Forbes, a railroad baron, who arranged for Waldo to take a cross-country trip on a private Pullman car in 1871 (and to have the travelers be greeted by George Pullman himself when they boarded). It was Forbes who repeatedly invited Waldo to his private retreat on Naushon Island in Maine. There the gaggle of grandchildren referred to Waldo as Grampa Moo Moo, since he lived in the country and therefore in some proximity to cows. I'm not suggesting that Waldo was seduced into wealth worship by his fancy accommodations. But it's easier to denounce an abstraction than a generous man with a starched collar and a bulky pocket watch, which led those same grandchildren to call him Grampa Tick Tick.

. . .

So Waldo rounded the corner into a new decade, aging but seemingly intact. His audience was bigger than ever. His ideas had begun to nourish, in the manner of an underground freshet, the next great school of American philosophy: Pragmatism Then came two calamities, one instantaneous, the other slow and stealthy.

The first: in the early hours of July 24, 1872, Waldo was awakened in his bedroom by a crackling sound in the wall. A fire had started in the attic, possibly caused by an overturned kerosene lamp, and now the house was burning. He ran outside and shouted for help, wearing only a nightgown in the heavy rain. This being the Victorian era, Lidian took the time to don a black alpaca dress, mantilla, and bonnet before she joined him. His neighbors soon arrived bearing fire buckets full of sand (Waldo's can still be seen hanging in the foyer of the house). As billows of black smoke poured out of the study on the first floor, the Concord fire department showed up as well.

Since the fire was burning slowly, neighbors managed to dart inside and rescue much of the furniture and personal effects. Yet it was understood, apparently, that the study was the vault of treasures—the intellectual epicenter of New England and beyond. Holding their breath, boys rushed into the smoke-filled room and threw books, manuscripts, and papers out the windows onto the wet grass. Aunt Mary's diaries survived, with just a few scorch marks, and most of Waldo's work was salvaged as well. Louisa May Alcott, by then the forty-year-old author of *Little Women* and a truckload of anonymous pulp fiction, stood guard over the pile of books and papers. At one point Waldo, still in his bare feet, approached her and said, "Could you tell me where my good neighbors have flung my boots?"

The process went on for hours. Waldo, in the grip of shock and fatigue and something much sadder, began a mission of his own. According to one witness, he took to throwing certain items back into the blaze: mementos of Ellen and Little Waldo. This assault on his own memories—literally feeding them into the fire—is hard to contemplate. Was it meant to lessen the pain of these unbearable losses by erasing the evidence, taking advantage of the conflagration to do what he never could have done in a moment of calm?

He was little better, if more tranquil, by morning, as the rain quenched the last of the flames. The lower walls of the house were standing; much of the roof was gone. Anna Alcott Pratt described "the Poet of America wandering forlornly around in an old muddy coat, & no stockings smiling serenely if any one spoke to him, & looking calmly on the wreck of his home as if it were of no special consequence to him." The image suggests a Yankee Lear—not the one raging on the heath, but the exhausted monarch of the morning after, contemplating the ruins.

Lidian had meanwhile stepped on the hem of her alpaca dress and torn it, not once but twice. In their louche and waterlogged outfits, the Emersons were loaded into a wagon, fed breakfast at a neighbor's house, then dropped off at the Old Manse, now tenanted by a cousin, Elizabeth Ripley. So did Waldo's life in Concord come full circle. He had retreated to the Old Manse to reconstruct his existence after losing both Ellen and his vocation. Now he retreated there again, with a more literal reconstruction to ponder.

The strange thing about a disaster, however, is not the disruption but the eerie continuity. Lidian, for example, claimed not to feel the full pathos of the fire until she saw the procession of homeless rats marching across the field in search of new lodgings. "There is this consolation," she allowed. "They are sure to find a home somewhere!" The animal lover had spoken again. The displacement of her own grief onto the rats was, at the very least, an impressive act of psychic legerdemain.

For his part, Waldo was set up in a duplicate study at the courthouse. There he spent hours each day, surrounded by mounds of damp, smoke-perfumed books and manuscripts, many of which had been dusty or decaying before the fire. All of his hair fell out, which must have given him that look of a wise infant. It's also possible that he had suffered a minor stroke: he told at least one friend that he "felt something snap in his brain" during the blaze.

Still, there was an effort to carry on as if nothing had happened. When his daughter Ellen, who had been at a seaside town about twenty miles north, rushed back to the Old Manse, she found her father nonplussed. Waldo seemed "just the same, and very happy," she wrote to her brother Edward six days after the blaze. She had no doubt that the fire had been a traumatic event, but understood that her father's smiling impersonality and distaste for melodrama would put a cap on any further discussion. "I suppose we shall never hear a word about that," she said. As far as we know, they never did.

In his own close-mouthed comments on the calamity, Waldo followed suit. His pertinent journal entry consisted of two words: "House burned." In September, he wrote to Charles Eliot Norton, the man of letters who would eventually edit his correspondence with Carlyle (and who was also the son of his old nemesis Andrews Norton). His description of the fire sounded more like an expedited form of spring cleaning. It had been, he said, a shock to find all his possessions "thrown out on the grass in his door-yard: but the ready & tender care of friends & neighbors saved all that could be rescued, & conveyed them into houses,

FIGURE 11. Ellen Emerson, circa 1855. Courtesy of the Houghton Library, Harvard University, MS Am 1280.235 (Box 63: 706.5).

or barns, or wagons." In addition, within a couple of days after the blaze, he "found himself richer than he had ever been before."

He wasn't kidding about the way the household goods had been scattered around town. When she visited some neighbors right after the fire, Ellen found the family's bedding and "odd bureau drawers" in the barn and her Chickering piano in the parlor.

Nor was he kidding about the benefaction. The house, valued at $5,000, had been insured for only $2,500. This represented a serious shortfall, just as Waldo's income from lecturing was likely to be interrupted. A group of friends and supporters stepped up at once. First the industrialist Francis Cabot Lowell discreetly handed him an envelope containing a check for $5,000. Then Rockwood Hoar swung by the Old Manse to inform Waldo that an even larger gift of $10,000 had been raised for him. When Waldo wondered aloud about accepting such a sum, Hoar responded: "I don't know what you can do about it. It is in the bank to your credit. The best use you can make of it is to go on to Egypt with it."

. . .

Judge Hoar had either advance intel or superb powers of suggestion. Egypt is exactly where Waldo went, with Ellen as his companion and aide-mémoire-in-crinoline. He did not leave right away, however. The aftershock of the fire caught up with him, laying him low with fever and fatigue for several weeks. He rotated from one recuperative spot to another, ending up in September at the Forbes compound on Naushon Island.

There the plan must have come into focus. In a brief note to his friend and literary executor James Elliot Cabot on September 25, Waldo mentions that he is "dreaming of Egypt." The idea, clearly, was that he could doze in the shadow of the pyramids while his house was rebuilt back in Concord. Yet Waldo had more in mind than simply soaking up the sun's rays and working on a tan. Egypt was for him a great locus of civilization—a place where the human soul had come to a high boil before lapsing back into room-temperature indolence. As far back as 1838, he had noted in his journal that the sphinxes had "an expression of health." In Waldo's weakened state, he must have liked the idea of a mythological rest cure.

The travelers departed on the steamship *Wyoming* on October 23. Given their pagan destination, and Waldo's rather oblique relationship to Christianity, it was a signal irony that they found themselves sur-rounded by a multidenominational horde of missionaries, many of them on their way to India. Aboard this floating revival meeting they heard two sermons and numerous hymns on Sunday. "But the liberal ocean sings louder," he assured Lidian in a letter, "& makes us all of one church."

They made stops in London (where Waldo received a final bear hug from Carlyle) and Paris (where Henry James was astounded by how quickly Waldo jogged through the Louvre). By December, they were in Cairo. There they boarded a dahabeah, a barge-like sailing vessel whose design had hardly changed over the past several millennia, and began their cruise down the Nile.

The enchanted river with its fringe of palm trees, the archaic vessel straight out of a pharaonic painting—these things should have made the ailing Waldo ecstatic. To a surprising degree, however, the initial leg of the trip seemed to confirm all of his old reservations about travel. At first the weather was cool, the scenery monotonous. The Nile was a turbid, loopy thing, suggesting to Ellen that they were "all the time in a large muddy pond." Why had he come here? The traveler, in Waldo's old formulation, was the ultimate sucker, fleeing his woes at home only to encounter them abroad in native dress:

> All this journey is a perpetual humiliation, satirizing and whipping our ignorance. The people despise us because we are helpless babies who cannot speak or understand a word they say; the sphinxes scorn dunces; the obelisks, the temple walls, defy us with their histories which we cannot spell.

This splenetic paragraph was committed to paper after Waldo's return to Cairo. In fact, he wrote almost nothing during the several weeks spent aboard the dahabeah. He subsequently noted to Lidian that he had been in the grip of a "long idleness," which involved an "incapacity to write any thing."

Ellen, who was having a whale of a time, suggested that her father's torpor was curative. The sun was finally shining, he was sleeping ten hours a night. His hair was growing back in snowy patches. He enjoyed going ashore to visit the copious ruins, traveling by donkey. On one such occasion, when they were inspecting the Valley of the Kings, the high-spirited Ellen plunged into the depths of a tomb, only to discover a petrified Waldo in her wake. "That poor man had been scared at seeing me disappear in the bowels of the earth," she wrote.

There was, in any case, something Waldo wanted to see, and badly. This was Philae, a flyspeck of an island located just north of the first cataract of the Nile—which is to say, near the modern-day Aswan Dam, which has since flooded the entire area. Waldo went so far as to renegotiate the itinerary, extending the trip by ten days, in order to see it.

Why? He had already expressed interest in the island before leaving America, having read that the god Osiris was buried there. Waldo was familiar with the mythology surrounding Osiris, the king of Egypt and consort of Isis who had been drowned by his jealous brother, resurrected by Isis, then slain once again by that same brother, who hacked his body to pieces. Like most such narratives, this one is a garden of forking paths. But in at least one version, poor Osiris was buried on Philae—only to have Isis break open the tomb and scatter his body parts.

There is a lot going on here. There is eros, sibling rivalry, resurrection, and a vexing question of identity. Is the body who you are, or only an incidental container, subject to change?

This last issue never stopped tantalizing Waldo. "Nothing is so fleeting as form; yet never does it quite deny itself," he wrote in his 1841 essay "History"—right before citing Isis and Osiris as the most mutable of beings. But I don't think mutability was the main issue here. I think something much more troubling was going on.

The fire had stirred up a deep reservoir of grief in Waldo. It had, in a sense, reopened the graves of Ellen and Little Waldo. No wonder he had thrown their effects back into the blaze, as if it had been a funeral pyre that would finally incinerate what remained of them. Let us recall, too, that Waldo was himself a man who had opened both his wife's coffin and that of his young son, when his remains were moved to Sleepy Hollow Cemetery in 1857. Presumably he had done so with a mixture of love, curiosity, and dread—yet the act still feels forbidden, even hubristic. All of this came to bear, I would argue, as he planned the trip to Egypt. Philae was where a goddess had broken into her husband's tomb, and that made it a necessary destination for a man newly frightened of his own death and that of his loved ones. Hence his panicky reaction when he saw Ellen disappear down the stairway into the underworld.

She apologized profusely, but he was too alarmed to say a word as they climbed the seventy stone steps back to the land of the living.

I'm talking, of course, about the role of Philae in Waldo's imagination. What role it played in daily life is another matter. The travelers reached there on January 28, and Waldo went ashore, riding a donkey supplied by the British consul. Yet he left no record of his encounter with the ghosts of Isis and Osiris.

It may be that the intrusion of American realities had distracted him. A few days before they reached this terminus of their voyage, he had heard that an entire flotilla of well-heeled tourists, numbering no less than seventeen vessels, was anchored at Aswan and Philae—socializing, dining, picnicking on the nearby islands. This miniature Newport-on-the-Nile included two close friends of his, Sam Ward and Anna Barker Ward, as well as the honeymooning Henry Adams and his bride Clover (who was just then sliding into a depressive funk). Adams had spent nearly a week exploring the temples on Philae and photographing them with the bulky equipment he had dragged all the way from London. Alas, by the time the Emersons arrived, the party had broken up and his countrymen had headed south to Nubia.

Yet America did rear its head once more as the dahabeah floated back downstream toward Cairo. At Luxor, a family of wealthy Americans invited Waldo and Ellen to join them for lunch, sending over a small boat for their guests. They boarded the craft and were rowed over by none other than the thirteen-year-old Theodore Roosevelt—"whose round red cheeks," Ellen noted, "honest blue eyes, and perfectly brilliant teeth make him a handsome boy, though plain." Waldo, who had chatted with John Adams and joshed with Abraham Lincoln, had now made the acquaintance of another (future) president. Let's dwell on this for a moment. Adams was born in 1735, and Roosevelt would live until 1919. Can there be a better illustration of the intense compression of American history, with its accordion folds and moiré patterns, and its key players forming a tiny repertory company, with Waldo as a frequent fixture?

In any case, he and Ellen now abandoned the dahabeah and took a train back to Cairo, then a steamer to Naples. They made stops at Florence, Rome, Paris, London, and Edinburgh, and Waldo was everywhere treated as a living monument, a good-natured American sphinx. They sailed from Liverpool on May 15 and eleven days later walked down the gangplank in Boston. The train that carried them to the depot in Concord began shrilling its whistle the moment it passed Walden woods, and the entire town turned out to welcome Waldo—on horse and on foot, in wagons and baby carriages, with the church bells ringing and a brass band ready to play "Home, Sweet Home" the moment his foot hit the platform. Ellen was nearly in tears at this display. "What a sight!" she later recalled. "My whole dear town all assembled." As for Waldo, he turned to his daughter in puzzlement and said, "Is today a public holiday?"

15

TERMINUS

I said before that there were two calamities. Now we can talk about the second one. During the last decade of his life, and probably earlier, Waldo had begun to lose his memory—and with it, his command of language. He almost certainly had Alzheimer's disease, which nobody recognized as such.

How could they? The disease wasn't even identified until 1906, when the German neuropathologist Alois Alzheimer examined the brain tissue of a deceased female patient whose cognitive state had atrophied while she was still in her early fifties. What he found was anatomical evidence—sticky plaques and neuronal tangles—of a novel malady. It was quite distinct from traditional dementia, not least because it was capable of afflicting people still in the prime of life.

The disease also entailed a terrible process of subtraction. It starts, as researchers would later learn, in the hippocampus, the seat of memory. From there, it spreads to other parts of the brain, progressively depriving the victim of language, logic, physical coordination, speech, understanding. The neurons, by the millions, blink off like bulbs. Identity, sustained by what is essentially a miniature power grid in the brain, begins to collapse. In the end, it is the self, the soul, the coherent thing built up out of decades of experience, that disappears.

Nobody looked at Waldo's brain after his death. No definitive diagnosis can be made. Still, what happened to him is completely consistent with Alzheimer's. As early as 1866, while he was still barnstorming across America as a Lyceum star, he felt a notable waning of his powers, both physical and mental. As I've already mentioned, Waldo was an old hand at anticipating his own decline, and it would be easy to write off these premonitory tremors as more of the same.

Still, in December of that year, he spent an evening with his son Edward in New York City, and shared a poem he had just written called "Terminus." The message (starting with the title) is unmistakable. "It is time to be old," Waldo writes. "To take in sail."

Edward was shocked by the valedictory tone, so at odds with the vigorous, cigar-smoking senior citizen who was about to depart for another freezing tour of the Midwest. But Waldo seemed to be renouncing his gift: "Fancy departs: no more invent." He also had plenty of tips for managing the depleted capital of his own existence:

> There's not enough for this and that,
> Make thy option which of two;
> Economize the falling river,
> Not the less revere the Giver,
> Leave the many and hold the few.

You could argue that an Alzheimer's patient would not be capable of writing such a sad and gnomic poem about having Alzheimer's. Correct, of course—except that the disease is a slow-moving and erosive thing. It starts by chipping away memories, words, facts, sensations, in such small quantities that they may be overlooked or, well, forgotten. So it was that Waldo began his gradual diminishment, in tiny increments. "Star by star," as he had written long ago, "his world resigning."

The decay of his memory was noted by others—and by himself. It was unlikely to be otherwise, if only because Waldo had long been fascinated by memory. In fact, he devoted an entire lecture to it in a much-revised series called *Natural History of Intellect*, which he was still fiddling with as late as 1871. Waldo stressed the centrality of memory, calling it the "the cement, the bitumen, the matrix in which the other faculties are embedded." Yet he offered several different models for how it might work.

On one hand, he views it as a mechanical device for the collection of sensory data, "as if the mind were a kind of looking-glass, which being carried through the street of time receives on its clear plate every image that passes; only with this difference, that our plate is iodized so that every image sinks into it, and is held there." This looks backward and forward. It simultaneously evokes John Locke's notion of the brain as a tabula rasa and the iodized silver on a daguerreotype plate. In both cases, though, memory is essentially passive. It does our bidding.

Yet Waldo also suggests that we are not necessarily in control of this magical power. Memory may deny us our precious recollections or destroy them entirely:

> One sometimes asks himself, Is it possible that it is only a visitor, not a resident? Is it some old aunt who goes in and out of the house, and occasionally recites anecdotes of old times and persons which I recognize as having heard before, and she being gone again I search in vain for any trace of the anecdotes?

By the time he revised these words for the last time, he probably felt himself searching in vain for any number of mnemonic treasures. It's hard to pinpoint exactly when the problems started. Ellen, in a report to her father's doctor after the fire, was pretty blunt about his faltering powers. "Memory went first," she wrote, adding that it had been five or six years "since that faculty failed," and that he was no longer able to remember, say, an errand he had been asked to perform, even after being reminded. That would date the initial slippage of Waldo's memory back to the mid-1860s—around the time he recited "Terminus" in that New York City hotel room, but also at the very climax of his lecturing career.

That would seem to be a contradiction. How could a man so constantly in the public eye hide his cognitive collapse from the audience? The answer is twofold. His decline was gradual, and for several years, his only mission was to read the text verbatim—his old habit of tinkering with the language in real time must have fallen by the wayside. To prevent him from mixing up the pages, Ellen took to sewing them together.

Eventually, she also accompanied him to most public appearances, sounding out words and sentences when he got stuck. She was, by the end, a kind of human teleprompter, whose assistance was so crucial that, as a reporter for the *Massachusetts Ploughman* noted in 1879, "it took two instead of one to read the lecture."

Waldo's peers, and even his subsequent biographers, were often reluctant to admit what was going on. They spoke of his affect as Olympian, serene, tranquil, lofty; they suggested, in the words of the scholar John McAleer, that he was "dwelling in the land of the ideal." It is tempting to think that Waldo was in a Platonic wonderland, amid the sheerest essence of things, rather than struggling to remember the name of his wife (which he did indeed forget). But once the process of subtraction was underway, it never really stopped.

It began with words. They were suddenly out of reach. An umbrella or a chair would stump him—what was this object called?—and he would resort to elaborate workarounds. He called his dressing gown "the red chandelier." He called a plough "the implement that cultivates the soul," either doubling down on his error or making poetic hay. This was in the early 1870s, when his loosening grip on nouns and verbs still seemed a little endearing, as if he were a visionary Mr. Magoo.

In a letter to her sister Edith in August 1872 (after the fire, that is, and before the trip to Egypt), Ellen wrote: "Poor man, how he struggles for words! The simplest escape him." She added that he had laughed the day before after finishing a sentence and said, "It is a triumph to remember any word." Any word! For most of his life, it had been the plenitude of words, the glory of syntax, the gamboling of sentences, that had kept him going. Words were the stepping stones into reality and what lay beyond it. He wasn't merely forgetting, now—his oxygen was being cut off.

Again, he knew what was happening. If "Terminus" was a kind of premonition, an early warning of weakening powers, Waldo came to grasp the specifics soon enough. His reluctance to write during the trip to Egypt, for example, was officially chalked up to idleness. But in a letter that he did manage to dash off to his son-in-law, a very different picture comes into view. He refers to himself as "an old scribe who, for the first time in his life, recoils from all writing." He continues: "Ellen sits daily by me vainly trying to electrify my torpid conscience & mend my pen, but the air of Egypt is full of lotus, & I resent any breaking of the dream." This is not a functioning writer on a holiday. This is a man repelled by the very thing that sustained him, almost certainly because language now hovered out of reach.

His condition grew steadily worse. Ellen, who never married and instead stayed at home to tend to her aging parents, became not only a performance coach but a secretary, amanuensis, editor, and actual collaborator. This is not an overstatement. At first she merely picked up the slack in his correspondence. By early 1876, however, he would inform Sam Ward that he had "ceased to write even notes—partly because my daughter Ellen is a skillful scribe and fast coming to absolute governance of her papa." She also began pitching in on editorial duties, which went far beyond inserting commas and mending solecisms. She and James Elliot Cabot produced his penultimate book, *Letters and Social Aims* (1875), via cut-and-paste. They dredged up materials from his earlier lectures and notes, assembled them, and sometimes tweaked the language to make it flow.

Ellen, who wanted no credit for this labor, was literally revising her father's work—channeling him, you might say. Cabot's contribution was no less substantial. In fact, when Waldo inscribed a copy of *Letters and Social Aims* for him, he wrote Cabot's name followed by two words: *His book*. The ironies here are thick on the ground. Waldo, always the great champion of singularity, was now acceding to a collaborative process. True, his notion of the universe had always included a kind of hive mind, an oceanic consciousness flowing in and out of every human being. But so much of his thinking had been devoted to cleansing the self of distractions, which often meant driving other people to the margins, avoiding the contamination of politics, history, daily life.

His deep dive into the abolition movement had signaled a change— he had turned a corner when it came to commingling with the herd. But in his final years, as his grip on language failed and his very self began to seep away, the multitude of other selves no longer struck him as alien. They were instead fellow creatures, participating in a giant and unending conversation, with no gold stars awarded for individual genius. Indeed, he (or Ellen, or James Elliot Cabot) declared in a late lecture that "there is no pure originality." God might well be within you, but so was everybody else. We were a horde of happy ventriloquists, begging and borrowing whatever words we needed to get through life. "All minds quote," Waldo insisted, finally relinquishing what had always been precious, and what had always been his.

He had curtailed his busy lecture schedule after his return from Egypt. Now he seldom appeared in public, and always under Ellen's watchful (and sometimes terrified) eye. His last such appearance seems to have been on February 11, 1882, when he spoke about the recently deceased Carlyle at the Massachusetts Historical Society in Boston. The *New York Times* reported the event with euphemistic discretion: "While Mr. Emerson was reading this interesting paper, with an occasional suggestion from his daughter, the members of the society gathered eagerly around him and listened to his words with close attention." My guess is that Ellen offered more than an occasional suggestion, and that the audience gathered around to encourage their fading oracle, whose speech may have been inaudible at times. They gave him a big round of applause at the end, for reasons too poignant to dwell on.

He had meanwhile cut back on receiving visitors at home, or even venturing out with any regularity. In 1876, when he was still lucid enough to explain his situation, he declined an invitation from Emma Lazarus, lamenting that

> an old man fears most his best friends. It is not them that he is willing to distress with his perpetual forgetfulness of the right word for the name of book or fact or person he is eager to recall, but which refuses to come. I have grown silent to my own household under this vexation, & cannot afflict dear friends with my tied tongue. Happily this embargo does not reach to the eyes, and I read with unbroken pleasure.

It is cheering to think that Waldo could still, at this late stage, immerse himself in the written word (even if he had trouble remembering what he had read). Yet the subtractive havoc of the disease went on and on. Alzheimer's does not merely dim the voltage of the self, or blur the contours of memory. Thanks to a process called retrogenesis, it ultimately returns the patient to childhood, peeling away everything we have learned since the cradle.

FIGURE 12. RWE in his study, 1879, photograph by A. H. Folsom. Courtesy of the Houghton Library, Harvard University, Autograph file, F (Box 69).

Waldo was lucky. He never lost the ability to walk, or eat, or hold up his head. Perhaps he simply didn't live long enough to shed these rudimentary skills. But he understood less and less, and withdrew into a shell of silence and outward amiability, which did strike many of his peers as a kind of splendid regression. Much was made of his supposedly wide-eyed demeanor in old age. Moncure Conway, one of his earliest biographers, noted his "playfulness, simplicity, and childlikeness," while Walt Whitman dwelled on the "benignant face, the clear eyes, the silently smiling mouth," specifically citing Waldo's "absence of decrepitude."

Perhaps there were moments of reprieve, shafts of cognitive sunlight, when Waldo regained a little of what he had lost. There is in fact a phenomenon, called paradoxical lucidity, which grants a tiny fraction of dementia patients some late-in-the-game access to their ravaged memories. For the most part, though, the progress of the disease, while seemingly reversing the flow of time and restoring us to a state of childish innocence—to a state of timelessness—moves in one direction only.

Who knows when Waldo forgot that he was forgetting? As late as 1882, Lidian was still teasing him for insisting that his watch was lost, suggesting that Ellen would simply "search all the hiding places in which she is accustomed to find your *daily lost wallet*." This sounds like the early stage of Alzheimer's, the era of verbal pratfalls and harmless confusions. But when a visitor showed up on Waldo's doorstep just a few months earlier, he observed a man who had lost not merely his wallet and watch, but his actual identity—who had lost himself.

The visitor was Edward Bok, an enterprising eighteen-year-old who had already discovered the allure of celebrity culture. Later on, he would be the editor of the *Ladies Home Journal*, a rock-ribbed conservative, and such a ceaseless booster of the suburban bungalow that Theodore Roosevelt, who had come a long way since rowing Waldo and Ellen across the Nile, declared him "the only man I ever heard of who changed, for the better, the architecture of an entire nation." For the moment, though, he was simply a Western Union office boy with lots of pluck and an autograph book.

Bok knew how to network. After charming Oliver Wendell Holmes and Henry Wadsworth Longfellow in quick succession, he found himself in Concord, charming Louisa May Alcott. She somewhat hesitantly agreed to walk him over to Waldo's house. Why she did so is a little puzzling—she surely knew the score.

At Bush, Ellen tried to turn them away. "Father sees no one now," she said, "and I fear it might not be a pleasure if you did see him." But Bok persisted, and eventually Alcott escorted him into Waldo's study, where the teenager's celebrity quarry stood up and shook his hand.

What followed was not, as Ellen had predicted, a pleasure. Bok thought he detected a flare of sentience in Waldo's eyes as they shook hands. After that, though, there were merely degrees of absence. Waldo urged his young visitor to sit down, stepped away to look out the window, and began whistling—he had clearly forgotten that Bok and Alcott were there. When he noticed them again, he no longer recognized Alcott. He was living, eerily, in a kind of eternal present, in which no memory can be retained for more than a few seconds: his old wish to escape the past had been granted.

When an increasingly nervous Bok asked for Waldo's autograph, his host was stumped for a moment. He no longer remembered who he was.

"Please write out the name you want," Waldo said, "and I will copy it for you if I can."

Bok picked up a slip of paper and wrote down *Ralph Waldo Emerson, Concord, November 22, 1881.* Slowly, and with difficulty, his hero obliged. *All minds quote.* He misspelled the name of the town in which he had lived for fifty years. He also forgot that he had signed the autograph book the moment that Bok slipped it into his pocket, and offered to do it again. This time, he managed to sign his name—to memorialize, in shaky script, his sublime and mostly dissipated self—without any coaching from his visitor.

. . .

As I have noted before, to recount a life is to omit almost everything about it. Biographers operate at a high altitude, like pipe-smoking, note-taking drones, capturing the terrain, the landmarks, the general drift of things. Waldo, of course, was just fine with this technique. He believed that any life could be boiled down to a handful of exemplary anecdotes. The rest, meaning the mountainous accumulation of detail, was dross.

He believed this to be especially true of great minds. For them, thinking made living just a tiny bit parenthetical. "As a good chimney burns up all its own smoke," he wrote, "so a good philosopher consumes all his own events in his extraordinary intellectual performances." As for writers, they simply disappeared into what they wrote. Once they had "put down their thoughts, [they] jumped into their book bodily themselves, so that we have all that is left of them in our shelves; there is not a pinch of dust beside."

The pinch of dust, the residue, the life so painstakingly lived from day to day, is what biographers (and readers of biographies) agree to ignore. Indeed, when the biographer swoops in to tell us exactly what happened in a minute-by-minute fashion, it feels suspect. We are being lulled with the smoke and mirrors and mendacity of fiction. We are being thrust into a scene with such swooning colors and retina-tickling detail that it must be a product of peak TV—it is high definition, and therefore fake.

Yet there are brief passages in any life that deserve such treatment. One of them is what happens before you die. Everything then operates under enormous (if retrospective) pressure. Everything means something, and sends a kind of backward irradiation into everything that preceded it.

That is why I will tell you some of the strange and salient details that led to Waldo's death. They fall into two chapters, roughly speaking: downstairs and upstairs. On Wednesday, April 19, 1882, he went to the bank in Concord to withdraw fifty dollars and got caught in the rain. "I have walked far today," he said that evening, "because I didn't feel well in my chair." The next morning, he seemed under the weather and was allowed to drowse in bed until nine o'clock, at which point Ellen went upstairs to help him dress, as she had done many times before. They descended the stairs and headed for the dining room. As they passed the storage closet under the front stairs, he stopped and cried out, "Oh dear!"

His frightened daughter embraced him. They stood there for a full minute, with Ellen uttering reassurance and Waldo saying nothing at all. Then, with a splayed and staggering gait, Waldo made his way to the dining room, and Ellen led him to the window, which she opened. Waldo was unable to convey what was happening to him. When he finally seated himself at the breakfast table, he said, "I hoped it would not come in this way." He would rather, he explained, have fallen down the cellar stairs.

After he ate, Ellen brought him to his study. There he sat and talked with her, using recognizable words in strange patterns or words that were simply unrecognizable. She sensed that he was talking about his impending death, and since the family considered him something of a hypochondriac, her tone was slightly teasing when she said, "Do you think you are going to die?" Waldo's response: "Yes." He tried to issue some instructions on how the household should be run when he was gone, but the words wouldn't come. He managed to say, "You must all be good." He slept on the sofa in the study for much of the day.

On Friday, his son Edward (who was, after all, a doctor) urged Waldo to stay in bed, but he insisted on dressing, coming downstairs, and sitting in the study. He napped up in the bedroom that afternoon, and was very grateful when Lidian covered him with a pile of quilts.

The next morning he was diagnosed with pneumonia and ordered to stay in bed. Again, he refused to comply—a born protestant, as he said of Thoreau, to the very end. He got dressed and proceeded to the study. He regarded the rocking chair, the round table, the burgundy carpets and the blue sofa whose protruding leg so often tripped visitors on their way in or out. He was weak. Perhaps he sensed that once he left the study, he would never see it again. After repeated pleas from the family, he agreed to go upstairs, but only after taking apart the fire, stick by stick, separating the glowing brands. He also insisted, quite vehemently, on carrying his own lamp. In fact, he ran with it up the stairs on his tiptoes, stumbling on the tenth step but managing not to fall.

This ended the first chapter of his dying—the part that had taken place downstairs. You could view the ground floor as a kind of annex or entryway to the great world. There people came and went, dropped off cans of milk or rolls of fabric, stomped the dust off their boots as they entered. They hung their hats on the rack in the hall (where Waldo's are hanging to this very day). It was where you died in public. But the rest of his death would take place upstairs, in private.

For several days, he stayed in bed and spoke in sentences that nobody could understand. Visitors sat beside him, grasping no more than an occasional phrase. Even in his weakened state, some of the old music could be heard—the baritone rising and falling, the rhetorical call to arms. Perhaps he imagined himself back on the Lyceum circuit. If so, it was a scenario he had anticipated four years earlier, when he described himself as "a lecturer who has no idea what he is lecturing about, and an audience who don't know what he can mean." His companions, in any case, understood little of what he said. The words meant everything to him and nothing to them.

Waldo's family and friends came to say goodbye. He recognized his visitors: Rockwood Hoar, Bronson Alcott, Ellery Channing. He was especially pleased to see James Elliot Cabot, who was not only his literary right-hand man but his authorized biographer. Having gotten out a few decipherable sentences for Alcott, he made a similar effort for Cabot, to little avail. He might have said, "This is that good man who has done so much for me," followed by more random syllables. After that the brightness seemed to go out of him. He was less pleased to see Franklin Sanborn, yet another future biographer, and the sentence he squeezed out for him was simpler and more tautological: "This is a man that is a man."

To be flanked by your biographers on your deathbed must be a strange sensation: they start the minute you stop. They impart an ink-and-paper immortality, even though Waldo was plenty skeptical about their mission to begin with. As soon as Sanborn departed, Waldo felt a sharp pain. The doctors ran upstairs and gave him ether.

For several hours he lay there, thinking whatever thoughts occur to an anesthetized brain—for we do dream in such a state, we do gather up, in magpie fashion, the shiniest and most disparate bits of reality we can find. It wasn't so different, really, from the way he wrote his essays. It may have seemed like an eternity to him, or just an instant. His son Edward was in the room. At a certain point, shortly before nine o'clock in the evening, Edward summoned the rest of the family: the end, he said, was near.

"This is the last breath, probably," he told them. "But he may breathe once more." They waited. It seemed as though a long time passed—Ellen later guessed that it was a full minute, maybe two. Another breath, and he was gone.

16

CIRCLES

What is gone is gone always. Or so we tell ourselves, melancholy materialists who have seen the disappearance of so many things we loved: people, objects, eras, ideas. Waldo, of course, was less certain about these matters. It was in "Nominalist and Realist" that he seemed to deny the reality of death itself. "Nothing is dead," he insisted. "Men feign themselves dead, and endure mock funerals and mournful obituaries, and there they stand looking out of the window, sound and well, in some new and strange disguise."

He wrote these sentences (or at least published them) in 1844. He was still reeling, in other words, from the death of his son. Was he soothing himself with the idea that he would someday see Little Waldo's eyes peering out at him from another face? Or was this a tribute to the power of memory, wrapped in another of his deadpan metaphors? Or simple denial?

His conviction that nothing truly ended—that extinction was illusory—ran very deep, and he never expressed it more beautifully than in "Circles," from his first collection of essays. "Our life is an apprenticeship to the truth, that around every circle another can be drawn; that there is no end in nature, but every end is a beginning; that there is always another dawn risen on mid-noon, and under every deep a lower deep opens."

His argument went far beyond the question of mortality. Regeneration was the engine of the universe. "Thus there is no sleep," he wrote, "no pause, no preservation, but all things renew, germinate, and spring."

Nor did human beings live in straight lines, but in a kind of glorious circularity. (In a moment of self-mockery, Waldo actually referred to himself as a "circular philosopher.") Has he not encouraged us, then, to turn directly from his death—with his body still warm—to his birth?

He entered the world on May 25, 1803. This was in Boston, the very city he would later condemn as a necropolis of dead ideas and faint hearts and mercantile mildew. But what he saw as a child was very different. The yellow wooden house on Summer Street sat on two acres of land, girdled with spreading elms and Lombardy poplars and with a view of the harbor down below. All around were leafy estates and open, cow-dotted pastures. It was a small bucolic paradise within the city limits, and probably defined Waldo's notion of tranquility forever.

Not that all was tranquil within the Emerson household, at least for Waldo. The third son in a rapidly growing family, he seemed to draw his father's ire or indifference from the time he was born. In his diary, the Reverend William Emerson jammed his arrival between a host of social engagements: "This day also, whilst I was at dinner at Governor Strong's, my son Ralph Waldo was born. Mrs. E. well. Club at Mr. Adams.'" He frequently carped about the boy's educational progress, complaining that he was "a rather dull scholar"—when Waldo was all of two years old! A few months later, with the boy just shy of three, his father continued in the same sniffy vein: "He cannot read very well yet."

He was also concerned, over the next few years, that Waldo spoke too freely, wolfed down his food, and got himself into mischief. It was to be hoped, wrote this flinty paterfamilias, that Waldo would soon be "resigning his impetuosity to younger boys."

. . .

There is a puzzle here. In so many ways, William Emerson should have been a role model for the young Waldo, and for the man he came to be. They had a lot in common. William was also the son of a revered clergyman who had little desire to follow his father into the ministry. After his ordination, when he found himself tending the flock in the tiny town of

Harvard, Massachusetts, he was undoubtedly a modernizer and quasi-maverick.

He asked, for example, to retire the old Calvinist custom of "making public confessions for the sin of fornication," and was soundly shouted down. He also offered to accompany the choir on bass viol—a smaller sibling of the cello that was increasingly employed in colonial churches for its deep sonority, and because it kept the wobbly-pitched singers in tune. Again, he was voted down.

The village, which just a generation earlier had stoned a congregation of Quakers, was having none of William Emerson's Unitarian-leaning bells and whistles. He felt besieged, and was regularly reviled at town meetings. His position in Harvard, he wrote a friend, isolated him "from the intercourse of all humanized beings." Meanwhile, his attempts to mollify his flock—he sold the bass viol—got him nowhere. He dreamed of fleeing the town to establish a post-Puritan church "in which there was to be no written expression of faith, no covenant, and no subscription whatever to articles, as a term of communion," where he would simply "administer the rituals of Christianity to all who would observe them."

Salvation finally arrived in the form of an offer from the First Church in Boston, which happened to be the oldest in America. There he was no longer a clay pigeon for a bunch of cranky Calvinists, but a pillar of Brahmin society. He sported a gold-topped cane and loved to show off his elegant ankles in their black stockings. He was also heavily involved in literary culture. The possessor of a frisky prose style—at times it suggests a tamer, less dirty-minded Laurence Sterne—he spent several years running the nation's first literary magazine, *The Monthly Anthology* (which would eventually morph into the *North American Review*). Meanwhile, having established a small public library in Harvard, he now became the motivating force behind the Boston Atheneum's collection. Shouldn't this double-decker paragon, with one foot in the pulpit and the other in literature, have inspired his son?

There were some flies in the ointment. William Emerson became a more cautious and conservative man as he ascended the social ladder. Having showed at least some radical tendencies during his miserable exile in Harvard, he quickly became part of the Establishment—a fact

that rankled Waldo as a young adult, although it would not have bothered him as a child. More to the point, William's glory days as a wig-
wearing ecclesiastical peacock were sadly short-lived. The family moved
to Boston in 1799. In 1808, he suffered a severe lung hemorrhage, then
spent the next three years struggling with tuberculosis and stomach
cancer. These dual maladies, which finally killed him in 1811, must have
cast a pall over the entire household.

Yet none of this completely explains Waldo's lifelong hostility toward
his father, which took the form, as he grew older, of flagrant erasure.
Asked later in life for memories of William Emerson, he insisted that
there were only two. He was nearly eight when his father died—old
enough to have retained at least the bare bones of a filial narrative. Instead there were two isolated anecdotes, the first involving the treatment of Waldo's eczema (then known as salt rheum):

> I know the doctor had advised him to have me go into the salt water
> every day because I had the salt rheum and he used to take me him-
> self to the Bath-house. I did not like it, and when in the afternoon he
> called me I heard his voice as the voice of the Lord God in the garden,
> and I hid myself and was afraid.

Pain, of course, is the first association here: the salt working its
excruciating magic on the boy's open wounds. But the phrasing in the
second half is straight out of Genesis. The voice of the Lord God in
the garden, let's recall, is what precedes nakedness, ruin, the expulsion
from Eden. Waldo could hardly have cast his father in a more punitive
role.

As for that other anecdote, it concerned his father's funeral. This affair
took place on May 16, 1811, and featured a lengthy procession of mourners
loaded into more than fifty coaches. The two oldest Emerson boys
marched directly behind the hearse, and while they must have been impressed by the solemnities, the elderly Waldo, recalling the event for his
daughter, stressed that he wasn't sad. Indeed, Ellen wrote, "he used to
smile as he recalled his delight in that funeral." It's absurd to expect
children to feel the appropriate emotions (whatever that means) at such
an event—they are old hands already at sublimation, and are most likely

to shunt their sorrow elsewhere. Yet Waldo's delight, decades after the fact, smacks just slightly of dancing on the grave.

So does his habit, in his twenties, of tearing the pages out of bound volumes of his father's sermons or notebooks, then using the binding to house his own compositions. In a family less devoted to the written word, this might have qualified as Yankee thrift—a slightly perverse sort of virtue. Among the Emersons, it was sacrilege, even if nobody noted it as such. Nor did Waldo, in his mellow old age, desist from this patricidal recycling. On one occasion late in the game, ripping the used pages out of an old notebook of his father's, he left the stubs throughout, some of them still covered with fragmentary scribbles.

Of course, he had already passed judgement on whatever was contained in those volumes, declaring in his journal that between 1790 and 1820, certainly the heyday of the Reverend William Emerson, "there was not a book, a speech, a conversation, or a thought" in the state of Massachusetts. Why save the mementos of such a wasteland, over which his father had so conspicuously presided?

I don't mean to stuff Waldo and his father into an Oedipal pigeonhole. But there is a mystery at the heart of that relationship, a friction and sharp sense of disappointment that is hard to ignore. Sons imitate fathers. Sons also struggle mightily, when the time comes, to differentiate themselves from those enormous and engulfing figures. Fathers meanwhile feel the draft of time on the back of their necks—the slight coolness of age and obsolescence—and sometimes they blame their sons.

There is, in other words, plenty of room for hostility. Much of that hostility is never expressed directly. It takes the form of slights, omissions, misunderstandings, betrayals: the emotional equivalent of paper cuts, which may nonetheless leave the relationship in anemic shape.

What stops the bleeding is the other elemental fact, that fathers and sons tend to love one another. The attachment is so deep, the recognition so mutual. You are approximations of each other, two versions of the same human being who happen to occupy different spots on the chronological continuum, sharing perhaps a nose and a funny gait and a widow's peak, the tossed salad of DNA making you different enough to view your sameness with real, joyful astonishment, that being the rough definition of love between a father and son. This eerie and beautiful identification is what supercharges so many other emotions: pride, sadness, loyalty, rage. It also, over a lifetime, puts to bed so much of that original, almost mythological hostility. Only Saturn devours his undoubtedly delicious sons. The rest of us, looking back on all the thoughtless things we said and the pain we never meant to inflict, eat our words instead.

But not in Waldo's case. William Emerson died young and the conflict between them was set in stone—there could be no armistice between this father and son, no loving recognition of their likeness. Waldo erased the man from his memory, pillaged the written record of his life and replaced it with his own.

Indeed, he began his career as a writer, in *Nature*, by impugning the age for its filial devotions: "It builds the sepulchers of the fathers." His great project, from the very start, was to cut himself loose from the past—from the demoralizing burden of his (like it or not) patrimony. I don't think this is accidental. He hated the distant figure of William Emerson and disdained to build him a memorial. Yet he couldn't help but note, in that very same book, that the divine spirit almost always came in a paternal package: "Man in all ages and countries, embodies it in his language, as the FATHER." The heart forgives, even for a moment, what the mind cannot.

. . .

Of course Waldo had a mother, too. She was Ruth Haskins Emerson, universally admired for her calm, piety, and grit—especially after her husband's death, which left her a pauperized widow with five sons to raise. She supplied at least some of the warmth that William Emerson had withheld. Yet her parental style was also straight out of the Calvinist playbook. Pleasure was kept in studiously short supply. When the infant Waldo sucked his thumb, a gratification-denying cloth mitten was sewed onto his nightgown. Breakfast consisted of toast, but no butter. The young children were dressed day and night in yellow flannel. Mary Russell Bradford, who lived with the family as a babysitter for several years starting in 1806, clearly viewed this last austerity measure as a bit much. ("I did not think it pretty enough for the pretty boys," she later recalled.)

The brothers were also kept on a short leash. When snow covered the sloping pasturage around the house, sledding was forbidden. In all seasons, Waldo was warned against mingling with his peers from Windmill Point and the South End, who frequently swarmed down the dirt road on their way to some lively kicking and punching on the Boston Common. Sometimes he would wander around the wharves and pick up shells, stones, and gypsum, which gave off a luminous glow when he rubbed two pieces together in a dark closet. But the magic, crucially, took place indoors—within the walls of the educational hothouse on Summer Street.

The Emerson boys, with allowances made for Bulkeley, were expected to be prodigies of learning. "They were born to be educated," declared their aunt Mary Moody Emerson, who monitored their reading and once berated the young Waldo for checking a novel out of a circulating library. "How insipid is fiction to a mind touched with immortal views!" she fumed.

It was never too early to expect academic miracles, as William Emerson had intimated more than once. When Mary Russell Bradford put Waldo to bed as a child, he would dutifully intone the Lord's Prayer, and also some of his favorite set pieces, including David Everett's "Lines Written for a School Declamation." Everett, a newspaperman who collected his prose in something called *Common Sense in Dishabille*, had written the poem for a seven-year-old. Waldo was likely quite younger when he recited this perky anthem to precocity:

> You'd scarce expect one of my age
> To speak in public on the stage,
> And if I chance to fall below
> Demosthenes or Cicero,
> Don't view me with a critic's eye,
> But pass my imperfections by.

It's a hilarious picture: the little orator in his yellow flannel, declaiming to a teenage girl. Sometimes he also recited a poem about Benjamin

Franklin, or the dialogue between Brutus and Cassius in the first act of *Julius Caesar*. Heady stuff, you might think, for a five-year-old with a superb memory. "Men at some time are masters of their fates," I imagine him piping up, perhaps in a sleepy tone. "The fault, dear Brutus, is not in our stars." He would include the entire dialogue, more than seventy years later, in an autumnal anthology he called *Parnassus*. But even as a child, he was doubtless storing up silent lessons in fate and freedom, not to mention the mouth-watering music of Shakespearean diction, which he may not have fully understood.

Except that he probably did. There really was no sense, in a family like this one, that children were different from adults, and might benefit from a separate intellectual diet. The Victorian notion of the child as a vessel of innocence was still some distance down the road. Wordsworth had already declared his own childhood a prelapsarian wonder ("Heaven lies about us in our infancy!"), but none of that penetrated the yellow house on Summer Street. There, John Locke was a more likely guide to parenting. Locke's pedagogical treatise, *Some Thoughts Concerning Education*, had been published in 1693, more than a century before Waldo's birth. Yet it had a lengthy vogue, both in England and abroad. It stressed the importance of tamping down infantile appetites, very much up Ruth Haskins Emerson's alley. Locke also described the child's mind as a blank slate—as "white Paper, or Wax, to be moulded and fashioned as one pleases."

In the Emerson household, those blank slates got a real workout. Life was an orgy of reading for the young brothers. They were pelted with texts like John Flavel's *On Keeping the Heart*, a Puritan guidebook to a sound relationship with God, and Charles Rollin's *Ancient History*, a multivolume monster frequently read aloud by the boys. Waldo also cut his teeth on Samuel Johnson's *Lives of the Poets* and, once he began attending the Boston Latin School in 1812, Jacob Cummings's *An Introduction to Ancient and Modern Geography*, whose globe-trotting author insisted that it would "not be profitable to confine the young mind long to any one part of the earth." As adolescents, the brothers already knew Alexander Pope and Thomas Gray well enough to produce decent parodies of both.

There was also John Mason's *A Treatise on Self-Knowledge*, in which Waldo would have learned that curiosity was a wonderful thing, but only up to a point. "A fatal instance of this in our first parents we have upon sacred record," Mason warned, "the unhappy effects of which are but too visible in all." Disobedience, in other words, was only half of the problem in the Garden of Eden. It was the desire to *know* that had ultimately done in poor Adam and Eve. In case the message wasn't clear, Mason also quoted Corinthians: "Knowledge puffeth up," a phrase that even a bored child must have relished.

Less weighty material had to be jammed in around the margins. In an 1837 journal entry, Waldo sketched out a domestic scene that was surely a backward glance at his own, complete with the ban on frivolous fiction. He noted the boys "hastening into the little parlor to the study of tomorrow's merciless lesson yet stealing time to read a novel hardly smuggled in to the tolerance of father & mother & atoning for the same by some pages of Plutarch or Goldsmith."

Political speech was also fed into the machine. While gathering wood, the boys traded passages by the long-winded Edward Everett (who would later drone on for more than two hours at Gettysburg) and their hero Daniel Webster, who lived in the neighborhood. They meanwhile tackled other languages. By the time Waldo was thirteen and Edward was eleven, they were not only reading French books together but corresponding in Latin.

True to Aunt Mary's credo, they were all educated to the hilt. Waldo, however, was something different: an inward, dreamy, language-drunk child. Later in life, he recalled sitting in a pew at church and repeating words over and over to himself until they lost all meaning. He made the shocking discovery that almost all bookish children make: words, the key to the universe, are also accidental. "I began to doubt which was the right name for the thing," he recounted, "when I saw that neither had any natural relation, but were all arbitrary. It was a child's first lesson in Idealism."

He was a youthful Idealist, then, dressed a little later in blue nankeen. He had the Idealist's tenuous grip on physical reality. The least robust of the Emerson boys, he seldom played, at least in the company of other children. He was not "vigorous in body," recalled one schoolmate. "He dwelt in a higher sphere," recalled another. "You have no *stamina*," the doctor told him when he was young, a remark that stung him deep into his old age.

Yet he had the strength to separate himself, little by little, from the expectations of his family. His destiny, he declared early on, was to be a poet. I have already mentioned the toddler's bedtime recitals for his babysitter. This habit seems to have persisted. After the family spent a season in Concord in 1814, and it was time for Waldo to depart the local school, he was asked to mount a barrel in the classroom and deliver a valedictory ode. He happily complied. Years later, he was still reciting scraps of the ode for his children.

There was apparently a similar routine at Deacon White's general store in Concord. The moment Waldo was hoisted onto a sugar cask like the miniature prodigy he was, he reeled off excerpts from Milton or Thomas Campbell's "Glenara." Most likely he delivered the latter in a faux-Scots accent. Of course it's funny—the boyish solemnity, the audience there to buy rum, nails, a ball of twine, the little kid going on about "the heath where the oak tree grew lonely and hoar." Of course Waldo was not the first child to amuse his listeners with such intimations of adulthood, like Brahms played on a pennywhistle.

Yet the moment seems to point backward and forward. Waldo must have seen, many times, his father in the pulpit at the First Church. Such things are etched into a child's brain. That daunting and distant figure was gone now, buried three years earlier. But surely the sugar barrel was a kind of pulpit, the poems a kind of sermon, the whole performance a gentle parody of what his father had done—and a commemoration. The reader, meanwhile, will see Waldo's future inscribed in his performance: the adult in the creaky boots, the lectures so numerous that they must have eventually blurred into just one. The infinitely private man opening that final door, sharing that final residuum, vanishing into his audience.

. . .

This sense of circularity was never far from Waldo's mind. In 1842, he sketched it out in his journal (with yet another example of his poetry-declaiming ways):

I was a little chubby boy trundling a hoop in Chauncy Place and spouting poetry from Scott and Campbell at the Latin School. But Time, the little gray man, has taken out of his vest pocket a great awkward house (in a corner of which I sit and write of him), some acres of land, several full grown and several very young persons, and seated them close beside me; then he has taken that chubbiness and that hoop quite away (to be sure he has left the declamation and the poetry) and here left a long lean person threatening soon to be a little gray man like himself.

The hoop is real, a child's toy. The hoop is also a figure for the wistful fusion of past and present, infancy and old age, since that is clearly where Waldo felt himself to be heading. There is Chauncy Place, at the corner of Summer Street, and there is Bush, on the Cambridge Turnpike—the essential geography of his life. Time has compensated Waldo for what he has lost with land, a house, children. It has transformed him, too, into a lanky middle-aged man who himself dabbled in eternity, made it his stock-in-trade: a Chronos on the village green.

But what was eternal? On his sixty-ninth birthday, engaged in some errands in Boston, Waldo found himself wandering by Summer Street. He was near the spot where he had spent his childhood, he later wrote in his journal, yet he could identify no familiar landmarks. In the "granite blocks" of the warehouses and stores he saw not a single hint of his "nearness to my native corner." Nathaniel Goddard's pasture was gone, he noted. So was the long fence that always ran along one side of it, painted the same shade of green that the owner, a shipping magnate, favored for his vessels.

In our childish moods, we expect what we remember to be there always. Waldo, pushing seventy, looked in vain for the yellow house. Instead there was Hovey's department store, and a jeweler's on the corner, and the twin awnings of the Mercantile Library across the street. Now these things, these plump specimens of reality and entrepreneurial zeal, seemed eternal.

The irony is that almost all of it would be gone just a few months later. The Great Boston Fire of 1872, which started on November 9, had its

FIGURE 13. RWE with his son Edward and his grandson Charles, 1876. Courtesy
of the Concord Free Public Library.

origins in the basement of a hoop-skirt factory on Summer Street. It devastated sixty-five acres of the city, including Waldo's old neighborhood. In the stereoscopic images taken from the roof of Hovey's—which happened to sit roughly on the spot where the yellow house had been—the ruins look apocalyptic, as if the structures had been not only scorched but taken apart brick by brick.

And what of Waldo's other habitat? Concord had already reinvented itself more than once before he lived there. Prior to 1825, the village center had been a noisy, mosquito-infested hub of light industry, stinking from the tanneries on the Mill Dam. But that year, the town fathers decided to relocate the factories and replace them with the chaste white Federal structures that we now identify with the place. Even the elms, sycamores, and maples on the main drag were hastily parachuted in by the Ornamental Tree Society. Concord itself, then, was to some extent a simulacrum. It was an imitation New England village erected by a New England village.

This self-conscious feedback loop only intensified once Concord acquired its reputation as the American Athens. I have mentioned the swelling tide of Transcendental pilgrims who thronged the town during Waldo's day. They came to stroll its visionary pavements and ambush its celebrities, and nobody was more scathing about Concord's role as a mystical theme park than Louisa May Alcott. In a satirical piece published in 1869, she advised visitors on the best souvenirs ("orphic acorns by the peck") and the most suitable lodgings, which were fitted out with "Alcott's rustic furniture, the beds made of Thoreau's pine boughs, and the sacred fires fed from the Emersonian woodpile."

But she, too, was a creature of Concord and a contributor to its mythology. She knew that the place was "one of the dullest little towns in Massachusetts" *and* something amazing. Its qualities as a tourist trap couldn't eclipse the slight, sublime, pollen-dusted, sometimes silly-making magic in the air. As Waldo once put it: "Things are, and are not, at the same time."

It's another of those statements that readers will never stop chewing over. It might be Waldo leaving himself an escape hatch, dodging any responsibility for the one million contradictions he had uttered in the course of a long career. It might be a nod to the Idealists, whose undermining of the material world so disturbed him during his youth. It might be a statement about immortality—a way of keeping his vanished loved ones close to him, putting the living and the dead on an equal footing. It might be all or none of these.

Yet Concord, the alpha and omega of Waldo's world, still endures. I was there on a June afternoon not so long ago, as I will certainly be there again. It was hot, bright, beautiful, and somehow oversaturated with itself. On the main street, young girls carried melting ice-cream cones in their hands, wearing skimpy outfits that probably would have made Waldo turn in his grave. And there, at 28 Cambridge Turnpike, itself a boring blacktop with a fresh yellow double-line painted down the middle, was Waldo's house. It was close to the road, like something in the suburbs. This seemed a token of modesty—a representative man lived in a representative house. The sign told you it was his, announced the hours of operation and phone number and some extra material that had been redacted with strips of black tape, which I itched to tear off.

I did not. I toured the house and was moved by every single object—even the stuff in the study, which I understood to be a duplicate, a simulacrum at the heart of a bigger simulacrum. Here were Waldo's hats, his walking stick, his engravings on the wall. Here was Little Waldo's leather pull toy—a heartbreaking memento that his father had failed to consign to the flames in 1872. Here was the rocking horse Waldo had shipped from Liverpool in 1848, with its mild, fixed, forgiving expression. Here was the physical evidence of his time on earth. But I wondered whether it was also incidental. Did everything here point to some spiritual fact, which required neither a modern HVAC system nor the efforts of devoted curatorial staff? Waldo might be here and not here.

That left the cemetery. There it was also hot. In the Sleepy Hollow parking lot, which looked big enough to accommodate an IKEA, the heat bounced off the asphalt. The grass and trees and shrubbery were green, extraordinarily so, as if they had just been dipped in boiling water, except in the deep shade, where they looked colorless, dull, like ghosts of themselves. Some of the monuments resembled enormous chess pieces. Others were low and rectangular and blunt about who lay beneath then: MOTHER or FATHER and nothing more.

You went up the hill to see the community's favorite sons and daughters. There was already a springy layer of dead pine needles on the path, which cushioned your feet and made your uphill progress mostly silent. Waldo himself had consecrated Sleepy Hollow when it opened in 1855. He praised the undulating layout of the cemetery, the woods and the water, the way each family chose its own clump of trees. "We lay the corpse in these leafy colonnades," he said, probably wondering where his own would come to rest.

Here, at the top of the ridge, was the entire cast of characters: Thoreau, Hawthorne, a small constellation of Alcotts. They had not always gotten along while they were alive. Their relations were prickly, erratic, full of disappointments—the price, perhaps, of truly Transcendental affections. Yet their adjacency up here, their *nearness*, was terribly moving.

Further down the path was the large Emerson family plot, marked off by rusty chains and stone bollards. I studied the gravestones—the low gray markers covered with words, lots of them, as if the living were under strict orders to explain the dead. They told what had happened; they were narrative objects of a kind, weathering away at the top of the hill. Waldo's was different. It was a jagged hunk of stone, which looked to have been deposited by some Neolithic glacier or dropped from outer space. It was a boulder, that is, scarcely domesticated by the greenish bronze plaque affixed to its side. It was bigger, odder, more outlandish. Yet there was nothing egotistical about that massive piece of rose quartz, which was sturdier than marble and whose thinner edges might allow a hint of light to pass through.

So this is where it ended, I told myself. There were bald patches on the ground, where the flow of visitors had worn away the grass. In the dappled shade I could hear the distant sound of car doors slamming and something like rushing water. Sometimes you are inhabited by things that you cannot explain. I had been thinking about Waldo for so long that his life now seemed to overlap my own, and I found myself stubbornly resisting the idea of an ending. *Nothing is dead*, he had written. I thought of the fire that had burned in his study every single day of his adult life, whose final heap of ashes had been reverently shoveled into his grave. I thought of the fire that had swallowed up the scene of his childhood—the apocalyptic aftermath, the scattered bricks and blackened timbers. I thought of my own father, too, who was alive when I wrote the first sentences of this book and who is gone as I write the last ones. If you could somehow run the footage of the Great Boston Fire in reverse, could you make the place whole again? If I read this book backward, will my father be there to greet me on the first page? These are fantasies, I know. Dreams of circularity, just like Waldo had, where beginning and end touch each other like two points on a hoop. But what of my own nearness to those who are supposedly vanished, consumed bit by bit by the conflagration of their own living? I don't know what to make of it. I walk back down to the bottom of the hill. There the oldest slabs—the sepulchers of the fathers—are just barely visible above the grass, and the black cars and silvery SUVs are idling in the sunshine, and I remind myself of the lesson I should have figured out in the first place, which is that nothing here is ever gone.

ACKNOWLEDGMENTS

This book took longer to write than planned, for reasons that would require another book to explain. I was lucky to have stalwart friends who urged me on whenever I started to flag, and my thanks are due to Kerry Fried, Mark Stein, Mike Sittenfeld, Gerald Lee, Peter Wortmann, David Hajdu, Virginia Pye, Lisa Zeidner, Bonnie Nadzam, Adrian Kneubuhl, Guinevere Turner, Daniel Smith, Dasha Kiper, Arthur Krystal, David Shields, Anthony Heilbut, Vivian Gornick, Lore Segal, Rochelle Gurstein, Jane Kupersmidt, Elizabeth Kunreuther, Phil Campbell, Jessica Bruder, Ted Conover, David Hafter, Mark and Amy Jockers, Carlin Romano, Karen Baicker, Spencer Finch, Tom Rayfiel, Carol Baker, Andrea Clearfield, Julia Klein, Daniel Asa Rose, Chris Hallman, Matthew von Unwerth, David Galef, Scott Sherman, and many others too numerous to mention. For roadside assistance when I needed it most: Art Winslow, Robert Sullivan, Stephen Koch.

I am indebted to my agent, Chris Calhoun, who suggested that I write this book in the first place, then stuck with it through thick and thin. Anne Savarese did me the honor of acquiring the book for Princeton, and I'm grateful to her and the entire team, including James Collier, Jaden Young, Leah Caldwell, Karl Spurzem, Erin Suydam, Alyssa Sanford and Carmen Jimenez. For their assistance in helping me run down the visual material in this book, I'd like to thank Anke Voss at the Concord Free Public Library, Jessica Desany Ganong at the Concord Museum, and Mary C. Haegert at the Houghton Library.

For the gift of time, space, quiet, and congeniality, I must thank Yaddo, MacDowell, and the Virginia Center for the Creative Arts. The Trustees of Reservations and the curatorial staff of the Old Manse were kind enough to allow me to work in the upstairs study for a few days, where perhaps I inhaled a few stray molecules of Emersonian oxygen. I am also indebted to Fred Whiting for inviting me to share part of this book at the University of Alabama in Tuscaloosa—as Emerson himself learned, there is nothing like a living, breathing audience to help you clean up your act.

Michael Maglaras and Terri Templeton generously invited me to collaborate on their Emerson documentary *Give All To Love*. They also helped me over a rough patch in the book's history, when their enthusiasm meant the world to me.

My family kept this project alive when it was running on fumes, which was pretty often. I couldn't have asked for more supportive siblings than Doug Marcus and Lisa Ross-Marcus, not to mention my excellent in-laws: Diane Mehta, Jerry Sticker, Lee Ross. Iris Marcus let me read a portion of the final chapter to her and told me to keep going. Last but not least, I would never have written a single word of this book without Nina Mehta. She welcomed a third wheel named Emerson into our lives for almost a decade, read everything I wrote, told me which jokes to take out and which facts to put in, and gave me the benefit of her brilliance and steadfastness and love. I can never thank her enough.

SELECTED BIBLIOGRAPHY

Ahlstrom, Sydney E. *A Religious History of the American People*. 2nd ed. New Haven, CT: Yale University Press, 2004.

Albee, John. *Remembrances of Emerson*. New York: Robert Grier Cooke, 1903.

Alcott, Bronson. *Concord Days*. Reprint of 1872 edition. Carlisle, MA: Applewood Books.

Allen, Gay Wilson. *Waldo Emerson*. New York: Penguin Books, 1982.

Baggini, Julian. *The Great Guide: What David Hume Can Teach Us about Being Human and Living Well*. Princeton, NJ: Princeton University Press, 2021.

Baier, Annette C. *The Pursuits of Philosophy: An Introduction to the Life and Thought of David Hume*. Cambridge, MA: Harvard University Press, 2011.

Ballou, Maturin M. "Gossip about Eating." *Ballou's Dollar Monthly Magazine* 3, no. 1 (January 1856).

Barish, Evelyn. *Emerson: The Roots of Prophecy*. Princeton, NJ: Princeton University Press, 1989.

Bauder, Bob. "Get Used to It: They Stink and Are Staying." *Beaver County Times*, October 1, 2008.

Bercovitch, Sacvan, ed. *The Cambridge History of American Literature*. 2 vols. Cambridge, UK: Cambridge University Press, 1994–1995.

Blight, David W. *Frederick Douglass: Prophet of Freedom*. New York: Simon & Schuster Paperbacks, 2018.

Bloom, Harold. *The American Canon: Literary Genius from Emerson to Pynchon*, edited and introduced by David Mikics. New York: The Library of America, 2019.

Blumenbach, Johann Friedrich. *The Anthropological Treatises of Johann Friedrich Blumenbach*, translated and edited from the Latin, German, and French originals by Thomas Bendyshe. London: Longman, Green, 1865.

Bode, Carl. *The American Lyceum: Town Meeting of the Mind*. Carbondale: Southern Illinois University Press, 1956.

Bok, Edward. *The Americanization of Edward Bok: The Autobiography of a Dutch Boy Fifty Years After*. New York: Charles Scribner's Sons, 1923

Bosco, Ronald A., ed. *The Complete Sermons of Ralph Waldo Emerson*. 3 vols. Columbia: University of Missouri Press, 1991.

Bosco, Ronald A., and Joel Myerson, eds. *Emerson in His Own Time: A Biographical Chronicle of His Life, Drawn from Recollections, Interviews, and Memoirs by Family, Friends, and Associates*. Iowa City: University of Iowa Press, 2003.

———. *The Emerson Brothers: A Fraternal Biography in Letters*. New York: Oxford University Press, 2006.

———. *The Selected Lectures of Ralph Waldo Emerson*. Athens, GA: University of Georgia Press, 2005.

Brown, David S. *The Last American Aristocrat: The Brilliant Life and Improbable Education of Henry Adams*. New York: Scribner, 2020.

Buell, Lawrence. *Emerson*. Cambridge, MA: Harvard University Press, 2003.

———. *Literary Transcendentalism: Style and Vision in the American Renaissance*. Ithaca, NY: Cornell University Press, 1973.

Burnett, Gene M. *Florida's Past: People and Events That Shaped the State*. Sarasota, FL: Pineapple Press, 1996.

Bynum, Helen. *Spitting Blood: The History of Tuberculosis*. New York: Oxford University Press, 2012.

Cabot, James Elliot. *A Memoir of Ralph Waldo Emerson*. 2 vols. Boston and New York: Houghton Mifflin Company/The Riverside Press, 1887.

Cameron, Kenneth Walter, ed. *The Massachusetts Lyceum during the American Renaissance: Materials for the Study of the Oral Tradition in American Letters*. Hartford, CT: Transcendental Books, 1969.

Carpenter, Delores Bird, ed. *The Selected Letters of Lidian Jackson Emerson*. Columbia: University of Missouri Press, 1987.

Castillo, Susan. "'The Best of Nations'?, Race and Imperial Destinies in Emerson's *English Traits*." *The Yearbook of English Studies* 34, Nineteenth-Century Travel Writing (2004): 100–111.

Charvat, William. *Emerson's American Lecture Engagements: A Chronological List*. New York: New York Public Library, 1961.

———. *Literary Publishing in America: 1790–1850*. Amherst: University of Massachusetts Press, 1959.

Chiasson, Dan. "Ecstasy of Influence." *New Yorker*, September 7, 2015.

Choi, Charles Q. "Peace of Mind: Near-Death Experiences Now Found to Have Scientific Explanations." *Scientific American*, September 12, 2011.

Clarkson, Thomas. *The History of the Rise, Progress, and Accomplishment of the Abolition of the African Slave Trade by the British Parliament*. London: Longman, Hurst, Rees and Orme, 1808.

Cole, Phyllis. *Mary Moody Emerson and the Origins of Transcendentalism*. New York: Oxford University Press, 1998.

Crain, Caleb. *American Sympathy: Men, Friendship, and Literature in the New Nation*. New Haven, CT: Yale University Press, 2001.

Cushman, Stephen. "When Lincoln Met Emerson." *Journal of the Civil War Era* 3, no. 2 (June 2013): 163–183.

Daniels, Bruce C. *Puritans at Play: Leisure and Recreation in Colonial New England*. New York: St. Martin's Griffin, 1995.

De Tocqueville, Alexis. *Democracy in America*. Vol. 1. New York: Vintage Books, 1954.

Delavan, Edward C., ed. *Temperance Essays and Selections from Different Authors*. New York: The National Temperance Society and Publication House, 1866.

Delbanco, Andrew. *The War Before the War: Fugitive Slaves and the Struggle for America's Soul from the Revolution to the Civil War*. New York: Penguin Books, 2019.

Delbanco, Andrew, and Alan Heimert, eds. *The Puritans in America: A Narrative Anthology.* Cambridge, MA: Harvard University Press, 2009.

Downes, Alan J. "The Legendary Visit of Emerson to Tallahassee." *Florida Historical Quarterly* 34, no. 4 (April 1956): 334–338.

DuBois, Ellen Carol. *Suffrage: Women's Long Battle for the Vote.* New York: Simon & Schuster, 2020.

Dubos, René, and Jean Dubos. *The White Plague: Tuberculosis, Man, and Society.* New Brunswick, NJ: Rutgers University Press, 1996.

Eichhorn, Johann Gottfried. *Introduction to the Study of the Old Testament: A Fragment Translated by George Tilly Gollop, Esq.* London: Printed for private circulation by Spottiswoode and Co., 1888.

Ellis, Allison. "Ralph Waldo Emerson's Grave Encounters." *Longform*, March 25, 2021.

Emerson, Edward Waldo. *A Chaplain of the Revolution.* Massachusetts Historical Society, 1922.

———. *Emerson in Concord: A Memoir.* Boston and New York: Houghton Mifflin Company / The Riverside Press, 1888 and 1916.

Emerson, Ralph Waldo. *The Annotated Emerson*, edited by David Mikics and with a foreword by Phillip Lopate. Cambridge, MA: The Belknap Press of Harvard University Press, 2021.

———. *Collected Poems and Translations.* New York: The Library of America, 1994.

———. *The Complete Works of Ralph Waldo Emerson, Volume X: Lectures and Biographical Sketches*, with a biographical introduction and notes by Edward Waldo Emerson. Boston and New York: Houghton, Mifflin and Company, 1904.

———. *Essays & Lectures.* New York: The Library of America, 1983.

———. *Journals of Ralph Waldo Emerson*, edited by Edward Waldo Emerson and Waldo Emerson Forbes. 10 vols. Boston: Houghton Mifflin Company, 1909–1914.

———. *The Journals and Miscellaneous Notebooks of Ralph Waldo Emerson*, edited by William H. Gilman, Alfred R. Ferguson, George P. Clark, and Merrell R. Davis. 16 vols. Cambridge, MA: Harvard University Press, 1960–1982.

———. *Letters and Social Aims*, edited by James Elliot Cabot. Boston: Houghton, Mifflin and Company, 1892.

———. *The Method of Nature: An Oration Delivered Before the Society of the Adelphi, In Waterville College, In Maine, August 11, 1841.* Boston: Samuel G. Simpkins, 1841.

———. *Natural History of Intellect and Other Papers*, edited by James Elliot Cabot. Boston and New York: Houghton, Mifflin and Company, 1893.

Emerson, Ellen Tucker. *The Letters of Ellen Tucker Emerson*, edited by Edith E. W. Gregg, with a foreword by Gay Wilson Allen. 2 vols. Kent, OH: Kent State University Press, 1982.

———. *The Life of Lidian Jackson Emerson*, edited and with an introduction by Delores Bird Carpenter. East Lansing: Michigan State University Press, 1992.

Emerson, Ralph Waldo, W. H. Channing, and J. F. Clark., eds. *Memoirs of Margaret Fuller Ossoli.* 2 vols. Boston: Roberts Brothers, 1884.

Feltenstein, Rosalie. "Mary Moody Emerson: The Gadfly of Concord." *American Quarterly* 5, no. 3 (Autumn 1953): 231–246.

Frothingham, Octavius. *Transcendentalism in New England: A History.* New York: Harper Torchbooks, 1959.

Gale, Robert L., ed. *A Henry Wadsworth Longfellow Companion.* Westport, CT: Greenwood Press, 2003.

Gerber, John C. "Emerson and the Political Economists." *New England Quarterly* 22, no. 3 (September 1949): 336–357.

Golden, Mason. "Emerson-Exemplar: Friedrich Nietzsche's Emerson Marginalia." *Journal of Nietzsche Studies* 44, no. 3 (2013): 398–408.

Goodman, Russell B. "East-West Philosophy in Nineteenth-Century America: Emerson and Hinduism." *Journal of the History of Ideas* 51, no. 4 (October–December 1990): 625–645.

Gougeon, Len. *Virtue's Hero: Emerson, Antislavery, and Reform.* Athens: University of Georgia Press, 2010.

Gougeon, Len, and Joel Myerson, eds. *Emerson's Antislavery Writings.* New Haven, CT: Yale University Press, 1995.

Gould, Stephen Jay. "The Geometer of Race." *Discover*, November 1, 1994.

Gozlan, Marc. "A Stopwatch on the Brain's Perception of Time." *The Guardian*, January 1, 2013.

Grayling, A. C. *The History of Philosophy.* New York: Penguin Books, 2020.

Gregg, Edith W., ed. *One First Love: The Letters of Ellen Louisa Tucker to Ralph Waldo Emerson.* Cambridge, MA: Harvard University Press, 1962.

Gross, Robert A. *The Transcendentalists and Their World.* New York: Farrar, Straus and Giroux, 2021.

Gura, Philip F. *American Transcendentalism.* New York: Hill and Wang, 2007.

———. *Jonathan Edwards: America's Evangelical.* New York: Hill and Wang, 2005.

Habich, Robert D. "Emerson's Reluctant Foe: Andrews Norton and the Transcendental Controversy." *New England Quarterly* 65, no. 2 (June 1992): 208–237.

Hanlon, Christopher. *Emerson's Memory Loss: Originality, Communality, and the Late Style.* New York: Oxford University Press, 2018.

Hanna, Alfred Jackson. *A Prince in Their Midst: The Adventurous Life of Achille Murat on the American Frontier.* Norman: University of Oklahoma Press, 1946.

Harvey, Karen. "Pleasantly Pink, the Murat House Is a Fine Example of Colonial Architecture." *St. Augustine Record*, September 9, 2018.

Haskins, David Greene. *Ralph Waldo Emerson: His Maternal Ancestors.* Boston: Cupples, Upham and Company, 1887.

Hawthorne, Nathaniel. *Mosses from an Old Manse.* New York: Modern Library Classics, 2003.

Hedin, Benjamin, ed. *Studio A: The Bob Dylan Reader.* New York: W. W. Norton, 2004.

Heywood, Colin. *A History of Childhood: Children and Childhood in the West from Medieval to Modern Times.* Cambridge, UK: Polity Press, 2001.

Higginson, Thomas Wentworth. *Cheerful Yesterdays.* Cambridge: The Riverside Press, 1898.

Hoeltje, Hubert H. "Emerson at Davenport." *The Palimpsest*, September 1, 1926.

James, Henry. *The American Essays of Henry James*, edited and introduced by Leon Edel. Princeton, NJ: Princeton University Press, 1956.

Jarvis, Edward. *Traditions & Reminiscences of Concord, Massachusetts, 1779–1878*, edited by Sarah Chapin and introduced by Robert A. Gross. Amherst: University of Massachusetts Press, 1993.

Jenkins, Sally. "Olympian Kerri Walsh Jennings Forgot What Top Athletes Know: Discipline Leads to Freedom." *Washington Post*, September 9, 2020.

Kazin, Alfred. *God and the American Writer*. New York: Alfred A. Knopf, 1997.

Knox, Robert. *The Races of Men: A Fragment*. Philadelphia: Lea & Blanchard, 1850.

Koch, Daniel. *Ralph Waldo Emerson in Europe: Class, Race and Revolution in the Making of an American Thinker*. New York: Bloomsbury Academic, 2012.

Kosman, Aryeh. "Beauty and the Good: Situating the *Kalon*." *Classical Philology* 105, no. 4 (October 2010): 341–357.

Krekelberg, Bart. "Saccadic Suppression." *Current Biology* 20, no. 5 (March 2010).

Lane, Marcia. "Ralph Waldo Emerson Came to St. Augustine for Treatment." *St. Augustine Record*, October 23, 2011.

Lehrer, Jonah. "The Self Illusion: An Interview with Bruce Hood." *Wired*, May 25, 2012.

Lemire, Elise. *Black Walden: Slavery and Its Aftermath in Concord, Massachusetts*. Philadelphia: University of Pennsylvania Press, 2009.

Leonard, George J. *Into the Light of Things*. Chicago: University of Chicago Press, 1994.

Lepore, Jill. *These Truths: A History of the United States*. New York: W. W. Norton, 2018.

Marshall, Megan. *Margaret Fuller: A New American Life*. New York: Houghton Mifflin Harcourt, 2013.

Mason, Shena. "Birmingham: The Toyshop of Europe." *West Midlands History*, April 2012.

Matteson, John. *Eden's Outcasts: The Story of Louisa May Alcott and Her Father*. New York: W. W. Norton, 2007.

Matthiessen, F. O. *American Renaissance: Art and Expression in the Age of Emerson and Whitman*. New York: Oxford University Press, 1968.

McAleer, John. *Ralph Waldo Emerson: Days of Encounter*. Boston: Little, Brown and Company, 1984.

McCarraher, Eugene. *The Enchantments of Mammon: How Capitalism Became the Religion of Modernity*. Cambridge: Belknap Press of Harvard University Press, 2019.

McClelland, Edward. "How Reagan's Childhood Home Gave Up on Reaganism." *Politico*, November 23, 2019.

McPherson, James M. *Battle Cry of Freedom: The Civil War Era*. New York: Oxford University Press, 1988.

Menand, Louis. *The Metaphysical Club: A Story of Ideas in America*. New York: Farrar, Straus and Giroux, 2001.

Miller, Perry, ed. *The Transcendentalists: An Anthology*. Cambridge, MA: Harvard University Press, 1950.

Morgan, Edmund. *Visible Saints: The History of a Puritan Idea*. Ithaca, NY: Cornell University Press, 1975.

Mott, Wesley T. *"The Strains of Eloquence": Emerson and His Sermons*. University Park: The Pennsylvania State University Press, 1989.

Myerson, Joel, ed. *A Historical Guide to Ralph Waldo Emerson*. New York: Oxford University Press, 2000.

———. *Ralph Waldo Emerson: A Descriptive Bibliography*. Pittsburgh, PA: University of Pittsburgh Press, 1982.

———. *The Selected Letters of Ralph Waldo Emerson*. New York: Columbia University Press, 1997.

Myerson, Joel, Sandra Harbert Petrulionis, and Laura Dassow Walls, eds. *The Oxford Handbook of Transcendentalism*. New York: Oxford University Press, 2010.

Newfield, Christopher. *The Emerson Effect: Individualism and Submission in America*. Chicago: University of Chicago Press, 1996.

Nickels, Cameron C. "'Roaring Ralph': Emerson as Lecturer." *New England Quarterly* 76, no. 1 (March 2003): 116–123.

Noll, Mark A. *America's God: From Jonathan Edwards to Abraham Lincoln*. New York: Oxford University Press, 2005.

Norton, Andrews. *A Discourse on the Latest Form of Infidelity*. Cambridge, MA: John Owen, 1839.

Norton, Charles Eliot, ed. *The Correspondence of Thomas Carlyle and Ralph Waldo Emerson*. 2 vols. Boston: James R. Osgood and Company, 1883.

Ozick, Cynthia. "She: Portrait of the Essay as a Warm Body." *The Atlantic*, September 1998.

Packer, Barbara. "Experience." In *Bloom's Modern Critical Interpretations: Emerson's Essays*. New York: Chelsea House, 2006.

———. *The Transcendentalists*. Athens, GA: University of Georgia Press, 2007.

Painter, Nell Irvin. *The History of White People*. New York: W. W. Norton & Company, 2010.

Petrulionis, Sandra Harbert. "'Swelling that Great Tide of Humanity': The Concord, Massachusetts Female Anti-Slavery Society." *New England Quarterly* 74, no. 3 (September 2001): 385–418.

Pickering, Henry Goddard. *Nathaniel Goddard: A Boston Merchant*. Cambridge, MA: The Riverside Press, 1906.

Porte, Joel. *Representative Man: Ralph Waldo Emerson in His Time*. New York: Columbia University Press, 1988.

Porte, Joel, ed. *Emerson in His Journals*. Cambridge, MA: The Belknap Press of Harvard University Press, 1982.

Reynolds, David S. *Beneath the American Renaissance: The Subversive Imagination in the Age of Emerson and Melville*. Cambridge, MA: Harvard University Press, 1988.

———. *Walt Whitman's America: A Cultural Biography*. New York: Alfred A. Knopf, 1995.

Richardson, Robert D. *Emerson: The Mind on Fire*. Berkeley: University of California Press, 1995.

———. *First We Read, Then We Write: Emerson on the Creative Process*. Iowa City: University of Iowa Press, 2015.

———. *William James: In the Maelstrom of American Modernism*. New York: Houghton Mifflin, 2006.

Rotundo, E. Anthony. *American Manhood: Transformations in Masculinity from the Revolution to the Modern Era*. New York: Basic Books, 1993.

Rusk, Ralph L. *The Life of Ralph Waldo Emerson*. New York: Columbia University Press, 1949.

Rusk, Ralph L., and Eleanor Tilton, eds. *The Letters of Ralph Waldo Emerson*. 8 vols. New York and London: Columbia University Press.

Russell, Bertrand. *The History of Western Philosophy*. New York: Simon & Schuster, 1945.

Sattelmeyer, Robert. "'When He Became My Enemy': Emerson and Thoreau, 1848–49." *New England Quarterly* 62, no. 2 (June 1989): 187–204.

Schlett, James. *A Not Too Greatly Changed Eden: The Story of the Philosophers' Camp in the Adirondacks*. Ithaca, NY: Cornell University Press, 2015.

Scudder, Townsend. *Concord: An American Town*. Boston: Little, Brown, 1947.

Seitz, Don C. *Artemus Ward: A Biography and Bibliography*. New York: Harper & Brothers, 1919.

Shenk, David. *The Forgetting: Alzheimer's: A Portrait of an Epidemic*. New York: Anchor Books, 2003.

Shrader, Erin. "Pilgrim's Pride." *Strings*, November 28, 2010.

Simmons, Nancy Craig, ed. *The Selected Letters of Mary Moody Emerson*. Athens: University of Georgia Press, 1993.

Sinha, Manisha. *The Slave's Cause: A History of Abolition*. New Haven, CT: Yale University Press, 2016.

Slavov, Matias. "No Absolute Time." *Aeon*, August 21, 2019.

Spector, Nicole. "Why Our Sense of Time Speeds Up as We Age—and How to Slow It Down." NBC News, November 26, 2018.

Spencer, Herbert. *An Autobiography*. Vol. 1. Boston: D. Appleton & Company, 1904.

Steegmuller, Francis. *Flaubert and Madame Bovary*. New York: NYRB Classics, 2004.

Strauch, Carl F. "Hatred's Swift Repulsions: Emerson, Margaret Fuller, and Others." *Studies in Romanticism* 7, no. 2 (1968): 65–103.

Sullivan, Robert. *The Thoreau You Don't Know*. New York: HarperCollins, 2009.

Thome, James, and Joseph Kimball. *Emancipation in the West Indies: A Six Month's Tour in Antigua, Barbadoes, and Jamaica, in the Year 1837*. New York: The American Anti-Slavery Society, 1838.

Thoreau, Henry David. *The Illustrated Walden: Thoreau Bicentennial Edition*, with an introduction by Bradford Torrey. New York: Tarcher Perigee, 2016.

———. *The Journal: 1837–1861*, edited by Damion Searls with a preface by John R. Stilgoe. New York: NYRB Classics, 2009.

Tomlin, Gregory. "Americans Still Believe Jesus Rose from the Dead." *Christian Examiner*, March 25, 2016.

Updike, John. "The Revealed and Concealed: An Extraordinary Love Token Holds the Key to America's Ambivalent Relationship with the Nude." *Art and Antiques* 15 (February 1993).

Von Cromphout, Gustaff. *Emerson's Ethics*. Columbia: University of Missouri Press, 1999.

Walls, Laura Dassow. *Emerson's Life in Science: The Culture of Truth*. Ithaca, NY: Cornell University Press, 2003.

———. *Henry David Thoreau: A Life*. Chicago: University of Chicago Press, 2017.

Wilentz, Sean. "Lincoln's Rowdy America." *New York Review of Books*, April 29, 2021.

Wilson, John B. "Darwin and the Transcendentalists." *Journal of the History of Ideas* 26, no. 2 (1965): 286–290.

Wortham, Thomas. "Did Emerson Blackball Frederick Douglass from Membership in the Town and Country Club?" *New England Quarterly* 65, no. 2 (June 1992): 295–298.

Wright, A. Augustus, ed. *Who's Who in the Lyceum*. Philadelphia: Pearson Brothers, 1906.

NOTES

Abbreviations for Frequently Cited Titles

I will give the full title the first time I cite these works, then revert to the abbreviations.

CAB: James Elliot Cabot. *A Memoir of Ralph Waldo Emerson*. 2 vols. Boston and New York: Houghton Mifflin Company/The Riverside Press, 1887.

EAW: *Emerson's Antislavery Writings*, edited by Len Gougeon and Joel Myerson. New Haven: Yale University Press, 1995.

E&L: *Ralph Waldo Emerson: Essays & Lectures*. New York: The Library of America, 1983.

EIHOT: *Emerson in His Own Time: A Biographical Chronicle of His Life, Drawn from Recollections, Interviews, and Memoirs by Family, Friends, and Associates*, edited by Ronald A. Bosco and Joel Myerson. Iowa City: University of Iowa Press, 2003.

JMN: *The Journals and Miscellaneous Notebooks of Ralph Waldo Emerson*, edited by William H. Gilman, Alfred R. Ferguson, George P. Clark, and Merrell R. Davis. 16 vols. Cambridge, MA: Harvard University Press, 1960–1982.

JRWE: *Journals of Ralph Waldo Emerson*, edited by Edward Waldo Emerson and Waldo Emerson Forbes. 10 vols. Boston: Houghton Mifflin Company, 1909–1914.

LRWE: *The Letters of Ralph Waldo Emerson*, edited by Ralph L. Rusk and Eleanor Tilton. 8 vols. New York and London: Columbia University Press.

OFL: *One First Love: The Letters of Ellen Louisa Tucker to Ralph Waldo Emerson*, edited by Edith W. Gregg. Cambridge, MA: Harvard University Press, 1962.

RLR: Ralph L. Rusk. *The Life of Ralph Waldo Emerson*. New York: Columbia University Press, 1949.

ROP: Evelyn Barish. *Emerson: The Roots of Prophecy*. Princeton, NJ: Princeton University Press, 1989.

TEB: *The Emerson Brothers: A Fraternal Biography in Letters*, edited by Ronald A. Bosco and Joel Myerson. New York: Oxford University Press, 2006.

TLLJE: Ellen Tucker Emerson. *The Life of Lidian Jackson Emerson*, edited and with an introduction by Delores Bird Carpenter. East Lansing: Michigan State University Press, 1992.

Introduction

Page

2   **Our day of dependence:** Emerson, *Ralph Waldo Emerson: Essays & Lectures*, 53.

2   **Like seven generations:** Five prior generations of Emersons had served the Congregational Church in Massachusetts and Maine: Joseph Emerson (1620–1680), Edward Emerson (who seems to have been a deacon rather than a minister) (1670–1743), Joseph Emerson (1700–1767), William Emerson (1743–1776), and William Emerson II (1769–1811). But intermarriage with other New England clans extended the lineage back another couple of generations. For example, when the first Joseph Emerson married Elizabeth Bulkeley, in 1665, the Emersons could add to their extended family tree the bride's father, Edward Bulkeley (before 1614–1696), and her grandfather, Peter Bulkeley (1583–1659), both pillars of the New England clergy. See Edward Waldo Emerson, *Emerson in Concord: A Memoir*, 2–4. See also Cabot, *A Memoir of Ralph Waldo Emerson*, 1: 7–12. Robert D. Richardson supplies a useful genealogical chart in *Emerson: The Mind on Fire*, 574–575.

3   **It was now the faith of well-heeled Bostonians:** See Ahlstrom, *A Religious History of the American People*, 400–402. Ahlstrom quotes but also attempts to debunk the famous jab at Unitarian parochialism, which held that the faith was devoted to "the fatherhood of God, the brotherhood of man, and the neighborhood of Boston." Mark A. Noll, meanwhile, calls the Unitarians the "elite bearers of reason, good taste, benevolence, and refined sensibility in Boston," in *America's God: From Jonathan Edwards to Abraham Lincoln*, 287. Margaret Fuller, observing a Unitarian congregation in its heyday, took a snarkier approach: "That crowd of upturned faces, with their look of unintelligent complacency!" For Fuller's remark, see Miller, *The Transcendentalists: An Anthology*, 8. None of this should be taken to impugn modern-day Unitarian Universalism with its long, honorable, and progressive tradition. What matters here is the institution in RWE's day and his allergic reaction to it, which is amply documented. For a good discussion of his deep debt to Unitarianism, see David Robinson, *Apostle of Culture: Emerson as Preacher and Lecturer* (Philadelphia: University of Pennsylvania Press, 1982), 11–47.

3   **explosive rise of evangelical Christianity:** Ahlstrom, *A Religious History of the American People*, 415–455.

3   **enjoy an original relation:** *E&L*, 7.

3   **to abhor and abominate R. W. Emerson:** Convers Francis, quoted in Bosco and Myerson, *Emerson in His Own Time: A Biographical Chronicle of His Life, Drawn from Recollections, Interviews, and Memoirs by Family, Friends, and Associates*, 6.

3   **The maker of a sentence:** *JMN*, 4: 363.

4   **A foolish consistency** ("Self-Reliance," *E&L*, 265), **An institution is the lengthened shadow** ("Self-Reliance," *E&L*, 267), **In every work of genius** ("Self-Reliance," *E&L*, 259), **There is a kind of contempt** (*Nature*, *E&L*, 11), **Every spirit builds itself a house** (*Nature*, *E&L*, 48), **A strange process too** ("The American Scholar," *E&L*, 60), **I pack my trunk, embrace my friends** ("Self-Reliance," *E&L*, 278), **Tobacco, coffee, alcohol, hashish, prussic acid** ("Old Age," *Society and Solitude: Twelve Chapters*, 319), **Crossing a bare common** (*Nature*, *E&L*, 10).

4   **infinitely repellent particle:** See Norton, *The Correspondence of Thomas Carlyle and Ralph Waldo Emerson 1834–1872*, 1: 161.

5   **anecdotes of the intellect:** Ralph Waldo Emerson, *Natural History of Intellect and Other Papers*, 10.

6   **desperate for titillation:** Daniels, *Puritans at Play: Leisure and Recreation in Colonial New England*, 31, 130.

6   **The climate and people:** *JMN*, 14: 27–28.

6   **undivided attention of his audience:** *EIHOT*, xv.

6   **spiritual prism though which we see:** *EIHOT*, 34.

7   **Man is an analogist:** *E&L*, 21.

7   **first surviving letters:** The letter is reproduced on two unpaginated leaves at the beginning of Rusk and Tilton, *The Letters of Ralph Waldo Emerson*, 1: unpaginated.

7   **the infinitude of the private man:** *JMN*, 7: 342.

9   **corpse-cold Unitarianism of Brattle Street:** *JMN*, 9: 381.

9   **in no sense a uniform group:** Packer, *The Transcendentalists*, 46–61, with Brownson's quote about Christ as "the prophet of the workingmen" on 53.

10   **They favored empiricists like John Locke:** For the pervasive influence of Locke, and some of the challenges eventually posed to his empiricism, see Packer, 7–31. Philip Gura discusses some of those early challenges in *American Transcendentalism*, 46–68. Writing about James Marsh, who attempted to close the gap between Unitarian rationalism and a more emotive version of faith, he notes how empiricism had at least temporarily triumphed over imagination in the generation preceding RWE's: "With the Enlightenment's emphasis on science and reason . . . and particularly after the seminal work of Locke in epistemology and Isaac Newton in physics, such poetic use of nature was subordinated to scientific understanding." See also "The Eighteenth-Century Enlightenment," in Grayling, *The History of Philosophy*, 268–278.

11   **Idealism as it appears in 1842:** *E&L*, 193.

11   **forever forming associations:** De Tocqueville, *Democracy in America*, vol. 1.

12   **The whole creation is made of hooks and eyes:** *E&L*, 1056.

12   **an Olympic gold medalist:** Jenkins, "Olympian Kerri Walsh Jennings Forgot What Top Athletes Know: Discipline Leads to Freedom."

14   **our faith in ecstasy consists with total inexperience:** *E&L*, 1061.

14   **"I am glad," he wrote, "to the brink of fear.":** *E&L*, 10.

15   **the pith of each man's genius:** *E&L*, 472.

16   **The last year has forced us all:** Gougeon and Myerson, *Emerson's Antislavery Writings*, 53.

16   **an 1839 letter to Margaret Fuller:** *LRWE*, 2: 197–198.

17   **A man is the faculty of reporting:** *E&L*, 747.

Chapter 1. Finding a Voice

Page

18   **towering figure of Peter Bulkeley:** Delbanco and Heimert, *The Puritans in America: A Narrative Anthology*, 117–120.

19   **"Come back, you graceless sinner, come back!":** *CAB*, 1: 10.

19   **There was Daniel Bliss:** Bliss's enthusiasm for the Awakening—he held outdoor revival meetings and preached sermons that left listeners "weeping on each other's shoulders"—was not shared by all of his parishioners. Some preferred the more staid Congregationalist approach. At one point twenty of these malcontents broke away to form a separate flock under the leadership of John Whiting, Bliss's predecessor and a man with what one local historian described as a "fondness for the flowing bowl" (i.e., a drunk). This splinter group met, perhaps unhelpfully, at the Black Horse Tavern. *CAB*, 1: 12. See also McAleer, *Ralph Waldo Emerson: Days of Encounter*, 188–189. Leslie Perrin Wilson mentions the Black Horse Tavern splinter group in "History of First Parish," at https://firstparish.org/wp/about/history-of-first-parish/.

19   **There is an inner satisfaction:** James, "Emerson," *The American Essays of Henry James*, 54.

19   **an amazing figure in her own right:** Cole, *Mary Moody Emerson and the Origins of Transcendentalism*, 7–12.

19   **It is my own humor to despise:** *JMN*, 2: 316.

20   **runt of the litter:** Allen, *Waldo Emerson*, 39.

20   **I find myself often idle:** *JMN*, 1: 39.

20   **a sense of vocation:** Barish, *Emerson: The Roots of Prophecy*, 61.

20   **the powerhouse of theological studies:** Bosco and Myerson, *The Emerson Brothers: A Fraternal Biography in Letters*, 75–77.

20   **merely theological use:** Eichhorn, *Introduction to the Study of the Old Testament: A Fragment Translated by George Tilly Gollop, Esq.*, ix.

21   **altogether human:** Eichhorn, *Introduction to the Study of the Old Testament*, 39.

21   **rubbed William the wrong way:** *TEB*, 94–95.

21   **theological complexities in private:** Allen, *Waldo Emerson*, 79. See also *TEB*, 111–112.

22   **purgatory of his mother's bedroom:** In a letter to Mary Moody Emerson, RWE referred to an impending teaching gig as a "fatal *Gehenna*." See *LRWE*, 1: 103. Details about his dreary spell as a schoolmaster can be found in Rusk, *The Life of Ralph Waldo Emerson*, 90–91, and also in Allen, *Waldo Emerson*, 60.

22   **grown up without sisters:** Allen, *Waldo Emerson*, 60.

22   **mock-Poetic Junior:** *LRWE*, 1: 89.

22   **dedicate my time, my talents:** For this quote and the self-analysis that follows, see *JMN*, 2: 237–242.

22   **the first step and degree toward knowledge:** John Locke, *An Essay Concerning Human Understanding*, 25th ed. (London: Printed for Thomas Tegg, 73, Cheapside, 1825), 85.

23   **deep and high theology:** Simmons, *The Selected Letters of Mary Moody Emerson*, 193. RWE quotes the letter, and cleans up his aunt's eccentric spelling and punctuation (as I too have done), in *JMN*, 2: 383.

24   **hardly any formal curriculum:** Allen, *Waldo Emerson*, 83–84.

24   **Waldo's health failed:** *ROP*, 177–186.

24   **lost the use of:** *RLR*, 110–111.

24   **unconscious but positive distaste:** *RLR*, 112. Rusk is not the only scholar to speculate along these lines. In *The American Canon: Literary Genius from Emerson to Pynchon*, Harold Bloom refers to "an episode of hysterical blindness during [RWE's] college years," 19.

Yet Barish's deep dive into RWE's health crisis (see above) pretty much trashes the notion of merely psychosomatic blindness or lameness.

24   **resumed his career:** Allen, *Waldo Emerson*, 84–85.

25   **I come with mended eyes:** *JMN*, 2: 340.

25   **Every defect:** *JMN*, 2: 341.

25   **dangerous empire:** *JMN*, 3: 9.

25   **significant testimonies:** RWE's letter to Mary Moody Emerson is quoted in Emerson, *Journals of Ralph Waldo Emerson*, 1: 85.

26   **fledgling minister:** Allen, *Waldo Emerson*, 93.

26   **I was born cold:** *JRWE*, 2: 123.

26   **the secret self:** *RLR*, 117.

26   **what we wish:** Allen, *Waldo Emerson*, 93.

26   **feared consumption:** Allen, *Waldo Emerson*, 93–94. See also *ROP*, 177–184, which quotes the assessment made by Oliver Wendell Holmes that half of the entire population of Boston was or would be infected with tuberculosis.

27   **sketched out in a letter:** *LRWE*, 1: 176.

27   **the most lethal ailment:** Dubos and Dubos, *The White Plague: Tuberculosis, Man, and Society*, 5–10, 69–73, 194–195. The quote from the 1768 edition of the Encyclopedia Britannica, along with much useful information about the disease, can be found at https://www.britannica.com/science/tuberculosis/Tuberculosis-through-history.

27   **bound for Charleston, South Carolina:** Allen, *Waldo Emerson*, 94–97.

28   **no scythe in St. Augustine:** *JMN*, 3: 115.

28   **Americans live on their offices:** *LRWE*, 1: 189.

28   **Sometimes I sail:** *LRWE*, 1: 189.

29   **glad tidings of great joy:** *JMN*, 3: 117.

29   **barking of dogs:** *JMN*, 3: 115.

29   **at the pink boardinghouse:** The tiny pink cottage, at the corner of St. George Street and Bridge Street, is still standing. Its former owner, the Daytona Beach Museum of Arts and Sciences, turned it into shrine, but not to Emerson—the place is known as Prince Murat's House. It is now part of a boutique hotel. See Lane, "Ralph Waldo Emerson Came to St. Augustine for Treatment," and Harvey, "Pleasantly Pink, the Murat House Is a Fine Example of Colonial Architecture."

29   **nephew of Napoleon:** Allen, *Waldo Emerson*, 99–100.

30   **wash his feet:** Hanna, *A Prince in Their Midst: The Adventurous Life of Achille Murat on the American Frontier*, 128–130. See also Burnett, *Florida's Past: People and Events That Shaped the State*, 102–104.

30   **owl, crow, alligator:** Ballou, "Gossip about Eating," 395.

30   **an atheist:** Allen, *Waldo Emerson*, 100.

30   **low-level infatuation:** *JRWE*, 2: 185.

30   **A new event is added:** *JMN*, 3: 77.

30   **broached some of these topics:** A brief entry in one of RWE's pocket notebooks (*JMN*, 3: 115) suggests that he visited Tallahassee with Murat prior to leaving St. Augustine. He describes the city itself, chosen as the state capital just three years before, as an eyesore, overrun with "public officers, land speculators & desperadoes." He also notes a very

specific detail: "I saw here a marble copy of Canova's bust of Queen Caroline of Naples"—
i.e., Murat's mother. Yet in a letter (*LRWE*, 1: 94) to his brother William, RWE says that
he "did not become much acquainted with [Murat] till we went to sea." The biographer
in me badly wants the trip to have occurred. It's all too easy to imagine the young men
camped out for the night under the stars, with a crackling fire of pine twigs and Murat in
the nude, debating the existence of God. It seems implausible, though, that Waldo would
have undertaken a three-day horseback trip through rough terrain without ever mention-
ing it in his journal or correspondence. So we've got one of those spectral episodes, which
can neither be proved nor disproved, stuck in a biographical limbo.

Which never kept anyone from trying. In a scholarly fusillade called "The Legendary
Visit of Emerson to Tallahassee," *The Florida Historical Quarterly* 34 (April 1956): 334–
338, Alan J. Downes dismisses the very notion of such a trip as absurd. RWE was a tubercular wreck, insists Downes, "physically incapable (according to his own belief at
least) of enduring the exhausting two-hundred-mile ride over a wheel-rut trail, sleeping
in the open in the middle of winter—even a Florida winter." Instead RWE must have heard
those scattered details about Tallahassee from Murat himself, during their fireside chats
at the pink house. Now, this is certainly possible. The one weak spot in the argument is
Downes's comment about the faux-Canova bust: "Obviously [RWE] saw it—could only
have seen it—exhibited by Murat at their hotel." Really? Murat, hacking his way through
the pine thickets and mangrove swamps of Florida, was carting around a seventy-pound
marble likeness of his mother?

To further complicate matters, there is an article about the Murat household in a
Kentucky newspaper ("Napoleon Achille Murat, Florida's Citizen Prince," *Kentucky New
Era*, August 16, 1913, p. 4), which leans heavily on the misty-eyed reminiscences of his
formerly enslaved house staff. In a description of Bellevue, the widow's retirement cottage near Tallahassee, the author notes the presence of a "marble bust of Caroline
Bonaparte." So did the bust usually reside in Tallahassee, or did Murat just park it there
after one of his many road trips?

I don't know what to make of an additional, crazily recursive detail. We have a miniature mystery here, which hinges on whether RWE saw a fake Antonio Canova sculpture
in the pink house in 1827. As it happens, the pink house was then owned by—Antonio
Canova. No, not the celebrated sculptor, but an American-born gentleman listed in the
Florida Census of 1850 as a farmer (see http://files.usgwarchives.net/fl/stjohns/census
/1850/pg0202a.txt). Of course it's a coincidence. But Waldo's conception of the universe
as a self-correcting entity and metaphorical echo chamber makes the notion of coincidence less, well, *coincidental*.

31   **a near neighborhood:** *JMN*, 3: 76.

31   **relations more intimate:** See RWE's letter to Mary Moody Emerson, *JRWE*, 2: 180.

Chapter 2. The Lives of Others

Page

33   **former King of Spain:** Allen, *Waldo Emerson*, 100.

33   **absolute notion of truth:** Murat's letter is quoted in *JRWE*, 2: 188.

34   **The night is fine:** *JMN*, 3: 78.

34   **jot better or worse:** *LRWE*, 1: 198.

34   **puking energetically:** Allen, *Waldo Emerson*, 103.

34   **blue wonder:** *JRWE*, 2: 208.

35   **pleasurable element:** RWE's letter to Mary Moody Emerson, *JRWE*, 2: 108.

35   **much of the summer:** Allen, *Waldo Emerson*, 105.

35   **enrich himself:** *RLR*, 123.

36   **tender eye of the mind:** Mott, *"The Strains of Eloquence": Emerson and His Sermons*, 20.

36   **eyes are not so strong:** *LRWE*, 1: 208.

36   **most popular preacher:** *RLR*, 125.

36   **ever saw him run:** Allen, *Waldo Emerson*, 108.

37   **mere soap bubbles:** *RLR*, 126.

37   **force of my love:** *LRWE*, 1: 214.

37   **his hero Daniel Webster:** E. Anthony Rotundo discusses Webster's intimate epistolary style, and the more fluid male friendships of the era, in *American Manhood: Transformations in Masculinity from the Revolution to the Modern Era*, 75–91. Caleb Crain also touches on Webster's endearments in *American Sympathy: Men, Friendship, and Literature in the New Nation*, 33.

37   **nervous collapse:** *RLR*, 127.

38   **not touch a book:** *LRWE*, 1: 235.

38   **eyes screwed shut:** Allen, *Waldo Emerson*, 117, including the "maniac" quote in the next paragraph.

38   **mixture of silliness:** *JMN*, 3: 137.

39   **the whole of August:** *LRWE*, 1: 238.

39   **His present idea:** *LRWE*, 1: 244.

39   **ancient and respectable church:** *JMN*, 3: 49.

40   **mightiest engine:** Mott, *"The Strains of Eloquence": Emerson and His Sermons*, 49.

40   **all for the Arminians:** Ahlstrom, *A Religious History of the American People*, 404, 438–439. See also Thomas H. McCall and Keith D. Stanglin, *After Arminius: A Historical Introduction to Arminian Theology* (New York: Oxford University Press, 2020), 23.

40   **Our life looks trivial:** *E&L*, 472.

41   **David Hume's severing of cause from effect:** *ROP*, 99–115. See also Julian Baggini, *The Great Guide: What David Hume Can Teach Us about Being Human and Living Well* (Princeton, NJ: Princeton University Press, 2021), 67–69. For a more specific discussion of Hume's notion of time, see Slavov, "No Absolute Time," *Aeon*, August 21, 2019.

41   **We wake and find ourselves:** *E&L*, 471.

42   **One recent study:** Gozlan, "A Stopwatch on the Brain's Perception of Time."

Chapter 3. One First Love

Page

43   **strange face:** *JMN*, 1: 22.

43   **Indian doctrine:** *JMN*, 1: 39.

43   **grant me still:** Crain, 155.

44   **lifelong affection:** *JMN*, 1: 44.

44   **nasty appetite:** *JMN*, 1: 133.

44   **Cotton Mather, who had published:** Daniels, *Puritans at Play*, 31, 130.

44   **ending up like King James I:** *JMN*, 2: 227–228, 241.

44   **fabulous description of a friend:** *LRWE*, 1: 225.

45   **It is hard to yoke:** *JMN*, 3: 146–147.

45   **from his humble beginnings:** Allen, *Waldo Emerson*, 111. See also the bibliographic notes in "Kent / Thomas Families (Concord, NH), Family Papers 1679–1888," New Hampshire Historical Society, https://www.nhhistory.org/finding_aids/finding_aids/Kent-Thomas_Family_Papers.pdf.

45   **easily imagined:** Gregg, *One First Love: The Letters of Ellen Louisa Tucker to Ralph Waldo Emerson*, 4.

46   **very beautiful by universal consent:** *LRWE*, 1: 256.

46   **raised blood a week ago:** *LRWE*, 1: 259.

46   **too lovely to live long:** Allen, *Waldo Emerson*, 127–129.

47   **taken sick in the old way:** *RLR*, 141.

47   **miniature portraits:** At least one of Waldo's biographers calls her "Goodrich," which was indeed the name she used, at least professionally. But she was born Sarah Goodridge, and her celebrated miniatures, which made her rich enough to live on Boston's Beacon Hill, captured many distinguished Americans of the day. While her miniatures of Waldo and Ellen seem fairly generic, her portrait of Gilbert Stuart is a small, vivid marvel. Then there is "Beauty Revealed," an image of her own bared breasts that she executed in watercolor on ivory and gave to her lover Daniel Webster, last seen in this narrative being violently seasick off the Baltimore coast. Erotic, mysterious, riveting, this suggestive gift prompted an Emersonian roundelay from breast-fancier John Updike in 1993: "They float ownerless and glow like ghosts, or angels, in some transcendental realm whose dark atmosphere lurks in the corners." See Updike, "The Revealed and Concealed: An Extraordinary Love Token Holds the Key to America's Ambivalent Relationship with the Nude," 71.

47   **reposing among its fellows:** *OFL*, 4.

47   **Dear Ellen, many a golden year:** RWE, *Collected Poems and Translations*, 322.

48   **Do you remember what I told you:** *OFL*, 27.

48   **I write a thousand letters:** *OFL*, 57.

50   **kind though annoying arm:** *OFL*, 59.

50   **I am inclined to believe:** *OFL*, 67.

50   **instant of meeting:** *OFL*, 75–76.

51   **According to Thomas Sydenham:** Bynum, *Spitting Blood*, 49–67.

51   **beauty of virginity:** *LRWE*, 1: 276.

51   **Ellen is sometimes smart:** *LRWE*, 1: 277.

51   **It is rather delightful to me:** *OFL*, 86–87.

52   **we botanize & criticize:** *LRWE*, 1: 283.

52   **that big house full of women:** Allen, *Waldo Emerson*, 144.

52   **eventually asked to leave:** *RLR*, 140.

53   **Fair land of bonnets:** *OFL*, 121.

53   **red wheezers:** *LRWE*, 1: 296.

53   **fair unruffled Friends:** *OFL*, 128.

53   **blue & shrill:** *RLR*, 145.

53   **thermometer at 6:** *OFL*, 135.

53   **A drop of vermeil:** *OFL*, 138.

54   **golden feather quivering:** *OFL*, 161.

54   **Is it possible for religious principle:** *JMN*, 3: 205–206.

54   **All history is an epitaph:** Bosco, *The Complete Sermons of Ralph Waldo Emerson*, vol. 3, 68–69.

55   **She saw no reason:** Allen, *Waldo Emerson*, 166–167.

55   **to heaven to see, to know:** *JMN*, 3: 226.

55   **This miserable apathy, I know:** *JMN*, 3: 227.

56   **pleasanter to me:** *LRWE*, 1: 319.

Chapter 4. The Shining Apparition

Page

57   **still contested:** See "Views About Global Warming Among U.S. Subgroups," which shows that 65 percent of U.S. adults believe climate change to be the result of pollution and human activities, leaving 35 percent who believe otherwise. The data is part of a 2021 Gallup poll: https://news.gallup.com/poll/355427/americans-concerned-global-warming.aspx.

58   **poplars and Balm-of-Gilead trees:** RWE mentions both in "May-Day," and I assume the poem reflects his own experience, in RWE, *Collected Poems and Translations*, 131.

59   **Truly in the fields:** *JMN*, 5: 179.

59   **calm and genial as a bridegroom:** *JMN*, 4: 199.

59   **not a form so grotesque:** *JMN*, 4: 199–200.

60   **using the cinders:** *E&L*, 24.

60   **There are no books:** *JMN*, 4: 82.

61   **I like my book about Nature:** *JMN*, 3: 196–197.

61   **My little book is nearly done:** *LRWE*, 2: 26.

61   **I send you the little book:** Norton, *The Correspondence of Thomas Carlyle and Ralph Waldo Emerson*, 1: 98–99. Carlyle's reply, quoted below, appears on 112.

62   **as in a disturbed dream:** Miller, *The Transcendentalists*, 173–174.

62   **albeit one whose first printing:** In a letter written to his brother William on October 23, 1836, RWE notes that *Nature* had sold five hundred copies in the first few weeks after publication, "which for a book purely literary or philosophical is a good deliverance" (*LRWE*, 2: 42). But in *Ralph Waldo Emerson: A Bibliography* (Pittsburgh: University of Pittsburgh Press, 1982), the editor, Joel Myerson, notes that according to the accounts of RWE's publisher, James Munroe and Company, there were still twenty-three copies of the original press run of *Nature* in stock as of January 17, 1844. See 15.

62   **Our age is retrospective:** *E&L*, 7.

63   **Standing on the bare ground:** *E&L*, 10.

64   **I conceive a man:** Emerson, *The Method of Nature*, 18.

64   **Dopamine makes us hallucinate:** Choi, "Peace of Mind: Near-Death Experiences Now Found to Have Scientific Explanations," *Scientific American*, September 12, 2011.

64   **Nature always wears the colors of the spirit:** *E&L*, 11.

64   **The eye is closed:** *JMN*, 5: 152. The following quote ("He sympathized wonderfully . . .") appears on 155.

66   **lose my human nature:** *JMN*, 5: 155.

66   **The misery of man appears:** *E&L*, 12.

66   **the mark God sets upon virtue:** *E&L*, 16.

66   **long philosophical tradition:** For Dionysius and the longstanding equation of beauty and virtue, see Kosman, "Beauty and the Good: Situating the *Kalon*," *Classical Philology*, 341–357. The conception of the universe as an "exfoliation of God's will" is discussed in Gura, *Jonathan Edwards: America's Evangelical*, 39–40. For RWE's description of natural beauty as a "herald," see *E&L*, 19.

67   **Words are signs of natural facts:** *E&L*, 20.

67   **There seems to be a necessity in spirit:** *E&L*, 25.

68   **Each particle is a microcosm:** *E&L*, 30.

68   **His earlier remark about the physical world:** For an excellent summary of Berkeley's thought, see Grayling, *The History of Philosophy*, 226–232, which includes Berkeley's remark about substance and spirit. The same author discusses Kant's quasi-immaterialism, 261–264, as does Bertrand Russell, rather sardonically at times, in *The History of Western Philosophy* (New York: Simon & Schuster, 1945), 706–710. For Emerson's immersion in Eastern thought, see Buell, *Emerson*, 169–180, and Goodman, "East-West Philosophy in Nineteenth-Century America: Emerson and Hinduism," 625–628.

68   **noble doubt:** *E&L*, 32–34.

69   **If it only deny the existence of matter:** *E&L*, 41.

69   **puts it forth through us:** *E&L*, 41.

69   **he starts in his slumber:** *E&L*, 46.

70   **Every spirit builds itself a house:** *E&L*, 48–49.

71   **dry run for the ecstasy:** *JMN*, 5: 168, 171.

72   **These were marmorated stink bugs:** Bauder, "Get Used to It: They Stink and Are Staying." See also this press release from Penn State: https://www.psu.edu/news/agricultural -sciences/story/stink-bugs-are-move-across-pennsylvania/.

72   **It makes me feel so tired:** Emerson, "Immortality," *Letters and Social Aims*, 314.

Chapter 5. Ruin and Resurrection

Page

74   **This is my body:** *E&L*, 1130.

74   **Christ's body is not in this sacrament:** See https://www.christianhistoryinstitute.org /study/module/aquinas-eucharist/.

74   **his position in chalk:** Ahlstrom, *A Religious History of the American People*, 76.

75   **Religion will become purer and truer:** Elisabeth Hurth, "William and Ralph Waldo Emerson and the Problem of the Lord's Supper: The Influence of German 'Historical Speculators,'" *Church History* 62 (June 1993): 196.

75   **many Unitarians continued:** Packer, *The Transcendentalists*, 7–9.

75   **denial of the existence of God:** Gura, *American Transcendentalism*, 110.

76   **Cold cold:** *JMN*, 4: 27.

77   **cantankerous guest:** Cole, *Mary Moody Emerson and the Origins of Transcendentalism*, 143.

77   **withering Lucifer doctrine of pantheism:** Cole, *Mary Moody Emerson and the Origins of Transcendentalism*, 215–216. The entire letter can be read in Simmons, *The Selected Letters of Mary Moody Emerson*, 313–315.

78   **administer the ordinance:** Allen, *Waldo Emerson*, 188.

78   **brow and shaggy lid:** Cole, *Mary Moody Emerson and the Origins of Transcendentalism*, 218.

80   **My solitude opens far distant views:** Simmons, *The Selected Letters of Mary Moody Emerson*, 318.

80   **There is nothing to be said:** *JMN*, 4: 27.

80   **The good of going into the mountains:** *JMN*, 4: 29–30.

81   **I will remember that after the ruin:** *JMN*, 4: 34.

81   **For the kingdom of God is not meat and drink:** *E&L*, 1129.

81   **reality, its boundless charity, its deep interior life:** *E&L*, 1139.

81   **The sensation caused by this step:** *EIHOT*, 97.

82   **The Lord's Supper was simply his excuse:** See, for example, Allen, *Waldo Emerson*, 187 and Richardson, *Emerson: The Mind on Fire*, 126.

82   **great principle of Undulation in nature:** *E&L*, 62.

83   **a cup of Madeira wine:** It seems that all sorts of wine-like substances and adulterated plonk were used for Holy Communion, but a well-heeled congregation like Waldo's would almost certainly have availed itself of Madeira. See Delavan, *Temperance Essays and Selections from Different Authors*, 69–70. In Edward Jarvis's *Traditions & Reminiscences of Concord, Massachusetts, 1779–1878*, 12, the author recalls Ezra Ripley's practice at Concord's First Parish Unitarian Church: "Dr. Ripley preferred Lisbon wine to Malaga, which was used in the communion service." But both of these were, like Madeira, fortified wines with a distinct sweetness to them.

83   **In this refulgent summer:** *E&L*, 75.

83   **There is an argument to be made:** Porte, *Representative Man: Ralph Waldo Emerson in His Time*, 131–133.

84   **The child amidst his baubles:** *E&L*, 76.

84   **Truly speaking, it is not instruction:** *E&L*, 79.

84   **The very word Miracle:** *E&L*, 80.

84   **the state of society is one in which the members:** *E&L*, 54.

84   **sorely tempted me to say:** *E&L*, 84–85.

85   **he runs through a rogue's gallery of atheistic enablers:** For Spinoza, see Grayling, *The History of Philosophy*, 211. Norton's critique of Schleiermacher can be found in his *A Discourse on the Latest Form of Infidelity*, 27–52, while his remark about the German theologian's name appears on 35.

85   **A man of talents has only to be obscure:** Norton, *A Discourse on the Latest Form of Infidelity*, 18.

86   **whip that naughty heretic:** Allen, *Waldo Emerson*, 323.

86   **vulgar mistake of dreaming that I am persecuted:** *JMN*, 7: 139–140.

86   **The ocean is a large drop:** *JMN*, 5: 169.

86   **This turns out to be a bad habit:** Habich, "Emerson's Reluctant Foe: Andrews Norton and the Transcendental Controversy," 208 fn.

87   **miscellaneous crowd:** Habich, 210.

87   **According to a 2021 survey:** https://research.lifeway.com/2020/09/08/americans-hold-complex-conflicting-religious-beliefs-according-to-latest-state-of-theology-study/.

87   **present generation will see Unitarianism:** Noll, *America's God*, 161–162.

87   **Just one glance at the scorecard:** Noll, *America's God*, 165–167.

87   **monstrous absurdities of the Methodists:** *JMN*, 3: 115.

88   **was bewailed as the age of Introversion:** *E&L*, 67

88   **Unitarian graft on the Methodist stock:** Reynolds, *Beneath the American Renaissance: The Subversive Imagination in the Age of Emerson and Melville*, 19–21.

88   **I have seen so many educated preachers:** Ahlstrom, *A Religious History of the American People*, 438.

88   **Any preacher who is a real preacher:** Hedin, *Studio A: The Bob Dylan Reader*, 149.

89   **over the 16,800 congregants:** Craig Hlavaty, "10 Years Ago: Lakewood Church, Joel Osteen Move into Houston's Compaq Center," *Houston Chronicle*, July 14, 2015.

90   **A strange process too:** *E&L*, 60.

Chapter 6. A Conjunction of Two Planets

Page

92   **There is one birth:** *JMN*, 3: 227.

92   **She didn't know a human being:** Ellen Tucker Emerson, *The Life of Lidian Jackson Emerson*, 43.

93   **divine rage and enthusiasm:** *E&L*, 327.

93   **as though a curtain:** *TLLJE*, 41.

94   **I have not deserved this!:** Allen, *Waldo Emerson*, 239.

94   **Home again from Plymouth:** *JMN*, 5: 14.

94   **deep and tender respect:** Allen, *Waldo Emerson*, 240.

95   **She was telling him something:** *TLLJE*, 48.

95   **very sober joy:** *LRWE*, 1: 436.

95   **the winds of heaven blow away:** *LRWE*, 1: 435.

95   **externally as well as internally:** Carpenter, *The Selected Letters of Lidian Jackson Emerson*, 25.

95   **sort of Sybil for wisdom:** *RLR*, 214–215. The same passage includes the Peabody, Clarke, and Fuller quotes.

96   **weaving them of golden-rod:** *RLR*, 223.

97   **Every society of Heaven:** Carpenter, *The Selected Letters of Lidian Jackson Emerson*, 28–30.

97   **heyday of the blood:** *E&L*, 327–328.

98   **In the noon and the afternoon of life:** *E&L*, 330–332.

99   **which is the deification of persons:** *E&L*, 334–335.

99   **I hope you will be able to find:** *RLR*, 213.

100   **For me to measure my influence:** *LRWE*, 1: 437.

100   **Mr E. thinks we must not deny ourselves bells:** Carpenter, *The Selected Letters of Lidian Jackson Emerson*, 32–36.

100   **Sometimes it comes over me:** Carpenter, *The Selected Letters of Lidian Jackson Emerson*, 40.

100   **conjunction of the two planets:** *RLR*, 225.

101   **One apostle thought all men:** *E&L*, 591.

101   **miseries of her hens:** *TLLJE*, 68.

102   **They are a bitter, sterile people:** *JMN*, 14: 166.

102   **They dined & took tea with [me] one day:** Carpenter, *The Selected Letters of Lidian Jackson Emerson*, 60–61.

102   **She was always more sensitive:** *TLLJE*, 83. Early in their marriage, at least, Lidian attributed to RWE her own hypersensitivity to human pain, noting in an 1839 letter, "I scarce ever saw the person upon whom the suffering of *others* made so real an impression." Carpenter, *The Selected Letters of Lidian Jackson Emerson*, 82.

103   **deeply cerebral husband:** Lidian's role as a reality check extended beyond RWE to the other Transcendentalists. On a Sunday evening in January 1843, for example, she hosted a meeting of "the wise men and their admirers" to discuss various schemes for utopian living. As she recounted in a letter to her husband, there would evidently be "no more hats or shoes—and I fear on reconsideration of the decision we must give up even linen and dress as did the sinless inhabitants of Eden." She goes on to report another priceless exchange with Bronson Alcott. "Mr Alcott proposes to abridge labour and live a life of ease and independence by certain ways of proceeding, one of which is to make your own chairs in a form of simple elegance and cover them with linen of your own spinning and weaving. When I said with a sigh that I would rather be excused from washing those linen covers[,] preferring to dust common painted chairs, he said 'O but we will contrive a way to simplify *washing*.'" Carpenter, *The Selected Letters of Lidian Jackson Emerson*, 114.

103   **There were communal prayers every morning:** Carpenter, *The Selected Letters of Lidian Jackson Emerson*, 35, 40.

103   **All despondency is founded on delusion:** Carpenter, *The Selected Letters of Lidian Jackson Emerson*, 82.

104   **that blessed nearness to God:** *TLLJE*, 83.

104   **Once I was in love:** *JMN*, 7: 372.

104   **brave ties of affection:** *JMN*, 7: 368.

105   **The writer ought not to be married:** *JMN*, 7: 420.

105   **married & chained through the eternity:** *JMN*, 7: 532.

105   **infinitude of the private man:** *JMN*, 7: 342.

105   **droll dream, whereat I ghastly laughed:** *JMN*, 7: 544.

106   **call this a wet dream:** Porte, *Representative Man*, 226.

106   **sadness was the ground-colour of her life:** *TLLJE*, 84.

107   **How intensely his heart yearns:** Carpenter, *The Selected Letters of Lidian Jackson Emerson*, 106.

108   **magnify our lost treasure to extort:** *LRWE*, 3: 9.

108   **cannot be a stove:** *LRWE*, 4: 33.

108   **Save me from magnificent souls:** *JMN*, 8: 242.

108   **Loathe and shun the sick:** *TLLJE*, 82–83.

109   **most excellent Jewish youth:** Carpenter, *The Selected Letters of Lidian Jackson Emerson*, 314.

109   **very charming of course to such as St. Ellen:** Carpenter, *The Selected Letters of Lidian Jackson Emerson*, 290.

Chapter 7. The Age of the First Person Singular

Page

110   **recreation to my other studies:** Harold Bayley, *The Tragedy of Sir Francis Bacon* (New York: Haskell House Publishers, 1970), 249.

110   **whose Augustan elegance:** See Buell, *Literary Transcendentalism*, 94–95. Granted, I am simplifying the history of the Anglo-American essay here, but in his introduction to *The Oxford Book of Essays* (Oxford and New York: Oxford University Press, 1991), John Gross proposes a similar genealogy, from Montaigne to Bacon to Steele and Addison (the latter of whom he calls "the father of the English essay") to Hazlitt and Lamb, xix–xxi. For a more capacious view of the form, stretching from ancient Babylonia to (basically) the day before yesterday, see John D'Agata's *The Lost Origins of the Essay* (St. Paul, Minnesota: Graywolf Press, 2009).

110   **leaned heavily on:** For Steele's launch of *The Tatler* and its initial flavor, see George S. Marr, *The Periodical Essayists of the Eighteenth Century* (London: James Clarke & Co., 1923), 22–23. When RWE praises the "excellence of Virtue" (*JMN*, 1: 331) in Addison's essays, he does not mention him by name, but by citing both *The Tatler* (half Addison's work) and *The Spectator* (mostly Addison's work), he seems to be inclining in that direction. He does mention Addison by name elsewhere in the same volume (*JMN*, 1: 14).

111   **Here I sit and read and write:** Norton, *The Correspondence of Thomas Carlyle and Ralph Waldo Emerson*, 1: 161.

111   **I am a rocket manufacturer:** *JMN*, 7: 245.

111   **The preacher should be a poet:** *JMN*, 5: 471.

112   **the hum of perpetual noticing:** Ozick, "She: Portrait of the Essay as a Warm Body."

112   **It makes no difference:** *EIHOT*, 59–60.

113   **cut-and-paste job:** RWE's cousin David Greene Haskins recounts a similar methodology: "The thoughts were entered one after another in the Thought Book, without regard to their connection. Whenever he wished to write an essay or a lecture, he made free use of the Thought Book, selecting and adapting such thoughts as seemed fitting, and stringing them together as a child strings beads on a thread. After this explanation, I was at no loss to account for the mosaic character of much of his writing." Haskins, *Ralph Waldo Emerson: His Maternal Ancestors*, 117.

113   **a string of mosaics or a house built of medals:** *The Essential Margaret Fuller*, edited by Michael Croland (Mineola, NY: Dover Publications, 2019), 207.

114   **elsewhere called the "age of the first person singular.":** *JMN*, 3: 70.

114   **To believe your own thought:** *E&L*, 259.

114   **voice of God himself which speaks to you:** Emerson, *The Annotated Emerson*, 160.

114   **"In every work of genius," he writes:** *E&L*, 259.

114   **There is a time in every man's education:** *E&L*, 259–260, including "Trust thyself."

115   **Society everywhere is in conspiracy:** *E&L*, 261.

115   **I shun father and mother:** *E&L*, 262.

115   **brethren, or sisters, or father:** *TAE*, 164.

115   **natives to turn piano-forte legs:** Charles Dickens, *Bleak House*, edited with notes and an introduction by Nicola Bradbury, preface by Terry Eagleton (London: Penguin Books, 1996), 57.

115   **I tell thee, thou foolish philanthropist:** *E&L*, 262–263.

116   **Madmen, madwomen, men with beards:** Emerson, *The Complete Works of Ralph Waldo Emerson, Volume X: Lectures and Biographical Sketches*, 374.

116   **For nonconformity:** *E&L*, 264–265.

117   **A foolish consistency is the hobgoblin of little minds:** *E&L*, 265.

117   **consciousness caught on a narrative treadmill:** For this, and for saccadic suppression below, see Lehrer, "The Self Illusion: An Interview with Bruce Hood."

118   **bound their eyes with one handkerchief or another:** *E&L*, 264.

118   **A character is like an acrostic:** *E&L*, 266.

118   **prospect or retrospect:** *E&L*, 266.

118   **quarry a new self:** Stephen E. Whicher produced a book-length exploration of this polarity in his classic *Freedom and Fate: An Inner Life of Ralph Waldo Emerson* (Philadelphia: University of Pennsylvania Press, 1953).

119   **Every true man is a cause, a country, and an age:** *E&L*, 267.

119   **At home I dream that at Naples:** *E&L*, 278.

120   **The moment you putty and plaster:** Richardson, *First We Read, Then We Write: Emerson on the Creative Process*, 36.

121   **each member of the community:** Alexis De Tocqueville, *Democracy in America* (New York: Everyman's Library, 1994), 98. De Tocqueville's use of the word is the very first citation supplied by *The Oxford English Dictionary*, vol. 5 (Oxford: Oxford University Press, 1978), 224.

121   **entirely within the solitude:** De Tocqueville, *Democracy in America*, 99.

121   **the vice of the age:** *JMN*, 8: 249.

121   **caricature of Romanticism:** Wesley T. Mott, "Emerson and Individualism," in *A Historical Guide to Ralph Waldo Emerson*, edited by Joel Myerson, 79.

122   **antinomian disdain for established religion:** Allen, *Waldo Emerson*, 379.

122   **Never have I felt so much at home:** Golden, "Emerson-Exemplar: Friedrich Nietzsche's Emerson Marginalia," 398.

122   **no reprint was required until 1849:** Myerson, *Ralph Waldo Emerson: A Descriptive Bibliography*, 16–17.

122   **Boston retained a certain cachet:** Charvat, *Literary Publishing in America: 1790–1850*, 17–20.

122   **Waldo's arrangement with Munroe was perilously close:** Myerson, *Ralph Waldo Emerson: A Descriptive Bibliography*, xvi, 43.

123   **I print them at my own risk:** *LRWE*, 3: 308.

123   **not press the sale of the book at a distance:** *LRWE*, 3: 350–351.

123 **a vanity & vexation:** *LRWE*, 3: 248.

123 **was astonished to learn:** Charvat, *Literary Publishing in America*, 30.

123 **The literacy rate in the United States:** By 1840, the literacy rate for adult whites (an important caveat) was 90 percent. There were also regional variations, with New England in the lead and the South bringing up the rear. Mary Kelley, "Educating the Citizenry: Introduction," *A History of the Book in America, Volume 2: An Extensive Republic: Print, Culture, and Society in the New Nation, 1790–1840*, edited by Robert A. Gross and Mary Kelley (Chapel Hill, NC: The University of North Carolina Press, 2010), 269–270. The total population for that same year can be found at: https://www.census.gov/history/www/through_the_decades/fast_facts/1840_fast_facts.html

124 **producing small-batch product for the neighborhood:** Charvat, *Literary Publishing in America*, 30–31.

124 **1,573 printing offices:** Jack Larkin, "'Printing Is Something Every Village Has In It': Rural Printing and Publishing," in Gross and Kelley, *A History of the Book in America: Volume 2*, 127.

124 **Henry Wadsworth Longfellow, for example, claimed to have sold:** Matthiessen, *American Renaissance: Art and Expression in the Age of Emerson and Whitman*, x.

124 **a New York newspaper paid him:** James Marcus, "The Public Poet," *New Yorker*, June 8 and 15, 2020, 75.

124 **magnificent absurdities:** Gale, *A Henry Wadsworth Longfellow Companion*, 69.

124 **I have always one foremost satisfaction in reading:** Myerson, *The Selected Letters of Ralph Waldo Emerson*, 386.

Chapter 8. Beautiful Enemies

Page

126 **always seemed to be on stilts:** Fuller's remark is cited in Bryan F. LeBeau, *Frederic Henry Hedge, Nineteenth Century American Transcendentalist: Intellectually Radical, Ecclesiastically Conservative* (Eugene OR: Pickwick Publishers, 1985), 177.

126 **We have a great deal more kindness:** *E&L*, 341.

126 **A new person is to me a great event:** *E&L*, 343.

127 **Is it not that the soul puts forth friends:** *E&L*, 344.

127 **Every man alone is sincere:** *E&L*, 347.

127 **Better be a nettle in the side:** *E&L*, 350.

128 **Friendship is something very delicious:** *JMN*, 3: 25.

128 **We walk alone in the world:** *E&L*, 352.

129 **His idol had already made some effort:** Walls, *Henry David Thoreau: A Life*, 79.

129 **teased for his green homespun coat:** See Walls, *Henry David Thoreau*, and also James Marcus, "Into the Wild," *Harper's Magazine*, October 2017, 90.

130 **What are you doing now?:** Thoreau, *The Journal: 1837–1861*, 3.

130 **My good Henry Thoreau made this else solitary afternoon:** *JMN*, 5: 453.

131 **I shouldn't know them apart:** *Letters of James Russell Lowell*, vol. 1, edited by Charles Eliot Norton (New York: Harper and Brothers Publishers, 1893), 27.

131 **Also, he liked to dance:** Sullivan, *The Thoreau You Don't Know*, 20.

131   **The highest condition of art:** Thoreau, *The Journal*, 10.

132   **The thoughts seem to me so out of their natural order:** Sullivan, *The Thoreau You Don't Know*, 86.

132   **the porcupine impossibility of contact:** *JMN*, 5: 325.

132   **I work with him as I should not without him:** *LRWE*, 2: 402.

133   **full of noble madness lately:** *LRWE*, 2: 447.

133   **eating the verdigris off pennies:** Steegmuller, *Flaubert and Madame Bovary*, 17.

133   **our American subsoil must be lead or chalk:** *LRWE*, 3: 75. For an excellent overview of the entire friendship, see Sattelmeyer, "'When He Became My Enemy,'" 187–204.

133   **old fault of unlimited contradiction:** Porte, *Emerson in His Journals*, 313.

134   **There was one other with whom I had 'solid seasons,':** Henry David Thoreau, *The Illustrated Walden: Thoreau Bicentennial Edition*, with an introduction by Bradford Torrey (New York: Tarcher Perigee, 2016), 285. Robert D. Richardson's characterization of this as "the saddest sentence" in *Walden* can be found in *Henry Thoreau: A Life of the Mind* (Berkeley, CA: University of California Press, 1988), 299.

135   **ban on "boisterous laughing" and card games:** *EIHOT*, 171.

135   **He very seriously asked me, the other day:** *The Correspondence of Henry D. Thoreau, Volume 1: 1834–1848*, edited by Robert N. Hudspeth (Princeton, NJ: Princeton University Press, 2013), 314. For RWE's letter in response, see 324–325.

136   **While my friend was my friend:** Sattelmeyer, "'When He Became My Enemy,'" 190.

136   **As for taking Thoreau's arm:** *JMN*, 10: 343.

136   **the ice on Walden Pond:** Allen, *Waldo Emerson*, 615.

137   **broken, tender voice:** *TAE*, 470.

137   **born protestant:** *TAE*, 472.

137   **This habit, of course, is a little chilling:** *TAE*, 473.

137   **had been made by Elizabeth Hoar:** *JMN*, 8: 375. Hoar's actual wording, at least as recorded in RWE's journal, was: "I love Henry, but do not like him."

137   **attorney of the indigenous plants:** *TAE*, 480.

138   **Instead of engineering for all America:** *TAE*, 488.

138   **owe us a new world:** *JMN*, 8: 375. Tellingly, RWE jotted down this indictment of "[y]oung men like H. T." right on the heels of Elizabeth Hoar's comment about not liking Thoreau, back in 1843. He then reused portions of the sentence not once, but twice. The first time was in "Experience" (*E&L*, 474), which appeared as part of RWE's second essay collection in 1844. There the sentence signified a more general exasperation at the wasted energies of the young. The second time was in Thoreau's funeral oration, in 1862, at which point RWE dropped the generalizing fog and aimed his shaft directly at his beloved friend. This seems like a sad move on his part. But it also illustrates just how renewable the journals were as a writerly resource—everything in them was available to RWE throughout his entire life, even if the context and actual meaning of a given sentence kept changing.

138   **I ask to be melted:** *TAE*, 491.

138   **What was the name of my best friend?:** *TAE*, 491.

139   **Presented with Margaret instead:** Marshall, *Margaret Fuller: A New American Life*, 6, and also Allen, *Waldo Emerson*, 283.

140   **She made me laugh more than I liked:** Emerson, Channing, and Clark, *Memoirs of Margaret Fuller Ossoli*, 1: 202.

140   **made up [her] mind to be bright and ugly:** Marshall, *Margaret Fuller*, 28.

140   **Her extreme plainness:** Emerson, Channing, and Clark, *Memoirs of Margaret Fuller Ossoli*, 1: 202.

140   **of any American mind:** Marshall, *Margaret Fuller*, 85.

140   **It is always a great refreshment to see:** *LRWE*, 2: 32.

141   **She loves you very much:** Allen, *Waldo Emerson*, 284.

141   **magnetic power over young women:** Marshall, *Margaret Fuller*, 99–105.

141   **Will you commission me to find you a boudoir:** *LRWE*, 2: 169.

141   **We are armed all over with these subtle antagonisms:** *LRWE*, 2: 168.

141   **views more in accordance with the Soul:** Bercovitch, *The Cambridge History of American Literature*, vol. 2, 442.

142   **whom she had come to love:** For some useful thoughts about these high-voltage emotions, see Strauch, "Hatred's Swift Repulsions: Emerson, Margaret Fuller, and Others," 70–71.

142   **two of these women:** See Strauch above and also Jeffrey Steele, "Transcendental Friendship," *The Cambridge Companion to Ralph Waldo Emerson*, edited by Joel Porte and Saundra Morris (Cambridge: Cambridge University Press, 1999), 126–131.

142   **Most of the persons whom I see:** *JMN*, 7: 301. The entire passage is worth reading for the way it nails RWE's sense of emotional privation (his word). It also introduces some ambiguity as to whether the remark about RWE being on stilts was uttered by Fuller or his Concord neighbor Sam Staples.

142   **old arctic habits:** Marshall, *Margaret Fuller*, 180.

143   **I need to be recognized:** Marshall, *Margaret Fuller*, 180–181.

143   **spirits can meet in their pure upper sky:** *JMN*, 7: 512.

143   **Humanity can be divided into three classes:** David Watson, *Margaret Fuller: An American Romantic* (Oxford: Berg Publishers, 1988), 109. Poe's quip is surprisingly hard to run down and Watson backs away from putting it in quotation marks.

143   **meet & treat like foreign states:** *LRWE*, 2: 336.

143   **You would have me love you:** *JMN*, 7: 400.

144   **strange, cold-warm, attractive-repelling conversations with Margaret:** Porte, *Emerson in His Journals*, 264.

144   **When I did go in:** Allen, *Waldo Emerson*, 404.

145   **as we almost always do, on Man and Woman:** Marshall, *Margaret Fuller*, 197.

145   **mutual degradation:** Marshall, *Margaret Fuller*, 192.

145   **I serve you not, if you I follow:** Emerson, *Collected Poems and Translations*, 65–66.

146   **Her attachments, one might say, were chemical:** Emerson, Channing, and Clark, *Memoirs of Margaret Fuller Ossoli*, 2: 217.

146   **Goethe for his essay, beautiful enemies:** Von Cromphout, *Emerson's Ethics*, 110–111.

146   **new and permanent covenants:** Emerson, Channing, and Clark, *Memoirs of Margaret Fuller Ossoli*, 2: 214.

Chapter 9. The Costly Price of Sons and Lovers

Page

147   **It had neither hair nor teeth:** *TLLJE*, 69.

147   **Blessed child!:** *JMN*, 5: 234–235.

148   **I call him so because:** *LRWE*, 2: 48.

148   **the most thrifty of babies:** *LRWE*, 2: 55.

148   **Waldo struggles, leaps; studies manipulation & palmistry:** *LRWE*, 2: 58.

148   **Ah! My darling boy, so lately received:** Porte, *Emerson in His Journals*, 160.

148   **I've been told that the child:** *TLLJE*, 70.

149   **The image vanished at once:** *TLLJE*, 85, 228 (footnote 192), as well as Michael Sims, *The Adventures of Henry Thoreau* (New York: Bloomsbury, 2014), 168–169.

149   **He crawled on the floor and blackened his tiny hands:** *TLLJE*, 73–77.

150   **At the circus:** Edward Waldo Emerson, *Emerson in Concord*, 129.

150   **When he was taken to view the body:** *TLLJE*, 90.

150   **He promised to build his sister:** *JMN*, 8: 165.

150   **He also planned to build:** *TLLJE*, 85.

150   **and by and by a slow smile:** *TLLJE*, 90.

151   **the passage of time is encoded shakily:** Spector, "Why Our Sense of Time Speeds Up as We Age—and How to Slow It Down."

151   **"The pith of each man's genius,":** *E&L*, 472.

151   **Yesterday night at 15 minutes after eight:** *JMN*, 8: 163.

151   **When a family friend, Judge Rockwood Hoar, showed up:** Edward Waldo Emerson, *Emerson in Concord*, 167.

151   **The morning of Friday I woke at 3 o'clock:** *JMN*, 8: 163–164.

152   **Sorrow makes us all children again:** *JMN*, 8: 165.

152   **What shall I say of the Boy?:** *LRWE*, 3: 6–8.

153   **of no more use in their New York than a rainbow:** Allen, *Waldo Emerson*, 399–401, and *LRWE*, 3: 18.

153   **We should not be surprised if he made:** Allen, *Waldo Emerson*, 401.

153   **the best apple on the tree thus far:** *LRWE*, 3: 26.

153   **greet his two-month-old son, the future philosopher William James:** Allen, *Waldo Emerson*, 401. In *William James: In the Maelstrom of American Modernism*, Robert D. Richardson recounts the same incident while wondering whether it really took place, 17.

153   **If I go down to the bottom:** *JMN*, 8: 165–166.

154   **little chieftain:** *JMN*, 8: 451–455.

154   **The South-wind brings:** Emerson, *Collected Poems and Translations*, 117.

155   **rude dirges to my Darling:** *LRWE*, 3: 239.

155   **one of the great elegies in the English language:** Allen, *Waldo Emerson*, 306.

155   **the poem quickly stifles its desperation:** Chiasson, "Ecstasy of Influence."

156   **gave those few words more pathos:** Patrick J. Keane, *Emerson, Romanticism, and Intuitive Reason* (Columbia, MO: University of Missouri Press, 2005), 490 and footnote on 489.

156   **writing down his first scattered notes:** *JMN*, 8: 166 (footnote 63).

156   **I am really trying to end my old endless chapters:** *LRWE*, 3: 252.

157 **Where do we find ourselves?:** *E&L*, 471.

157 **Speak your latent conviction:** *E&L*, 259.

157 **All things swim and glimmer:** *E&L*, 471.

157 **Every ship is a romantic object:** *E&L*, 471–472.

158 **What opium is instilled into all disaster!:** *E&L*, 472.

158 **Souls never touch their objects:** *E&L*, 472.

159 **The suggestion that the loss of his son:** See, for example, Packer, "Experience," in *Bloom's Modern Critical Interpretations: Emerson's Essays*, 84.

159 **On the surface, he viewed his wife's bequest:** *TEB*, 316–320.

159 **Mr. E. had refused all compromise:** *LRWE*, 1: 349.

159 **lingered behind the newer, more transactional one:** *The Oxford English Dictionary*, vol. 3 (Oxford: Oxford University Press, 1978), 299–300.

160 **Waldo used it in this sense:** See *Representative Men* in *E&L*, 637 ("they meet someone so related as to assist their volcanic estate") and "Fate" in *E&L*, 948 ("he knows himself to be a party to his present estate").

160 **Nothing is left to us now but death:** *E&L*, 473.

160 **this occurs in the pituitary gland:** Adam Sprouse-Blum et al., "Understanding Endorphins and Their Importance in Pain Management," *Hawaii Medical Journal* 69, no. 3 (2010): 70–71.

160 **Dream delivers us to dream:** *E&L*, 473.

161 **snaps its rainbow fingers in the face:** Vladimir Nabokov, *The Man from the U.S.S.R. & Other Plays* (New York: Harcourt Brace Jovanovich, 1984), translated and introduced by Dmitri Nabokov, 326.

161 **a certain uniform tune which the revolving barrel:** *E&L*, 474.

161 **Like a bird that alights nowhere:** *E&L*, 477.

161 **What help from these fineries or pedantries?:** *E&L*, 478.

162 **We live amid surfaces, and the true art of life:** *E&L*, 478–479.

162 **find the old world:** *E&L*, 480.

162 **invert the visible world:** His exact prescription in *Nature* (*E&L*, 34) is: "Turn the eyes upside down, by looking at the landscape through your legs, and how agreeable is the picture, though you have seen it any time these twenty years!"

162 **The middle region of our being is the temperate zone:** *E&L*, 480.

163 **eating and drinking and sinning:** *E&L*, 481.

163 **A man is a golden impossibility:** *E&L*, 482.

163 **Grief too will make us idealists:** *E&L*, 473.

164 **the house philosopher of the Unitarians:** Packer, *The Transcendentalists*, 7–13.

164 **But Hume was more rigorous in paring away:** For a good overview of Hume's effect on RWE's thinking, see *ROP*, 99–115. As for the theological implications of severing the link between cause and effect, see Baier, *The Pursuits of Philosophy: An Introduction to the Life and Thought of David Hume*, 141.

164 **does not deny the presence of this table, this chair:** *E&L*, 193–194.

165 **It is very unhappy, but too late to be helped:** *E&L*, 487.

165 **ruins the kingdom of mortal friendship and love:** *E&L*, 487.

165 **It is the secret of the world that all things subsist:** *E&L*, 584.

165 **Oh, that beautiful boy!:** Allen, *Waldo Emerson*, 699.

Chapter 10. The Metaphysician on Tour

Page

166   **A man must ride alternately on the horses:** *E&L*, 966.

166   **This circuit was a relatively recent invention:** Bode, *The American Lyceum: Town Meeting of the Mind*, 8–15. See also Wright, *Who's Who in the Lyceum*, 16–20.

167   **everyone who could stoop or talk:** Wright, *Who's Who in the Lyceum*, 19.

167   **one annual fee shall be two dollars:** Wright, *Who's Who in the Lyceum*, 20–21. For Daniel Webster's supersized fee, see also: https://salemghosts.com/lyceum-hall/.

167   **Holbrook himself helped to found:** Cameron, *The Massachusetts Lyceum during the American Renaissance: Materials for the Study of the Oral Tradition in American Letters*, 26–30.

167   **ninety-eight lectures:** In *Emerson's American Lecture Engagements*, 9, William Charvat pegs the number of lectures in Concord at 126. This includes the ninety-eight delivered at the Lyceum and others delivered elsewhere. For example, RWE spoke on several occasions at the Social Circle, which Robert A. Gross describes as a "self-selecting club of the local elite." See *The Transcendentalists and Their World*, 260.

167   **come for the five dollars offered:** Wright, *Who's Who in the Lyceum*, 25–26.

168   **My pulpit is the Lyceum platform:** Wright, *Who's Who in the Lyceum*, 26.

168   **expenses of rent, lights, doorkeeper:** *JMN*, 6: 242 footnote.

168   **still scheming my lectures:** *LRWE*, 2: 42–43.

168   **everyone from Harvard professors to phrenologists:** Bode, *The American Lyceum*, 49.

168   **I found so much audience for my opinions:** *LRWE*, 2: 60.

169   **delivered a total of 1,469 lectures:** Charvat, *Emerson's American Lecture Engagements*, 7. See also Nickels, "'Roaring Ralph': Emerson as Lecturer," 116–123.

169   **It is because I am so ill a member of society:** *LRWE*, 7: 522–523.

169   **I am no very good economist:** *LRWE*, 2: 64.

170   **A lecture is a new literature:** *JMN*, 7: 224–225.

171   **Artemus Ward, whose goofy dialect stories convulsed:** Seitz, *Artemus Ward: A Biography and Bibliography*, 113–114.

172   **perpendicular coffin:** Ward made his comment in the *Cleveland Plain Dealer*, January 21, 1859. For more on Ward's life and his career at the paper, see: https://pressbooks.ulib.csuohio.edu/cleveland/chapter/ix-artemus-ward-his-town/.

172   **driving imaginary stakes:** Bosco and Myerson, *The Selected Lectures of Ralph Waldo Emerson*, xviii.

172   **I do not recall the subject of that lecture:** *EIHOT*, 227–228.

172   **We do not go to hear what Emerson says:** *EIHOT*, 55.

172   **He was not merely reading:** Bosco and Myerson, *The Selected Lectures*, xvii–ixix.

172   **lets off mental skyrockets:** Bosco and Myerson, *The Selected Lectures*, xvi.

173   **No, I do not oscillate in Emerson's:** *EIHOT*, 35.

173   **high-heeled grammar and three-storied Anglo-Saxon:** *EIHOT*, 50.

173   **Let us call him a fool:** *EIHOT*, 336.

173   **In fact, Kelly made the connection to Old West:** Nickels, "'Roaring Ralph,'" 119–121.

174   **Cut these words and they would bleed:** *Emerson's Literary Criticism*, edited and with a new introduction by Eric W. Carlson (Lincoln: University of Nebraska Press, 1995), 83.

174   **could no more have deciphered, or translated Mr. Ralph's:** Nickels, "'Roaring Ralph,'" 121.

174   **And I understood 'em, too:** Albee, *Remembrances of Emerson*, 14.

175   **I am too closely promised, day by day:** *LRWE*, 4: 534–535.

175   **a great deal of jolting, a great deal of noise:** Charles Dickens, *American Notes / Pictures from Italy / A Child's History of England* (London: Chapman and Hall, 1891), 52.

175   **Railroad iron is a magician's rod:** *E&L*, 213.

175   **I was got by & by into a railroad car:** *JMN*, 14: 20.

176   **The old Father is considered as brought into subjection:** Hoeltje, "Emerson at Davenport," 268.

176   **He treated laconically upon many subjects:** Hoeltje, "Emerson at Davenport," 269–270.

176   **His fee was forty dollars:** Charvat, *Emerson's American Lecture Engagements*, 31.

176   **A cold raw country this:** *LRWE*, 5: 4.

177   **was as sweet and idyllic as it could be:** McClelland, "How Reagan's Childhood Home Gave Up On Reaganism." See also Madeline Buckley, "Troubled Times at Reagan's Boyhood Home in Dixon," *Chicago Tribune*, September 13, 2019.

177   **correct quiet man:** *JMN*, 14: 26.

177   **the town elected him its first mayor:** Some useful information about John Dixon can be found at: http://genealogytrails.com/ill/lee/leefather.html.

177   **We will walk on our own feet:** *E&L*, 71.

177   **He who has made so many rich is a poor man:** *JMN*, 14: 26–27.

178   **clearly one of his favorites, which he subsequently reprinted:** *LRWE*, 5: 4–5.

178   **The spiral tendency of vegetation infects education also:** *E&L*, 1099.

178   **what the social birds say, when they sit in autumn council:** *E&L*, 1099.

178   **Our reliance on the physician is a kind of despair:** *E&L*, 1101.

178   **Beauty is the moment of transition:** *E&L*, 1105.

179   **are a record in sculpture of a thousand anecdotes:** *E&L*, 1105.

179   **Beauty without grace is the hook without:** *E&L*, 1108–1109.

179   **The feat of the imagination is in showing the convertibility:** *E&L*, 1111.

180   **these sinewy farmers of the north:** *LRWE*, 4: 4.

180   **The lecture bore evidence of ripe scholarship:** B. F. Shaw, *Dixon Evening Telegraph*, January 5, 1856.

180   **vastly superior to any lecture we have yet had:** *LRWE*, 5: 4.

180   **The French and the Fox Indians:** For a detailed history of Galena and its economy, see "Galena and Its Lead Mines," *Harper's New Monthly Magazine* XXXII, May 1866, 681–695. The yield of ore for 1845 (54,494,850 pounds) can be found on 692. The anonymous author notes on 693 that a "decrease of the mining interest" had shrunk the local economy. For DeSoto House, see "Historical Notes: De Soto House: Hundred-Year-Old Galena Hotel," *Journal of the Illinois State Historical Society* 47, no. 3, Autumn 1954, 315–321. See also https://web.archive.org/web/20070205042551/http://www.cityofgalena.org/history.cfm.

181   **hardly speak:** *LRWE*, 5: 6.

181   **Mercury below zero 22° and this the twelfth day:** *LRWE*, 5: 6.

181   **we had no cold weather in Illinois, only now & then:** *JMN*, 14: 27–28.

182   **cold fortnight's adventures on the prairie:** *LRWE*, 5: 7.

182   **long be remembered as the finest lecture ever delivered:** *LRWE*, 5: 9.

182   **A large proportion of those who were present:** *Summit County Beacon*, January 23, 1856, 5.

182   **There are times when the intellect is so active:** *JMN*, 14: 29.

183   **Every operator has his own manner:** *JMN*, 14: 28.

183   **When he was introduced to Abraham Lincoln:** Cushman, "When Lincoln Met Emerson," 163–183.

183   **We don't know exactly when Lincoln:** Bode, *The American Lyceum*, 97.

Chapter 11. Visit to a Cold Island

Page

184   **Hoosiers are good to begin:** *JMN*, 14: 29.

184   **Some of his peers, such as Bronson Alcott, regretted that he never:** Alcott, *Concord Days*, 39.

184   **consists in a little fire, a little food, but enough:** *JMN*, 14: 30.

185   **It is probable you left some obscure comrade:** *E&L*, 768.

185   **The visit was rather a spectacle than a conversation:** *E&L*, 773.

185   **newspapers are atrocious, and accuse members of Congress:** *E&L*, 776–778.

186   **England is a garden:** *E&L*, 784.

187   **telescope on every street:** *JMN*, 4: 25.

187   **theory of nature:** See Walls, *Emerson's Life in Science*, 4. Walls quotes the cited phrase and provides a wonderfully rich overview of RWE's involvement with scientific theory and practice.

187   **The axioms of physics:** Walls, *Emerson's Life in Science*, 5. Waldo's line is actually a paraphrase of Anne Louise Germaine de Staël-Holstein, better known as Madame de Staël.

187   **split into two camps:** Menand, *The Metaphysical Club*, 104–107.

188   **feeble argument:** Walls, *Emerson's Life in Science*, 185.

188   **he was a transmutationist:** Walls, *Emerson's Life in Science*, 168–175. RWE's relationship to these theories of race is extremely complicated, synthesizing bits of many different writers he had read. He was particularly fascinated by *Vestiges of the Natural History of Creation*, a bestselling study published by the Scottish journalist and fellow transmutationist Robert Chambers in 1844. Chambers argued that during its embryonic period, every organism recapitulated the forms of its evolutionary predecessors. A human embryo, for example, successively resembled a fish, reptile, bird, and primitive mammal. Evolutionary change occurred when the embryonic period ended too quickly (meaning a step backward) or went on too long (meaning a step forward). The process was reversible, in other words, encompassing what RWE called both "arrested and progressive development." Yet it was mostly progressive, in his view, "indicating

the way upward from the invisible protoplasm to the highest organisms." Walls, 169–171. See also Menand, 124–125. The appeal of such a system to RWE, with its encapsulation of biological history within a single living being, is not hard to imagine. It was a triumph of metaphor. An ocean was a drop of water, and a man was a zoological menagerie—while still in the womb, no less.

188   **Striving to be a man:** *E&L*, 5.

188   **Race is everything: literature, science, art:** Knox, *The Races of Men: A Fragment*, 7.

188   **no more a white man than an ass:** Knox, *The Races of Men*, 162–163.

188   **Blumenbach was a quintessential Enlightenment polymath:** Blumenbach, *The Anthropological Treatises of Johann Friedrich Blumenbach*, 13 (for the tapeworm and kangaroo), 20 (for melancholy and Alpine crevasses). For an overview of Blumenbach's race theories, see Painter's rollicking evisceration in *The History of White People*, 72–88. See also Justin E. H. Smith's more generous assessment In Nature, Human Nature, and Human Difference: Race in Early Modern Philosophy (Princeton: Princeton University Press, 2017), 253–263, as well as Stephen Jay Gould, "The Geometer of Race."

189   **Knox in particular:** Knox had a long eclipse, both because of his flagrant racism and because this irascible man had a gift for alienating his colleagues and superiors. There was also a body-snatching scandal in Edinburgh that tainted his reputation for centuries. Yet it was John D. Orr, a latter-day president of the Royal College of Surgeons of Edinburgh, who declared Knox to be the "foremost anatomist of his age" in the foreword to A. W. Bates's *Anatomy of Robert Knox: Murder, Mad Science and Medical Regulation in Nineteenth-Century Edinburgh* (Liverpool: Liverpool University Press, 2010), viii. See also the author's introduction (1–11) for a useful overview of Knox's career, and for an interesting postcancellation bulletin: Knox's waxwork likeness has been restored to the RCS's museum. The tableaux shows him seated at his desk, with various pickled specimens in jars and a grinning skeleton behind him.

189   **a library entirely composed of books:** Blumenbach, *The Anthropological Treatises of Johann Friedrich Blumenbach*, 57.

189   **Other countrymen look slight and undersized beside them:** *E&L*, 801.

189   **It is race, is it not?:** *E&L*, 792.

189   **It is a great shame, exactly as Painter says:** Painter, *The History of White People*, 151–189.

190   **Though we flatter the self-love of men and nations:** *E&L*, 792–793.

190   **author and geologist Robert Chambers:** See Chambers note above, plus John B. Wilson, "Darwin and the Transcendentalists," *Journal of the History of Ideas* 26, no. 2 (1965): 288.

190   **If we are composite creatures:** Castillo, "'The Best of Nations'?, Race and Imperial Destinies in Emerson's *English Traits*," 107–110.

190   **nothing can be praised in it without damning exceptions:** *E&L*, 793–795.

191   **full of thoughts like winged arrows:** Norton, *The Correspondence of Thomas Carlyle and Ralph Waldo Emerson*, 2: 304.

191   **are jealous of minds that have much facility of association:** *E&L*, 809.

191   **Steam is almost an Englishman:** *E&L*, 817.

191   **Their system of education is factitious:** *E&L*, 819.

191   **A terrible machine has possessed itself:** *E&L*, 822.

191   **Nothing savage, nothing mean resides in the English heart:** *E&L*, 842.

192   **Their religion is a quotation; their church is a doll:** *E&L*, 887.

192   **a term he coined, for better or worse:** *E&L*, 59.

192   **He must be treated with sincerity and reality, with muffins:** *E&L*, 893.

192   **mainly of England:** *JMN*, 5: 210–211. Given RWE's disparagement of Pope as a cake decorator, it's amusing to see that Shakespeare and Pope are listed here as the giants to avoid: they "destroy all."

192   **living index of the colossal British power:** *E&L*, 913.

193   **The old sphinx put our petty differences of nationality:** *E&L*, 918.

193   **rattlesnakes in the city of New York:** *JMN*, 10: 197.

193   **There I thought, in America, lies nature sleeping:** *E&L*, 923.

194   **moral peculiarity of the Saxon race:** *E&L*, 934–936.

194   **gimcracks known collectively as Birmingham toys?:** Mason, "Birmingham: The Toyshop of Europe."

195   **by which time his prediction had begun to come true:** There are, of course, many different measures of economic might. "America began to challenge Britain in economic terms as early as 1861," writes Peter J. Hugill in "The American Challenge to British Hegemony, 1861–1947," *Geographical Review* 99, no. 3 (July 2009): 404. Labor productivity, at least in the manufacturing sector, was already higher in the United States than in Britain, argues S. N. Broadberry in "Comparative Productivity in British and American Manufacturing during the Nineteenth Century," *Explorations in Economic History* 31 (1994): 521–522. America's GDP per person, on the other hand, was just 75.3 percent of Britain's in 1870—not until the turn of the century would the United States surpass its old rival, at which point the gap opened up fairly quickly. See Nicholas Crafts, "Forging ahead and Falling behind: The Rise and Relative Decline of the First Industrial Nation," *Journal of Economic Perspectives* 12, no. 2 (Spring 1998): 200.

195   **Patagonians of beef and beer:** *JMN*, 10: 181.

Chapter 12. Knocking Down the Hydra

Page

196   **The fact that William Emerson was a fierce proponent:** Lemire, *Black Walden*, 72–73, 84–89. Lemire draws her account of Phebe Emerson's swoon from *Diaries and Letters of William Emerson 1743–1776*, edited by Amelia Forbes Emerson (Madison: University of Wisconsin Press, 1972), 72. The suggestion that the lady of the house fainted at the sight of Frank with an axe, rather than at the approach of British troops, is Lemire's surmise. She argues that Phebe Emerson already *knew* the British were on the march, and that her panic attack was more likely connected to recent fears of a slave rebellion in the nearby town of Natick. Phebe may have also had in a mind an incident during the previous year, when an enslaved man in Concord named Casey Feen had thrown his axe at his owner's son, then fled. Edward Waldo Emerson tells the same story in a pamphlet-length life of his ancestor, "A Chaplain of the Revolution" (Boston: Massachusetts Historical Society, 1922), 15. This version omits Frank's name and hints that William Emerson may have been somewhere on the premises, perhaps to avoid the suggestion that he had left his wife and family unprotected.

197 **population of free Black people:** Gross, *The Transcendentalists and Their World*, 98–107. See also Lemire, *Black Walden*, 119–127.

197 **half-obliterated cellar hole:** *Walden*, 271.

198 **one of the only documented artifacts of this vanished:** Lemire, *Black Walden*, 144.

198 **gain some traction:** Gross, *The Transcendentalists and Their World*, 328–329.

198 **among the sixty-one women:** See Petrulionis, "'Swelling that Great Tide of Humanity': The Concord, Massachusetts Female Anti-Slavery Society," *New England Quarterly* 74, no. 3, September 2001, 387-39.

199 **introduce political and social equality between:** Reynolds, *Walt Whitman's America: A Cultural Biography*, 572.

199 **an Anglo-Saxon with common sense does not like:** Mark D. Morrison-Reed, *Darkening the Doorways: Black Trailblazers and Missed Opportunities in Unitarian Universalism* (Boston: Skinner House Books, 2011), 3.

199 **Is not America for the Whites?:** Reynolds, *Walt Whitman's America*, 572.

199 **had beaten white women to the ballot box:** DuBois, *Suffrage: Women's Long Battle for the Vote*, 73.

199 **power of an unsophisticated mind:** Blight, *Frederick Douglass: Prophet of Freedom*, 119.

199 **Lincoln, for example, moved far beyond his early:** Wilentz, "Lincoln's Rowdy America," 25–26.

199 **Garrison surely countermanded his crack:** See http://theliberatorfiles.com/douglasss-north-star/.

200 **No ingenious sophistry can ever reconcile:** *JMN*, 2: 57.

200 **I saw ten, twenty, a hundred large lipped:** *JMN*, 2: 48–49.

200 **there were only 1,726 Black Bostonians:** Robert L. Hall, "Boston's African American Heritage," *Footnotes* 36, no. 3 (March 2008). The overall population of Boston in 1820 can be found at http://www.demographia.com/db-bos1790.htm.

200 **had already squeezed out most of its people of color from Walden woods:** Gross, *The Transcendentalists and Their World*, 102.

201 **no melody, no emotion, no humor:** *E&L*, 688.

201 **Napoleon had the nerve to smash:** *E&L*, 744–745.

201 **It is natural to believe in great men:** *E&L*, 616.

202 **We swim, day by day, on a river of delusions:** *E&L*, 624.

202 **The ideas of the time are in the air:** *E&L*, 627.

202 **the slave's misery as they cross his path in life:** Gougeon, *Virtue's Hero: Emerson, Antislavery, and Reform*, 33.

202 **He also invited such abolitionists as Samuel May:** Gougeon, *Virtue's Hero*, 4. RWE's parishioners were probably no less appalled by his declaration of pan-racial solidarity in an 1832 sermon: "Let every man say then to himself—the cause of the Indian, it is mine; the cause of the slave, it is mine." As Mott notes in *"The Strains of Eloquence": Emerson and His Sermons*, 137, "This was heady stuff in 1832 Boston in a congregation whose individual members were benefitting at least indirectly from the slave trade."

202 **May had a particular gift for riling up the audience:** *In Memoriam: Samuel Joseph May* (Syracuse: The Journal Office, 1871), 26.

203   the "gag rule" of 1836 decreed that any antislavery: Delbanco, *The War Before the War: Fugitive Slaves and the Struggle for America's Soul from the Revolution to the Civil War*, 127, 134–138.

203   A friend of the slave shows me the horrors: *JMN*, 5: 437.

203   On November 7, 1837, a mob in Alton, Illinois: Delbanco, *The War Before the War*, 135, plus http://www.altonweb.com/history/lovejoy/.

203   The brave Lovejoy has given his breast: *JMN*, 5: 437.

204   Even the platform of the lyceum: *CAB*, 2: 425–428.

204   the lords of the lash and the lords of the loom: Sinha, *The Slave's Cause: A History of Abolition*, 352.

204   narrow, self-pleasing, conceited men, and affect us: *E&L*, 162.

204   redeem their own race from the doom: Gougeon and Myerson, *Emerson's Antislavery Writings*, 2–3.

205   this stirring in the philanthropic mud: *JMN*, 5: 479–480.

205   armed with all the weapons of a great Apostle: *JMN*, 7: 281.

205   noble woman: Gougeon, *Virtue's Hero*, 66–67.

206   But Garrison, for example, had dealt with: Blight, *Frederick Douglass*, 119–120.

206   agent of good: *JMN*, 9: 134.

207   whipped until unconscious, then dragged by her legs: Clarkson, *The History of the Rise, Progress, and Accomplishment of the Abolition of the African Slave Trade by the British Parliament*, 269.

207   the ebon hue of the negro: Thome and Kimball, *Emancipation in the West Indies: A Six Month's Tour in Antigua, Barbadoes, and Jamaica, in the Year 1837*, 22.

207   gave the immense fortification of a fact—of gross history: *EAW*, 7.

208   The blood is moral: *EAW*, 10.

208   The habit of oppression: *EAW*, 17.

208   If any mention was made of homicide: *EAW*, 20.

209   A man is added to the human family: *EAW*, 29–31.

209   It was not of that cold, clear: Gougeon, *Virtue's Hero*, 84–87.

Chapter 13. Higher Laws

Page

210   I do not and can not forsake my vocation: *JMN*, 9: 64 footnote.

210   the Creator of the Negro has given him up: Gougeon, *Virtue's Hero*, 98.

211   the true successors of that austere Church: *EAW*, 43–44.

211   revolution broke out: Koch, *Emerson in Europe*, 108, 111–113. See also Eric Hobsbawm, *The Age of Capital: 1848–1875* (New York: Vintage Books, 1996), 9–26.

211   fled Vienna in a panic: Koch, *Emerson in Europe*, 123.

211   petition to Parliament: Koch, *Emerson in Europe*, 36.

212   Every man a ballot: Koch, *Emerson in Europe*, 127.

212   remove the motive: *JMN*, 10: 312.

212   the hour to test his genius: *JMN*, 10: 310.

212 **arrived there on May 6:** Koch, *Emerson in Europe*, 131–135.

212 **The deep sincerity of the speakers:** *LRWE*, 4: 73–74.

212 **When I see changed men:** *JMN*, 10: 311.

213 **could not articulate, & the edge of all:** *JMN*, 10: 320.

213 **From this windfall would be carved:** Delbanco, *The War Before the War*, 201–204.

213 **The United States will conquer Mexico:** *JMN*, 9: 430–431.

214 **We prefer Old Zack with his sugar and cotton:** McPherson, *Battle Cry of Freedom: The Civil War Era*, 63.

214 **those exciting topics of a sectional character:** Delbanco, *The War Before the War*, 216–217.

214 **frequent brawls on the floor of the U.S. Congress:** McPherson, *Battle Cry of Freedom*, 68–69.

214 **allowing the cannonballs to pass between his legs:** Allan B. Schwartz, "Medical Mystery: Did This President Suffer Death by Cherries?" *Philadelphia Inquirer*, May 6, 2018. As the title suggests, the article also addresses Taylor's mysterious demise and proposes salmonella as the culprit.

214 **solution to preserve the imploding Union was to back:** McPherson, *Battle Cry of Freedom*, 70–75.

214 **It ultimately admitted California as a free state:** Lepore, *These Truths: A History of the United States*, 260.

214 **This was a provision dearly desired by:** Delbanco, *The War Before the War*, 19.

215 **the wreck of the universe:** McPherson, *Battle Cry of Freedom*, 71–72.

215 **final settlement:** McPherson, *Battle Cry of Freedom*, 76.

215 **It fell apart just four years later:** Lepore, *These Truths*, 261–263.

215 **Lidian read Daniel Webster's March 7:** *TLLJE*, 115.

215 **This was a day of petticoats:** *JMN*, 11: 249.

216 **in the mouth of Mr. Webster:** *JMN*, 11: 346.

216 **person held to service or labour:** Delbanco, *The War Before the War*, 81.

216 **came to be known as personal liberty laws:** McPherson, *Battle Cry of Freedom*, 79.

216 **fugitives frequently took the opportunity:** Delbanco, *The War Before the War*, 169–173.

216 **The new statute was an attempt to close all such loopholes:** McPherson, *Battle Cry of Freedom*, 80–81.

216 **which spilled out over more than eighty pages:** Painter, *The History of White People*, 186.

217 **a point Waldo had made, somewhat airily:** *CAB*, 2: 426.

217 **This is not meddling with other people's affairs:** *JMN*, 11: 411–412.

217 **For a very brief period, this appeared to be true:** Gougeon, *Virtue's Hero*, 150–152.

217 **He was marched to a waiting ship nine days later:** McPherson, *Battle Cry of Freedom*, 83.

217 **a stinging reminder to people like Waldo:** Gougeon, *Virtue's Hero*, 155.

218 **"The last year has forced us all into politics," he began:** *EAW*, 53–63.

219 **They have torn down his picture from the wall:** *EAW*, 65–70.

220 **whose great claim to fame was cheerleading:** Lepore, *These Truths*, 268.

220 **The two had traded barbs in the past:** Gougeon, *Virtue's Hero*, 166.

220   **a freshly hatched minister at Boston's Brattle Street Church:** *TLLJE*, 38.

220   **a reliable authority on questions of morals:** Gougeon, *Virtue's Hero*, 169.

220   **spiritual harangues, anniversaries, lectures, [and] laughing gas:** *New York Herald*, April 27, 1857, 5.

221   **It was a question, whether man shall be:** *EAW*, 79.

221   **they had no memory for what they had been saying:** *EAW*, 74.

221   **These things show that no forms, neither Constitutions:** *EAW*, 83.

221   **I was most thankful to those who stayed home:** Gougeon, *Virtue's Hero*, 198–199.

221   **One must write with a red hot iron:** *EAW*, 91.

221   **It is so delicious to act with great masses:** *EAW*, 105.

222   **Gunpowder sometimes smells good:** *CAB*, 2: 601.

222   **Pay ransom to the owner:** RWE, *Collected Poems and Translations*, 163–165.

222   **I vividly recall the thrill that went through me:** Gougeon, *Virtue's Hero*, 305–306.

223   **negro soldier lying in the trenches:** Gougeon, *Virtue's Hero*, 306.

223   **The German and Irish millions, like the Negro:** *E&L*, 949–950. It's worth noting that the scholar Eduardo Cadava, in a striking essay called "The Guano of History" (in *The Other Emerson*, edited by Branca Arsić and Cary Wolfe [Minneapolis: University of Minnesota Press, 2010], p. 101–129), views this passage as a fiery denunciation of American social reality rather than a grimacing acceptance of it. Cadava points to an 1852 journal entry in which RWE deconstructs one of the perennial defenses of slavery: "Abolition. The argument of the slaveholder is one & simple: he pleads Fate. Here is an inferior race requiring wardship,—it is sentimentality to deny it." Fate in this sense is anything but neutral, natural, inexorable: it is a rhetorical convenience and instrument of evil.

224   **Higginson suggests in his memoirs that Waldo:** Higginson, *Cheerful Yesterdays*, 172–175.

224   **With regard to color, I am of the opinion:** Wortham, "Did Emerson Blackball Frederick Douglass from Membership in the Town and Country Club?" 295–298. Even if Wortham *hadn't* examined the Town and Country minutes for his excellent article, I would have doubted the story about RWE blackballing Douglass. The mutual esteem between the two men makes it seem unlikely (although not impossible). For an excellent overview of the relationship, see Len Gougeon, "Militant Abolitionism: Douglass, Emerson, and the Rise of the Anti-Slave," *New England Quarterly* 85, no. 4 (December 2012), 622–657. When RWE gave his pivotal address about West Indian emancipation in 1844, he shared the platform with Douglass, who spoke later the same afternoon. But RWE was already well aware of the ex-slave and abolitionist firebrand. In an earlier draft of that day's speech, he cited Douglass as a model of self-made heroism. "So now it seems to me that the arrival of such men as Toussaint if he is of pure blood, or Douglas[s] if he is pure blood, outweighs all the English & American humanity. The Antislavery of the whole world is but dust in the balance, a poor squeamishness & nervousness [;] the might & the right is here. Here is the Anti-Slave." See *JMN*, 9: 125. (His remarks about "pure blood" were meant to bat away the Southern argument that a man like Douglass must owe his talents to an admixture of white ancestry.) The admiration flowed in both directions. Douglass copied passages from Emerson's speeches into his diary, reprinted snippets of them in his newspapers, and mentioned him by name in one of his most celebrated lectures, "Self-Made Men"

(1872). He wrote RWE in 1850 to request a copy of *Representative Men* (Gougeon, 642). He was also a fan of *English Traits*, which he read during an ocean passage to Britain in 1886. "I have been reading *English Traits* by Emerson," he wrote in his diary, "and have been glad to find my own views of the civilization of England supported by one so thoughtful and able as the sage of Concord." What did he think of the race theory? Alas, we'll never know. (Douglass's 1886 diary is in the Library of Congress and the scanned page including his comment about *English Traits* can be found here: https://www.loc .gov/resource/mss11879.01001/?sp=6&st=image.)

224   **men who confessed to a mild natural colorphobia:** Higginson, *Cheerful Yesterdays*, 174.

224   **contradicts itself in tone and in word:** Painter, *The History of White People*, 181.

225   **A man finds out that there is somewhat in him:** *JMN*, 14: 259.

225   **We are all boarders at one table:** *JMN*, 7: 382.

Chapter 14. An Inspection of the Wreck

Page

226   **Toys, dancing school, Sets, parties, picture galleries:** *JMN*, 8: 114.

226   **the life expectancy for a typical American:** See https://www.statista.com/statistics /1040079/life-expectancy-united-states-all-time/.

226   **In early 1862, for example, he visited the capital:** Cushman, "When Lincoln Met Emerson," 163–183.

226   **who told him a "smutty" story that Lincoln himself:** *JMN*, 15: 188.

226   **while Lincoln's two young sons were having their hair cut:** *JMN*, 15: 194.

227   **It was as if a creature from some fairer world:** *JMN*, 16: xi.

227   **despite his panting eagerness to shoot a deer:** Schlett, *A Not Too Greatly Changed Eden: The Story of the Philosophers' Camp in the Adirondacks*, 97–98.

227   **Instead of an avenue, it is a barrier:** *JMN*, 16: 123, 125.

228   **a practical question of the conduct of life:** *E&L*, 943.

228   **We fancy men are individuals; so are pumpkins:** *E&L*, 586.

229   **Providence has a wild, rough, incalculable road:** *E&L*, 946.

229   **the tyrannous circumstance:** *E&L*, 949.

229   **hooped in by a necessity, which, by many experiments:** *E&L*, 952.

229   **Fate has its lord:** *E&L*, 953.

229   **Every jet of chaos which threatens to exterminate:** *E&L*, 958.

229   **plaintiff and defendant, friend and enemy, animal and planet:** *E&L*, 967.

230   **The instinct of the people is right:** *E&L*, 975.

230   **Practice is nine tenths:** *E&L*, 984.

230   **applications of the mind to nature:** *E&L*, 989.

230   **Will a man content himself with a hut:** *E&L*, 991.

231   **main use of surplus capital:** *E&L*, 993.

231   **susceptibility to metaphysical changes:** *E&L*, 999.

231   **a "book of wisdom" on par:** Gerber, "Emerson and the Political Economists," 345.

231   **Wealth brings with it its own checks and balances:** *E&L*, 997–998.

232   **regulation of trade was not only a drag on prosperity but against nature:** Newfield, *The Emerson Effect: Individualism and Submission in America*, 179.

232   **met Waldo during his British tour:** Koch, *Ralph Waldo Emerson in Europe: Class, Race and Revolution in the Making of an American Thinker*, 84.

232   **who likened the experience to "distant thunder.":** Herbert Spencer, *An Autobiography*, vol. 1, 279.

232   **When Spencer hung out with Andrew Carnegie:** Andrew Carnegie, *Autobiography of Andrew Carnegie* (Boston and New York: Houghton Mifflin Company, 1920), 335. Their conversation, as reported by Carnegie, was essentially a lesson in anger management: "Mr. Spencer said: 'I feel just so myself, but I will tell you how I curb my indignation. Whenever I feel it rising I am calmed by this story of Emerson's: He had been hooted and hustled from the platform in Faneuil Hall for daring to speak against slavery. He describes himself walking home in violent anger, until opening his garden gate and looking up through the branches of the tall elms that grew between the gate and his modest home, he saw the stars shining through. They said to him: 'What, so hot, my little sir?' I laughed and he laughed, and I thanked him for that story. Not seldom I have to repeat to myself, 'What, so hot, my little sir?' and it suffices."

232   **You are responsible only for action in obedience to the judge within:** W. Ross Winterowd, "Capitalism and Culture: John and John and Scripture; Andy and Adam, Herb, Matt, and Waldo," *JAC* 27, no. 3/4 (2007): 555.

233   **It's quite likely that Waldo's vogue:** This is certainly the argument of Eugene McCarraher in *The Enchantments of Mammon: How Capitalism Became the Religion of Modernity*, 169. Emerson's "divinization of capitalist power," he writes, "would resound through the next two American centuries: in the nostrums of philosopher-businesspeople, in the casuistry of management writers, in the pieties of cheerfully merciless executives, journalists, and libertarians."

233   **to laugh at Transcendentalism as an incomprehensible folly:** Frothingham, *Transcendentalism in New England: A History*, xxvi.

233   **cheerless anxiety and hopeless dependence:** Matteson, *Eden's Outcasts*, 387.

233   **The stockholder has stepped into the place of the warlike baron:** Emerson, *The Complete Works of Ralph Waldo Emerson, Volume X: Lectures and Biographical Sketches*, 328.

233   **As the owner of sixty-seven shares in the City Bank:** *TEB*, 319–320.

234   **The counting-room maxims liberally expounded:** *E&L*, 1010.

234   **A dollar is not value:** *E&L*, 998.

234   **the prose of life:** *E&L*, 578.

234   **As long as our civilization is essentially one of property:** *E&L*, 745.

235   **can bear such a creature:** Emerson, *Letters and Social Aims*, 100.

235   **There the gaggle of grandchildren referred to Waldo:** These details about life on Naushon Island come from a now vanished blog by the author and art dealer Sukey Forbes, who also happens to be RWE's great-great-great granddaughter and a tenant, at least part of the time, of the Forbes compound that RWE repeatedly visited. However, the detail about RWE being called Grampa Moo Moo also occurs in Sukey Forbes, *The Angel in My Pocket: A Story of Love, Loss, and Life after Death* (New York: Penguin Publishing Group, 2015), 11.

235   **school of American philosophy:** The relationship between RWE and Pragmatism is much contested. It depends, to some degree, on which of the three pillars of Pragmatism—William James, C. S. Pierce, John Dewey—we're discussing. William James had a lifelong relationship with RWE and a clear intellectual debt to him. He argued that truth was not a static thing but a constantly unfolding *process*: "Truth *happens* to an idea. It *becomes* true, it is *made* true by events." Allen, *William James*, 436. With its vision of experiential and cognitive flux, this has an Emersonian ring to it. C. S. Pierce entered the conversation from an entirely different angle—like his father, he was a celebrated mathematician—and considered Transcendentalism an unfortunate contagion. And yet he couldn't dismiss it entirely. "It is probable," he wrote, "that some cultured bacilli, some benignant form of the disease was implanted in my soul, unawares, and that now, after long incubation, it comes to the surface, modified by mathematical conceptions and by training in physical investigations." See Charles S. Pierce, *Chance, Love and Logic: Philosophical Essays* (New York: Harcourt, Brace & Company, Inc., 1923), 203. Dewey, the furthest from RWE's actual orbit, insisted later in his career that we should think of "Emerson as the one citizen of the world fit to have his name uttered in the same breath with that of Plato." See Cornel West, *The American Evasion of Philosophy: A Genealogy of Pragmatism* (Madison: The University of Wisconsin Press, 1989), 76. West traces a straight line from RWE to the great Pragmatists, arguing that his stress on experience—on *how life was lived*—fed directly into their mode of thought. Rather than drilling down into the verities of truth, beauty, and mind, American philosophers would traffic in something closer to cultural criticism, as well as political engagement. West, 9–41. A similar argument is made by Carlin Romano in *America The Philosophical* (New York: Alfred A. Knopf, 2012), 66–78. For a remarkable history of Pragmatism and its role in American culture, see the entirety of Menand, *The Metaphysical Club*. While his explanation of Pragmatism is kaleidoscopic (to say the least), he does locate it in an Emersonian context. "Pragmatism," he writes, "belongs to a disestablishmentarian impulse in American culture—an impulse that drew strengths from the writings of Emerson, who attacked institutions and conformity, and from the ascendancy, after the Civil War, of evolutionary theories, which drew attention to the contingency of all social forms." Menand, 89.

235   **Lidian took the time to don a black alpaca dress, mantilla, and bonnet:** *TLLJE*, 159.

236   **Could you tell me where my good neighbors have flung:** *EIHOT*, 90.

236   **This assault on his own memories:** Hanlon, *Emerson's Memory Loss: Originality, Communality, and the Late Style*, 18.

236   **the Poet of America wandering forlornly around:** Hanlon, *Emerson's Memory Loss*, 18.

236   **In their louche and waterlogged outfits, the Emersons:** *TLLJE*, 159–160.

237   **felt something snap in his brain:** McAleer, *Ralph Waldo Emerson: Days of Encounter*, 612.

237   **just the same, and very happy:** Ellen Tucker Emerson, *The Letters of Ellen Tucker Emerson*, 1: 676.

237   **House burned:** *JMN*, 16: 278.

237   **thrown out on the grass in his door-yard:** *LRWE*, 6: 219.

238   **odd bureau drawers:** Ellen Tucker Emerson, *The Letters of Ellen Tucker Emerson*, 1: 680.

239   **I don't know what you can do about it:** *TLLJE*, 160, 240 footnote, plus *CAB*, 2: 654–655.

239   **dreaming of Egypt:** *LRWE*, 6: 221.

239   **an expression of health:** *JMN*, 7: 62.

239   **But the liberal ocean sings louder:** *LRWE*, 6: 225.

240   **all the time in a large muddy pond:** Ellen Tucker Emerson, *The Letters of Ellen Tucker Emerson*, 2: 40.

240   **All this journey is a perpetual humiliation:** *JMN*, 16: 285.

240   **incapacity to write any thing:** *LRWE*, 6: 234.

240   **That poor man had been scared at seeing me disappear:** Ellen Tucker Emerson, *The Letters of Ellen Tucker Emerson*, 2: 44.

241   **Nothing is so fleeting as form:** *E&L*, 242.

241   **remains were moved to Sleepy Hollow Cemetery:** *JMN*, 14: 154. For a fascinating meditation on the role of burial and unearthing in RWE's life, see Ellis, "Ralph Waldo Emerson's Grave Encounters."

242   **The travelers reached there on January 28:** *JMN*, 16: 287, plus Ellen Tucker Emerson, *The Letters of Ellen Tucker Emerson*, 2: 45–49.

242   **the honeymooning Henry Adams and his bride Clover:** Natalie Dykstra, *Clover Adams: A Gilded and Heartbreaking Life* (Boston: Houghton Mifflin Harcourt, 2012), 66–68, and Brown, *The Last American Aristocrat: The Brilliant Life and Improbable Education of Henry Adams*, 143–144. Adams mentions dragging his photographic arsenal all the way from London in *Letters of Henry Adams* (Boston: Houghton Mifflin, 1930), 239.

242   **honest blue eyes, and perfectly brilliant teeth:** Ellen Tucker Emerson, *The Letters of Ellen Tucker Emerson*, 2: 56–57.

243   **My whole dear town all assembled:** Ellen Tucker Emerson, *The Letters of Ellen Tucker Emerson*, 2: 90.

243   **Is today a public holiday?:** Townsend Scudder, *Concord: An American Town*, 269.

Chapter 15. Terminus

Page

244   **when the German neuropathologist Alois Alzheimer examined:** Shenk, *The Forgetting: Alzheimer's: A Portrait of an Epidemic*, 12–25.

244   **It starts, as researchers would later learn, in the hippocampus:** Shenk, *The Forgetting*, 37, 121–123.

245   **It is time to be old:** Emerson, *Collected Poems and Translations*, 191–192. Edward Waldo Emerson recounts hearing the poem in *Emerson in Concord*, 183.

245   **the cement, the bitumen, the matrix:** Emerson, *The Complete Works of Ralph Waldo Emerson, Volume XII: Lectures and Biographical Sketches*, 90.

245   **as if the mind were a kind of looking-glass:** Emerson, *The Complete Works of Ralph Waldo Emerson, Volume XII: Lectures and Biographical Sketches*, 93.

246   **One sometimes asks himself, Is it possible:** Emerson, *The Complete Works of Ralph Waldo Emerson, Volume XII: Lectures and Biographical Sketches*, 97.

246   **Memory went first:** Hanlon, *Emerson's Memory Loss*, 19–21.

247   **dwelling in the land of the ideal:** McAleer, *Ralph Waldo Emerson: Days of Encounter*, 653. William James, who should have known better, delivered a nasty assessment of

RWE's condition after a Cambridge dinner party in 1874. "Emerson looks in magnificent health," he wrote his brother Henry, "but the refined idiocy of his manner seems as if it must be affectation." *The Selected Letters of William James*, edited with an introduction by Elizabeth Hardwick (New York: Anchor Books, 1961), 99.

247   **the red chandelier:** Ellen Tucker Emerson, *The Letters of Ellen Tucker Emerson*, 2: 75.

247   **Poor man, how he struggles for words!:** Ellen Tucker Emerson, *The Letters of Ellen Tucker Emerson*, 1: 691.

247   **an old scribe who, for the first time in his life:** *LRWE*, 6: 235.

248   **ceased to write even notes—partly because my daughter:** Hanlon, *Emerson's Memory Loss*, 40.

248   **They dredged up materials from his earlier lectures:** Hanlon, *Emerson's Memory Loss*, 13–14, 33–36.

248   **he wrote Cabot's name followed by two words:** An antiquarian in Fleetwood, Pennsylvania, has been attempting to sell Cabot's copy of *Letters and Social Aims* for the past few years. The current price is a mere $25,000, and the offering (with photos of RWE's inscription) can be examined here: https://www.biblio.com/book/letters-social-aims -emerson-ralph-waldo/d/6939713.

248   **there is no pure originality:** Hanlon, *Emerson's Memory Loss*, 12.

249   **While Mr. Emerson was reading this interesting paper:** *New York Times*, February 13, 1881, 7.

249   **an old man fears most his best friends:** *LRWE*, 6: 296.

250   **playfulness, simplicity, and childlikeness:** "Emerson Extolled at Authors' Dinner," *New York Times*, May 26, 1903, 5.

250   **benignant face, the clear eyes, the silently smiling mouth:** Hanlon, *Emerson's Memory Loss*, 18.

250   **There is in fact a phenomenon, called paradoxical lucidity:** Alex Godfrey, "'The Clouds Cleared': What Terminal Lucidity Teaches Us about Life, Death, and Dementia," *The Guardian*, February 2021. See also George A. Mashour et al., "Paradoxical lucidity: A Potential Paradigm Shift for the Neurobiology and Treatment of Severe Dementias," *Alzheimer's & Dementia* 15, no. 8 (2019): 1107–1114.

251   **search all the hiding places in which:** Carpenter, *The Selected Letters of Lidian Jackson Emerson*, 320.

251   **the only man I ever heard of who changed, for the better:** Kenneth T. Jackson, *Crabgrass Frontier: The Suburbanization of the United States* (New York: Oxford University Press, 1987), 186.

251   **charming Oliver Wendell Holmes and Henry Wadsworth Longfellow:** Bok, *The Americanization of Edward Bok: The Autobiography of a Dutch Boy Fifty Years After*, 35–41.

251   **where the teenager's celebrity quarry stood up:** Bok, *The Americanization of Edward Bok*, 54–60.

252   **As a good chimney burns up all its own smoke:** Porte, *Representative Man*, 11.

252   **put down their thoughts, [they] jumped into their book:** *JMN*, 10: 350.

253   **That is why I will tell you some of the strange and salient:** Almost everything that follows comes from a summary of her father's final days that Ellen Emerson prepared

for his biographer and executor James Elliot Cabot (who used very little of it). It is reprinted in Ellen Tucker Emerson, *The Letters of Ellen Tucker Emerson*, 2: 670–677. Details that come from other sources are footnoted individually.

254   **In fact, he ran with it up the stairs on his tiptoes:** Ellen Tucker Emerson, *The Letters of Ellen Tucker Emerson*, 2: 462.

254   **the baritone rising and falling, the rhetorical call to arms:** *CAB*, 2: 683.

254   **a lecturer who has no idea what he is lecturing about:** *CAB*, 2: 670.

254   **He recognized his visitors:** Ellen Tucker Emerson, *The Letters of Ellen Tucker Emerson*, 2: 464–465.

Chapter 16. Circles

Page

256   **Nothing is dead:** *E&L*, 585.

256   **Our life is an apprenticeship to the truth:** *E&L*, 403.

256   **Thus there is no sleep:** *E&L*, 412.

257   **circular philosopher:** *E&L*, 411.

257   **This day also, whilst I was at dinner:** *CAB*, 1: 27.

257   **a rather dull scholar:** *ROP*, 26.

257   **William was also the son of a revered clergyman:** *CAB*, 1: 13.

258   **offered to accompany the choir on bass viol:** *ROP*, 11–12, plus Shrader, "Pilgrim's Pride."

258   **from the intercourse of all humanized beings:** *CAB*, 1: 13.

258   **in which there was to be no written expression of faith:** *CAB*, 1: 21–22.

258   **loved to show off his elegant ankles:** *ROP*, 10.

259   **I know the doctor had advised him to have me go:** *ROP*, 27. In an 1850 letter to his brother William, RWE described the same incident in even more bitter terms. He recalled his father as "a somewhat social gentleman, but severe to us children, who twice or thrice put me in mortal terror by forcing me into the salt water off some wharf or bathing house, and I still recall the fright with which, after some of this salt experience, I heard his voice one day, (as Adam that of the Lord God in the garden,), summoning us to a new bath, and I vainly endeavouring to hide myself." *LRWE*, 4: 179.

259   **phrasing in the second half is straight out of Genesis:** Genesis 3:8, in RWE's beloved King James Version, reads: "And they heard the voice of the LORD God walking in the garden in the cool of the day: and Adam and his wife hid themselves from the presence of the LORD God amongst the trees of the garden."

259   **He used to smile as he recalled his delight in that funeral:** *ROP*, 29–30.

260   **tearing the pages out of bound volumes of his father's sermons:** *ROP*, 32.

260   **there was not a book, a speech, a conversation, or a thought:** *ROP*, 33.

261   **"It builds the sepulchers of the fathers.":** *E&L*, 7.

261   **Man in all ages and countries, embodies it:** *E&L*, 21.

261   **parental style was also straight out of the Calvinist playbook:** *ROP*, 16–24.

261   **Breakfast consisted of toast, but no butter:** Haskins, *Ralph Waldo Emerson*, 58.

262   **I did not think it pretty enough for the pretty boys:** Haskins, *Ralph Waldo Emerson*, 55.

262   **which gave off a luminous glow when he rubbed:** *JMN*, 16: 263.

262   **They were born to be educated:** Cole, *Mary Moody Emerson and the Origins of Transcendentalism*, 147. See also Feltenstein, "Mary Moody Emerson: The Gadfly of Concord," 241–242.

262   **Everett, a newspaperman who collected his prose:** See the mini-bio of Everett in the *Boston Evening Transcript*, March 1, 1849, 1.

262   **You'd scarce expect one of my age:** The text of Everett's poem, which has never quite gone out of style, can be found at: https://www.theotherpages.org/poems/everett1.html.

263   **There really was no sense, in a family like this one:** Heywood, *A History of Childhood: Children and Childhood in the West from Medieval to Modern Times*, 23–27.

263   **white Paper, or Wax, to be moulded and fashioned:** Heywood, *A History of Childhood*, 23.

263   **not be profitable to confine the young mind long to any one part:** J. A. Cummings, *An Introduction to Ancient and Modern Geography* (Boston: Cummings and Hilliard, 1815), xi.

264   **A fatal instance of this in our first parents we have:** John Mason, *A Treatise on Self-Knowledge* (London: Thomas Tegg, 1821), 2, and *CAB*, 1: 25.

264   **Knowledge puffeth up:** Mason, *A Treatise on Self-Knowledge*, 9.

264   **hastening into the little parlor to the study of tomorrow's:** *JMN*, 5: 438. In the same passage, RWE recalls declaiming Webster and Everett while doing household chores.

264   **I began to doubt which was the right name for the thing:** *CAB*, 1: 14.

264   **vigorous in body:** *CAB*, 1: 43 (and for "dwelt in a higher sphere," 48).

265   **You have no:** *JMN*, 10: 110.

265   **hoisted onto a sugar cask like the miniature prodigy he was:** Edward Waldo Emerson, *Emerson in Concord*, 17.

266   **I was a little chubby boy trundling a hoop in Chauncy Place:** *JMN*, 8: 258.

266   **Waldo found himself wandering by Summer Street:** *JMN*, 16: 274.

266   **painted the same shade of green that the owner:** Pickering, *Nathaniel Goddard: A Boston Merchant*, 146.

266   **The Great Boston Fire of 1872, which started on November 9:** "Carleton," *The Story of the Great Fire: Boston, November 9–10, 1872* (Boston: Shepard and Gill, 1872), 10–11. See also "Site of the Great Boston Fire of 1872," The Historyist, at https://thehistoryist.com/site-of-the-great-boston-fire-of-1872/.

268   **Hovey's—which happened to sit roughly on the spot where:** Edward Waldo Emerson, *Emerson in Concord*, 4.

268   **Even the elms, sycamores, and maples on the main drag:** See Gross, *The Transcendentalists and Their World*, 88–92, and Walls, *Henry David Thoreau*, 53.

268   **orphic acorns by the peck:** Eve LaPlante, *Marmee & Louisa: The Untold Story of Louisa May Alcott and Her Mother* (New York: Simon & Schuster, 2013), 143.

268   **Things are, and are not, at the same time:** *E&L*, 585.

270   **We lay the corpse in these leafy colonnades:** See https://www.nps.gov/places/sleepy-hollow-cemetery.htm.

INDEX

Note: Page numbers in *italic* refer to figures.

A NOTE ON THE TYPE

This book has been composed in Arno, an Old-style serif typeface in the classic Venetian tradition, designed by Robert Slimbach at Adobe.